KEEPSAKE
Ornaments

A Collector's Guide
Fourth Edition

Clara Johnson Scroggins

ISBN 0-87529-626-2

CONTENTS

Dedication

To all organized Hallmark collector's clubs, especially "NASA Noelers." To the Murphys — Jody, Ellery and Lara. To Mary Jones, Adele and Bill Hanson, Meredith and Hal, Pat Anderson and John, Joan Ketterer, David Kirschke, and Teen Challenge. To the super staff at Hallmark and to all those who collect out of love for the ornaments and love and respect for the reason for this wonderful season.

To Joe, Michael, Kathy, Michelle, Terrence, the Johnson Family and my new "expected" grandchild, Baby Watkins.

NOTE TO THE COLLECTOR: This Fourth Edition of the *Keepsake Ornament Collector's Guide* provides a way for you to keep a record of your ornaments. You will find a small box beside each ornament description. Use the boxes to check off the ornaments in your collection.

Hallmark Keepsake Ornaments:
A Collector's Guide

Written by Clara Johnson Scroggins
Editor: Tina Hacker
Contributing Editors: Lynn Poe, Nancy Cox
Cover Design: Kathy Shulteis
Page Design: Sarah Taylor

Dear Collector Friends,

As I've traveled across the country in the last two years, I've had the wonderful opportunity to meet and spend time with many of you. It's been so gratifying to hear how much you enjoy reading and using my *Collector's Guides*.

This fourth edition of the *Keepsake Ornament Collector's Guide* has been updated to include all the new Keepsake Ornaments offered in 1988 and 1989. Of course, this includes the immensely popular Keepsake Miniature Ornaments, the latest technological wonders inside Keepsake Magic electronic ornaments, and the ornaments that were part of special Hallmark promotional programs such as Baby Celebrations and Open House.

As you explore this book, you'll discover that it's actually a history of ornament collecting. Before Hallmark introduced Keepsake Ornaments in 1973, people didn't have many decorating options when it came to ornaments. Most of us purchased boxes of plain glass balls and attempted to personalize our trees by trimming them with ornaments of one color or a combination of colors on alternate years.

The arrival of the Keepsake Ornament collection changed this situation dramatically. The designs were beautiful, and included a variety of subjects and art styles. We stopped buying ornaments in bulk and chose instead to collect Hallmark designs that reflected our own tastes, traditions, and lifestyles.

Now, many collectors count on Hallmark to offer ornaments each year that are meaningful, varied, and filled with intriguing surprises. And we haven't been disappointed yet!

Christmas ornaments have gone from being viewed as merely cute trinkets to being treasured as fine art objects. And no longer are they relegated to the tree only. Ornaments are displayed on shelves, mantels, and tabletops; on wall trees and bell pulls; in wreaths and floral arrangements; and in shadow boxes. Collectors have also discovered that many designs are suitable for decorating on other holidays such as Thanksgiving, Valentine's Day, and Easter.

Hallmark Keepsake Ornaments can be collected and cherished by the entire family. They're truly joy bringers and memory makers. As the numbers of Keepsake Ornament collectors grow, more and more local collector's clubs are being formed. The membership of the national club continues to swell — and for good reason — our sincere love for these unique ornaments.

Happy Collecting!

Clara Johnson Scroggins

Clara Johnson Scroggins

DESIGNING A TRADITION

The introduction of Hallmark Keepsake Ornaments in 1973 created a new look for the American Christmas tree and led to a meaningful tradition for millions of people — the tradition of collecting Keepsake Ornaments.

Before 1973, most American trees were trimmed primarily with plain glass balls. Hallmark offered people something more — a new way to decorate the tree as well as the entire home — by introducing ornaments that were varied in design and materials.

People enjoyed decorating their homes with these unique new ornaments so much that they began collecting them year after year. Keepsake Ornaments are now among the most widely collected in the country. The American tree has become a dazzling showcase of Keepsake designs that reflect not only the season's beloved symbols, but also individual tastes and lifestyles.

These introductory pages will trace the debut of popular new Keepsake Ornament designs and subjects that have appeared throughout Keepsake history. You'll be able to see the impact of these "firsts" on today's Keepsake Ornament line.

1973

The Keepsake Ornament premiere set the stage for collectibility. The '73 line featured ornaments with the first sentiment, year date and Property. It also had the first Collectible Series, which was a ball series featuring designs by Betsey Clark. All of these innovations, particularly series, continue to be of major interest to collectors. Since 1978, not one year has passed without the introduction of a new ornament series. There's even an active Betsey Clark ball series called "Home for Christmas."

1974

The spotlight was on Properties this year and in the two following years. Nearly every glass ball featured a design by a famous artist, including Hallmark artists. Properties remain an important part of the Keepsake offer because many ornament collectors also collect the works of their favorite designers.

1975

The handcrafted format — now the most popular with collectors — debuted in two collections: "Nostalgia Ornaments" and "Adorable Adornments." The subjects in these early groups — Santa and Mrs. Claus, a rocking horse, drummer boy, locomotive, Alpine scene, and Nativity — are as much in demand today as they were in 1975.

1976

Commemorative ornaments celebrate the special times and people in our lives. The first Keepsake commemorative was a ball ornament for "Baby's First Christmas." The number of commemorative captions increased greatly in the next few years, continuing on glass balls until 1979, when a handcrafted "Baby's First Christmas" ornament was introduced.

1977

Everyone loves PEANUTS®! Charles Schulz' gang joined the Keepsake family in 1977 and has made an annual appearance ever since. Both the '88 and '89 lines include two PEANUTS® designs — one glass ball and one handcrafted ornament.

1978

As long as there have been thimbles, there have been thimble collectors who were fascinated with these tiny and useful objects. The Keepsake Ornament artists incorporated this collectible into one of the very first handcrafted series. The "Thimble" series was one of the longest running and continued through 1989.

1979

When Santa Claus appeared in an antique car in 1979, Keepsake collectors knew the jolly old elf would be widening his horizons. In the '81 design, "Space Santa," he entered the space race, and in '82 and '83 enjoyed such sports as jogging and mountain climbing. These early lifestyle ornaments were forerunners of the contemporary lifestyle Santas seen in '88 and '89.

1980

The mystery and appeal of owls have made them valued collectibles through the ages. The first hand-crafted Keepsake Ornament version was the '80 "Christmas Owl." A wide variety of these special birds have followed this first design, including the 1989 bone china limited edition "Christmas is Peaceful." Some of the owl designs have featured puns such as the '86 "Happy Christmas to Owl."

continued on next page

1981

Even though penguins don't live at the North Pole, Santa can almost always find one in the Keepsake line. Since the first handcrafted penguin appeared in a 1981 ornament called "Perky Penguin," these appealing creatures have been delighting collectors. In fact, penguins star in two series: the '88 Keepsake Miniature "Penguin Pal," and '89 Keepsake Ornament "Winter Surprise."

1983

The 1986 limited edition, fine porcelain "Magical Unicorn" was one of the most sought after ornaments in Keepsake history. That lovely design had ancestors in earlier Keepsake lines. The first three-dimensional "Unicorn" appeared in 1983, in a porcelain design accented with gold.

1984

Politics and Christmas go together — at least in the Keepsake line. One of the first political ornaments was the 1984 "Uncle Sam," created to commemorate the election year. In 1988, two ornaments were mementos of the elections: "Americana Drum" and "Uncle Sam Nutcracker."

1982

Music is one of the loveliest joys of the season. Keepsake Ornaments have played favorite melodies since 1982 in designs that were offered in the Hallmark Musical and Gift Collections. (See Added Attractions.) The '89 Keepsake Magic line introduced two designs that combine music with light and motion.

1985

History repeated itself! The "firsts" in the '85 Keepsake Magic line nearly duplicated those of the original Keepsake Ornament line of 1973. The '85 Magic collection included the first dated design, the first Property, the first Collectible Series and the first commemorative. It's an interesting coincidence that underscores the continuing interest in collectibility.

1986

The year the ornaments talked! The first Keepsake "talky" was the plush "Chatty Penguin," which made a squeaky sound when you shook it. In '87, collectors discovered the even more talkative "Mistletoad." One of the most popular ornaments of the collection, this fellow opened his mouth and croaked a froggy greeting when you pulled the cord on the design.

1987

The '87 Christmas season was especially bright for collectors — in more ways than one! This Keepsake line was the first to include the CRAYOLA® Crayon Property. In response to the collectors' enthusiasm for this design, named "Bright Christmas Dreams," Keepsake Ornament planners started a "CRAYOLA® Crayon" Collector's Series in '89.

1988

When you touch the bounce toy in the '88 "Child's Third Christmas" ornament, you might think it could actually bounce. It can't, of course, but the bouncer was fashioned of a special flexible material that made it feel like a real ball. The material was so much fun to work with that the Keepsake artists used it to design a flexible, bendable "Rodney Reindeer" for 1989.

1989

All that glitters is perfect for the tree. The '89 line featured a unique, three-dimensional brass format. Layers of brass were curved to form the elegant flowing shapes of the "Festive Angel" and "Graceful Swan." The first brass Keepsake Ornament — a 1978 design called "Reindeer Chimes" — didn't look like brass at all. It was plated with chrome! Since then, brass has been etched, pierced, and embedded into acrylic.

KEEPSAKE MINIATURE ORNAMENTS DEBUT FOR COLLECTORS

Endearing, appealing, delicate, precious ...collectible. These are only some of the words collectors have used to describe Keepsake Miniature Ornaments.

Launched in 1988, this new collection was an instant hit with collectors. They loved the size, the quality, and most of all, the designs in the miniature ornament line.

Hallmark had been considering the idea of adding a line of miniature designs to the Keepsake family of ornaments for several years. But it was the enthusiasm of Hallmark sculptor Donna Lee that really set the plans in motion. Donna fashioned a group of miniature ornaments and a miniature tree for a design project.

"You can't find exquisite little ornaments anywhere," she said. "I knew they would be something our collectors would treasure."

Lee and the other Keepsake Ornament artists find working on the miniature line a very enjoyable though challenging experience.

"The major challenge is including as much detail in a really small design as you would in a larger ornament," Lee said. "We're constantly discovering what kinds of designs look best in the miniature size. Just because a certain shape or color looks attractive in a larger ornament doesn't mean it will have the same appeal in a smaller one."

In order to sculpt such minute detail, Lee often wears a magnifying lens attached to a headset. Other sculptors hold the ornament under large magnifying lenses attached to stands. Some of the ornaments are too tiny to hold at all!

"When we're sculpting original designs in wax, just one touch of your finger can blot out an entire side of a design," Lee explained. To avoid this kind of disaster, the artists often attach their wax originals to the end of a long stick. They hold the stick in one hand and sculpt with the other.

Shown two times larger than actual size to reveal the intricate details that make up these masterpieces in miniature.

Who says Keepsake Miniature Ornaments are just for the tree? Adorn yourself with these cherished collectibles. Their small scale is just right for accessories such as charm necklaces, drop earrings or laced with ribbon to barrettes. You may even want to stitch some of your favorites to a holiday sweatshirt. For best results, stitch on ribbon ties to secure your Keepsake Miniature Ornaments to the sweatshirt, then remove the ornaments before laundering or pressing.

Sculpting in miniature stretches the already considerable ingenuity of the Hallmark design staff. The artists use a variety of materials to create the detailing on the ornaments. Lee mentioned wire, string, tiny strips of paper and metal, beads, paper clips, nuts, dried leaves, tiny pinecones, wooden sticks, and chips — in other words — practically anything that can simulate the needed detail in a design.

Size is also crucial. The artists must constantly measure their designs to make sure they are not too large. Hallmark sculptor Bob Siedler came up with a handy way of measuring his designs. He took a piece of cardboard and cut out a square in the center. He then wrote measurements on all four sides of the square. When he suspends an ornament from the top of the cut-out, he can see exactly how large — or small — it is.

Although all of the artists have different methods for designing Keepsake Miniature Ornaments, they're all committed to creating ornaments that are worthy of the Keepsake name in uniqueness, appeal, and quality.

Hallmark designer Linda Sickman uses magnification as her way of judging the quality of a design. "If the ornament looks perfect under the magnifying lens," she said, "then I know I have the exact detail and finish I wanted in the design."

Collectors, through their letters and comments, have told Hallmark that the artists' efforts have resulted in a line that is wonderfully collectible. Indeed, the places collectors displayed miniature ornaments seem practically endless. In addition to every room in the home, ornaments were put in the foyer, gazebo, and even the sundeck. They also found their way into college dorm rooms, retirement homes, hospitals, and offices.

Hallmark planners created a miniature ornament offering that included everything collectors would need to display the new Keepsake Miniature Ornaments: a tree-topper, beaded garland, tiny glass balls, ornament hooks, and two kinds of miniature "Memory Trees." One of the trees was an artificial fir, and the other was a tree-shaped shadow box fashioned out of walnut. Both were designed by Hallmark artists to give the new ornaments an attractive and unique setting.

Many collectors have said that they plan to display their miniature ornaments year-round. This is exactly what artist Donna Lee hoped for when she first presented the idea for miniature ornaments to Hallmark management.

"Every design should create a sense of wonder," she said. "The ornaments are like jewels. They're something you cherish and like to look at year after year."

COLLECTOR'S CLUB BRINGS SURPRISES EVERY YEAR

We've got excitement!

That's what members say about the Hallmark Keepsake Ornament Collector's Club. Launched in 1987, the Club has heightened the fun and excitement of ornament collecting for more than 125,000 members.

Collectors enjoy being part of this special group of people who share a unique interest in Keepsake Ornaments. And they like to read about the ornament artists and other subjects of interest in the quarterly Club newsletter, the *Collector's Courier.*

But for many members, the most exciting part of belonging to the Collector's Club is receiving the annual Membership Kit.

Club members were surprised that the Kit contained so many different items.

Each 1987 Charter member received a personalized membership card, an ornament brochure, a Club folder and a Keepsake Ornament Registry.

The Registry, in particular, was fashioned in direct response to collectors' requests. Many collectors said they needed a handy place to make a list of their own ornaments. The Registry's pages are designed to hold ornament names and other information collectors may want to record.

The Club's sensitivity to members' needs is clearly reflected in the contents of the '87 Kit and of each Kit that followed.

Collectors told Hallmark that they like having items that are exclusive — items that only Club members can obtain.

To meet this need, the Club included an exclusive Keepsake Ornament in the '87 Membership Kit. Members were especially impressed with the beauty and exquisite detail of the Charter year design, "Wreath of Memories." Decorated with tiny reproductions of Keepsake Ornaments from past years, this Club ornament was personally meaningful.

The 1988 Membership Kit continued the excitement! Members were delighted with the '88 Club ornament, "Our Clubhouse" and the exclusive members only Christmas cards featuring a photo of Keepsake Ornaments.

In addition to these items and the annual Kit contents such as the membership card, the '88 Kit contained a carefully designed *Keepsake Ornament*

A collecting tradition that is growing in popularity is starting a Keepsake Ornament collection for a child. The decorating idea below shows you how Keepsake Ornaments can be used to add enchantment to a nursery all year-round. This idea features from left to right: the 1986 "Wynken, Blynken and Nod" handcrafted Keepsake Ornament, the 1988 "Baby's First Christmas" Keepsake Magic Ornament, and the 1987 "Heavenly Harmony" musical Keepsake Ornament.

Soft and sweet is this vignette of beloved Keepsake Ornaments. Reminscent of a Victorian boudoir, this tabletop display highlights ornaments from the 1984 and 1985 collections. This enchanting grouping is ideal for a Valentine's Day decoration or a year-round display for the romantic at heart.

For a gala dinner, let the shimmering beauty of brass and dimensional brass Keepsake Ornaments set a festive mood. Brass ornaments are hung from frothy lace bows on the back of each chair. Dimensional brass ornaments such as the 1989 "Graceful Swan" and "Festive Angel," as well as the 1983 "First Christmas Together" brass locket, add a warm glow to the tabletop. For truly special occasions, you may wish to give each guest an ornament for a keepsake.

Good things come in small packages —
especially when those packages are bedecked
with Keepsake Ornaments. The lucky gift
recipient will enjoy getting an extra gift, and
your present is sure to be the hit of the baby
shower or housewarming party!

This is such a cute idea that it's also a fun
way to display Keepsake Ornaments. Simply
gather together empty boxes, gift wrap, gift
bags, ribbons, tissue paper and trims, plus some
of your prized Keepsake and Keepsake
Miniature Ornaments. As you can see by the
photos, just grouping some ornaments around
the packages adds a lot of charm. Then, you can
use your cheerful creations as little tabletop
tableaus for parties, entryways or even hospital
rooms.

A small space is just the right spot for a
miniature shelf decorated with Keepsake Miniature
Ornaments. You can leave this shelf up year-round
and create a new display by simply changing the
ornaments on view.

Yippee-tie-yay! Add a little Southwest flavor to your home with Keepsake Ornaments. Start with a terra cotta bowl filled with sand and a few cacti (some real and some made of construction paper). Add a festive, fiesta touch with a bare branch tree bedecked with the 1989 "Feliz Navidad" piñata design. Next, add Keepsake Ornaments that complete the theme. From left to right: the 1989 "Cactus Cowboy," the 1988 "Feliz Navidad" burro, the 1983 "Hitchhiking Santa" and the 1989 "Kringle Coach" add atmosphere. Other Keepsake Ornaments that work well in a Southwest-inspired display are the first edition of the "Windows of the World" series (1985, "Feliz Navidad") and the spring-action "Doc Holiday" from the 1987 Christmas Pizzazz Collection.

Once you try displaying Keepsake Ornaments in other ways than hanging them on a tree, you'll discover all sorts of imaginative ways to showcase your "treasures." Many spaces ideal for displaying these colorful designs already exist in your home. Take a second look at a bookcase or china cabinet and eureka! the perfect niche for your collection.

For the young and the young-at-heart, decorate your home with everyone's favorite jolly old elf — Santa Claus! From the first offering in 1973 to the present collection, Keepsake Ornaments have offered a fascinating variety of Santa ornaments. From the dignity of St. Nicholas to the merriment of Kris Kringle, these popular Yuletide designs add just the right touch to theme trees, garlands, mantels, packages, and more! No wonder he is the most popular character in the Keepsake line, having appeared in over 180 designs.

THE 1973 COLLECTION

The year 1973 heralded a new dimension in Christmas tree decorating. Until then, Americans had few real choices when decorating their holiday trees. Red, blue, green, silver, and gold glass ball ornaments were the standard. The only way one could "dress up" the family tree was to use tinsel, angel hair, flocking, or garlands of some type.

But in 1973, Hallmark Cards introduced its newest product line — a selection of eighteen specially designed Keepsake Ornaments. Drawing from the talents of its large staff of artists, Hallmark offered six glass ball ornaments with decorative bands and twelve yarn ornaments. More expensive than the basic red, blue, green, silver, and gold balls (and more decorative), Hallmark ornaments were anything but run-of-the-mill. They definitely were destined to become keepsakes. And with this simple beginning, a new holiday tradition of ornament collecting was born.

The 1973 collection included, in the glass ball format, two Betsey Clark designs. One was dated and was first in the series of Betsey Clark ornaments (the longest collectible series made by Hallmark). Another Betsey Clark design was not dated. The four remaining ball ornaments included a manger scene, a Christmas Is Love theme, a drawing of elves, and a design featuring Santa with some of his helpers. The charmingly detailed Yarn ornaments, between four and five inches tall, all retailed for $1.25 (except the Soldier at $1).

Betsey Clark (Musicians), Betsey Clark (First Edition)

Manger Scene, Christmas is Love, Santa with Elves, Elves

Yarn Ornaments: *Mr. Santa, Mrs. Santa, Mr. Snowman, Mrs. Snowman, Angel, Elf, Choir Boy, Soldier, Little Girl, Boy Caroler, Green Girl, Blue Girl*

Betsey Clark

Five wistful little girls are caroling around a sparse Christmas tree.

White Glass, 3¼″ diam.
250XHD100-2, $2.50 ☐

Betsey Clark—First Edition

On the first Betsey Clark design bearing a year date, one little girl is feeding a deer; the other is cuddling a lamb. Caption: "1973."

White Glass, 3¼″ diam.
250XHD110-2, $2.50 ☐

Manger Scene

Ornately designed scene on deep red background shows the stable at Bethlehem with the Holy Family and two sheep.

White Glass, 3¼″ diam.
250XHD102-2, $2.50 ☐

Christmas Is Love

Front — two angels playing mandolins in a design executed in shades of green and lavender. Caption: "Christmas is love — Christmas is you."

White Glass, 3¼″ diam.
250XHD106-2, $2.50 ☐

Santa with Elves

Balding, graying elves are busy with Christmas activities.

White Glass, 3¼″ diam.
250XHD101-5, $2.50 ☐

Elves

Elves are enjoying the winter sport of ice skating.

White Glass, 3½″ diam.
250XHD103-5, $2.50 ☐

Yarn Ornaments

Each yarn figure measures 4½″ tall with retail price of $1.25 except for the soldier which was $1.00

125XHD74-5	Mr. Santa	☐
125XHD75-2	Mrs. Santa	☐
125XHD76-5	Mr. Snowman	☐
125XHD77-2	Mrs. Snowman	☐
125XHD78-5	Angel	☐
125XHD79-2	Elf	☐
125XHD80-5	Choir Boy	☐
100XHD81-2	Soldier	☐
125XHD82-5	Little Girl	☐
125XHD83-2	Boy Caroler	☐
125XHD84-5	Green Girl	☐
125XHD85-2	Blue Girl	☐

THE 1974 COLLECTION

The tremendous popularity of the 1973 Keepsake Ornaments prompted Hallmark to offer sixteen new designs in 1974.

Dating became more common in 1974 and three ornaments (including the second Betsey Clark 3¼″ ornament) carried a holiday date. In addition, Hallmark offered new packaging and introduced two new sizes — 2¼″ and 1¾″ ball ornaments. The new smaller sizes were offered in sets of two or four, depending upon the ornament design.

Norman Rockwell

On one side Santa is wearing an apron with pockets filled with tools. He is napping in a chair while elves on his lap, shoulder, and all around him are trying to complete the dollhouse that he was building. The other side, "Santa's Good Boys," shows two pajama-clad children engrossed in whatever Santa is telling them.

White Glass, 3¼″
250QX111-1, $2.50 ☐

Norman Rockwell

Father has that "special" tree over his shoulder and his son carries an ax as they triumphantly return from the woods. Caption: "1974."

White Glass, 3¼″ diam.
250QX106-1, $2.50 ☐

Betsey Clark - Second Edition

Orchestra and choir of Betsey Clark children are making music. A little girl directs, a boy plays a bass fiddle, a girl plays the banjo, and three are caroling. A garland of holly circles the ornament just above their heads. This is the second dated design in the Betsey Clark series. Caption: "1974."

White Glass, 3¼″ diam.
250QX108-1, $2.50 ☐

Charmers

A child decorates a tree; three children are caroling; a girl seems to be reaching for a little bird perched on a branch. Each scene is circled with a garland. Caption: "1974."

White Glass, 3¼″ diam.
250QX109-1, $2.50 ☐

Snowgoose

A powerful snowgoose flies above white capped waves with a sailboat in the background. Inspired by Paul Gallico's book, *The Snowgoose.*

White Glass, 3¼″ diam.
250QX107-1, $2.50 ☐

Norman Rockwell (Santa), Norman Rockwell (Christmas Tree)

Betsey Clark (Second Edition), Charmers

The Snowgoose, Angel

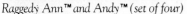
Raggedy Ann™ and Andy™ (set of four)   Little Miracles (set of four)

Buttons and Bo (set of two), Currier and Ives (set of two)

Yarn Ornaments: Santa, Angel, Elf, Snowman, Soldier, Mrs. Santa

Angel

A beautiful Renaissance-type angel is featured on the front and back.

White Glass, 3¼" diam.
250QX110-1, $2.50   ☐

Raggedy Ann™ and Raggedy Andy™

Famous pair get ready for Christmas by trimming their tree and exchanging gifts with friends. All ornaments are trimmed at bottom and top with holly garland.

White Glass, 1¾" diam.
450QX114-1, 4 per box $4.50   ☐

Little Miracles

Angelic little boy and his rabbit playmate are pictured in four Christmas scenes.

White Glass, 1¾" diam.
450QX115-1, 4 per box $4.50   ☐

Buttons & Bo

On one side Buttons & Bo are entwined in ribbon while wrapping a gift. The other side depicts Buttons & Bo leaning against each other with Buttons holding a poinsettia blossom.

White Glass, 2¼" diam.
350QX113-1, 2 per box $3.50   ☐

Currier & Ives

Two winter scenes picture a snow-blanketed farmstead and horse-drawn sleigh passing a colonial home.

White Glass, 2¼" diam.
350QX112-1, 2 per box $3.50   ☐

Yarn Ornaments

Six colorfully detailed yarn character ornaments, approximately 4¾" tall, were offered in 1974 at $1.50 each.

150QX100-1	Mrs Santa	☐
150QX101-1	Elf	☐
150QX102-1	Soldier	☐
150QX103-1	Angel	☐
150QX104-1	Snowman	☐
150QX105-1	Santa	☐

THE 1975 COLLECTION

In 1975, Hallmark expanded its Christmas ornament line to thirty-two models and introduced two new design formats — decorated satin ball ornaments and handcrafted ornaments. Two handcrafted groupings were offered: figurines call "Adorable Adornments" and "Handcrafted Nostaglia Ornaments."

The new satin ball ornaments featured a decorated band. Both of the handcrafted groups were made of sturdy, molded material and were individually hand painted. The colorful figurines had lively expressions, and the Nostalgia collection was distinguished by its antique wood look. Raggedy Ann and Andy™ were added to the Yarn Ornaments collection during this year.

Property Ornaments

Betsey Clark
Four different scenes of Betsey Clark children and the animals and birds associated with Christmas adorn fronts of this set. Backs are dated "Christmas 1975."

White Satin, 2" diam.
450QX168-1, 4 per box $4.50 ☐

Betsey Clark
These paired motifs show a stocking-capped little girl on one ornament and two struggling young skaters on the other. On the backs of both, "Christmas 1975" is surrounded by stars.

White Satin, 2½" diam.
350QX167-1, 2 per box $3.50 ☐

Betsey Clark
Appealing, pajama-clad toddler says bedtime prayers framed by a ring of stars. Caption: "1975."

White Satin, 3" diam.
250QX163-1, $2.50 ☐

Betsey Clark — Third Edition
Front — three little girls dressed in pink, blue, and yellow calico are singing from a songbook they are holding. Back — the book from the front with "Christmas 1975" on the cover. This is the third ornament in the Betsey Clark series.

White Glass, 3¼" diam.
300QX133-1, $3.00 ☐

Currier & Ives
Panoramic snowscene of farmhouse and farm buildings.

White Satin, 3" diam.
250QX164-1, $2.50 ☐

Betsey Clark (set of four), Betsey Clark (set of two)

Betsey Clark Satin Ball, Betsey Clark (Third Edition)

Currier and Ives Satin Ball, Currier and Ives (set of two)

Raggedy Ann™ and Andy™ (set of two), Raggedy Ann™ Satin Ball,

Norman Rockwell Satin Ball,
Norman Rockwell Glass Ball

Charmers, Marty Links™

Currier & Ives

Two Currier & Ives winter scenes are shown on this boxed pair: one of an old mill, the other of a merry group of Victorian ice skaters.

White Glass, 2¼" diam.
400QX137-1, 2 per box $4.00 ☐

Raggedy Ann™ and Raggedy Andy™

Front — the colorful pair are seated side-by-side in a green wreath which is tied at the top with a red bow. Back — they hold "Merry Christmas" banner. Front of second ornament — they decorate their Christmas tree. Back — garland of holly leaves circles "Christmas 1975."

White Glass, 2¼" diam.
400QX138-1, 2 per box $4.00 ☐

Raggedy Ann™

Front — Raggedy Ann™ in a ring of poinsettias. Caption on the back: "Christmas 1975" circled by poinsettias.

White Satin, 3" diam.
250QX165-1, $2.50 ☐

Norman Rockwell

Front — Santa writes in "Good Boys" book while checking on them through a telescope. Back — Santa emerges from a chimney carrying his bag of toys.

White Satin, 3" diam.
250QX166-1, $2.50 ☐

Norman Rockwell

Front — two small boys are asleep in a wingback chair as Santa peeks from behind. Back — youngster kneels at his bed to say a good-night prayer. Caption: "1975."

White Glass, 3¼" diam.
300QX134-1, $3.00 ☐

Charmers

Front — tiny barefoot girl in a deep rose-colored dress stands among boughs laden with ornaments. Back — bough and ornaments with "1975" on large center ornament.

White Glass, 3½" diam.
300QX135-1, $3.00 ☐

Marty Links™

Front — on a beautiful green background, a little girl is kissing an embarrassed little boy's hand as he stands under the mistletoe. Back — in mistletoe wreath center, "Merry Christmas 1975."

White Glass, 3¼" diam.
300QX136-1, $3.00 ☐

Buttons & Bo

In this coordinated grouping, Buttons &
Bo engage in a variety of Christmas activities.
The ornaments are dated on the back.

White Glass, 1¾″ diam.
500QX139-1, 4 per box $5.00   ☐

Little Miracles

Charming set depicts a wee cherub and his
forest friends sharing the joys of Christmas.

White Glass, 1¾″ diam.
500QX140-1, 4 per box $5.00   ☐

Yarn Ornaments

Raggedy Ann and Andy™ joined this
group of deftly styled yarn characters for the
first time in 1975. All are 4½″ tall,
individually packaged, and priced at $1.75.

175QX121-1	*Raggedy Ann™*	☐
175QX122-1	*Raggedy Andy™*	☐
175QX123-1	*Drummer Boy*	☐
175QX124-1	*Santa*	☐
175QX125-1	*Mrs. Santa*	☐
175QX126-1	*Little Girl*	☐

Handcrafted Ornaments

Nostalgia Ornaments

The Nostalgia Ornaments are "rings"
crafted of sturdy, molded material and
individually hand-painted to resemble
antique wood. Motifs evoke memories of
Christmas long ago. All are 3¼″ in
diameter and priced at $3.50.

350QX127-1	*Locomotive (dated)*	☐
350QX128-1	*Rocking Horse*	☐
350QX129-1	*Santa & Sleigh*	☐
350QX130-1	*Drummer Boy*	☐
350QX131-1	*Peace on Earth (dated)*	☐
350QX132-1	*Joy*	☐

Adorable Adornments

Six individually hand-painted characters
of intricate design were another first created
by Hallmark in 1975. Each are 3½″ tall
and $2.50

250QX155-1	*Santa*	☐
250QX156-1	*Mrs. Santa*	☐
250QX157-1	*Betsey Clark*	☐
250QX159-1	*Raggedy Ann™*	☐
250QX160-1	*Raggedy Andy™*	☐
250QX161-1	*Drummer Boy*	☐

Buttons and Bo (set of four)   *Little Miracles (set of four)*

Yarn Ornaments: Drummer Boy, Raggedy Ann™, Raggedy Andy™, Little Girl, Santa
Mrs. Santa,

Nostalgia Ornaments: Locomotive, Rocking Horse, Santa and Sleigh

Adorable Adornments: Santa, Mrs. Santa, Drummer Boy

Nostalgia Ornaments: Drummer Boy, Peace on Earth, Joy

Adorable Adornments: Raggedy Ann™, Raggedy Andy™, Betsey Clark

THE 1976 COLLECTION

In 1976, Hallmark added a fourth dimension to its handcrafted ornament offerings — movement. Called "Twirl-Abouts," the unique ornaments had a three-dimensional figure in the center that rotated on a brass pin. Three of the four different Twirl-About designs were dated.

To mark the Bicentennial year, Hallmark also offered a special commemorative ornament in 1976. The glass ball ornament featured Hallmark Charmers characters in 1776 dress and retailed for $2.50.

Also in 1976, Hallmark introduced the Baby's First Christmas ornament, a personalized design that in future years would prove to be the most popular captioned ornament in the Keepsake line.

The first Baby's First Christmas commemorative ornament.

First Commemorative Ornament

Baby's First Christmas

The original Baby's First Christmas ornament, designed to commemorate the birth of babies born in 1976, was a record best seller and introduced a new Christmas tradition to many families. Front — animals and birds are placing gifts for baby under the decorated tree. Caption: "Baby's First Christmas." Back — animals and birds visit smiling baby. Caption: "1976."

White Satin, 3″ diam.
250QX211-1, $2.50   □

Bicentennial Commemoratives: Bicentennial '76 commemorative, Bicentennial Charmers Colonial Children (set of two)

Betsey Clark (Fourth Edition), Betsey Clark Satin Ball, Betsey Clark (set of three)

Bicentennial Commemoratives

Bicentennial '76 Commemorative

Charmers dressed in the fashions of Christmas 1776, grace the Hallmark Bicentennial special commemorative ornament. Both the ornament and its package are marked "1976 Commemorative."

White Satin, 3″ diam.
250QX203-1, $2.50 ☐

Bicentennial Charmers

Front — three Charmers in colonial costume admire a tiny Christmas tree in front of their log cabin homes. Back — a Charmer girl gathers holly leaves. Caption: "Merry Christmas 1976."

White Glass, 3¼″ diam.
300QX198-1, $3.00 ☐

Colonial Children

Front — a boy and girl in colonial clothing have made and dressed a snowman. Back — garland, bird, flag, and "Christmas 1976." Front of second design — a group of colonial children brings home a Christmas tree. Back — garland, Christmas tree, squirrel, and "Merry Christmas 1976."

White Glass, 2¼″ diam.
400QX208-1, 2 per box $4.00 ☐

Property Ornaments

Betsey Clark — Fourth Edition

Front — two little dressed-up, bonnet-clad girls are framed by floral and ribbon circle. Back — wintry scene of snow-covered homes in a countryside setting. Caption: "Christmas 1976." This is fourth ornament in the Betsey Clark series.

White Glass, 3¼″ diam.
300QX195-1, $3.00 ☐

Betsey Clark

Front — little girl warms herself at a potbellied stove. Back — "Christmas 1976."

White Satin, 3″ diam.
250QX210-1, $2.50 ☐

Betsey Clark

The three front designs are: Santa and little girl caroling; little girl snow skiing; and a fiddling duet of children. All are dated on the back.

White Satin, 2″ diam.
450QX218-1, 3 per box $4.50 ☐

Currier & Ives

Front — a horse-drawn sleigh and skaters on a pond in front of a snow-covered colonial house. A farmyard in winter is shown. Back — Caption: "To Commemorate Christmas 1976."

White Satin, 3" diam.
250QX209-1, $2.50

Currier & Ives

Two snow scenes entitled "American Winter Scene" and "Winter Pastime." Caption: "To Commemorate Christmas 1976."

White Glass, 3¼" diam.
300QX197-1, $3.00

Norman Rockwell

Front — Santa is recuperating from his travels; it's "December 25." Back — Santa feeds his reindeers. Caption: "Christmas 1976."

White Glass, 3¼" diam.
300QX196-1, $3.00

Rudolph and Santa

Front — Rudolph with his "nose so bright" frolics in the snow as Santa watches. Caption: "Rudolph the Red-Nosed Reindeer." Back — a green garland and "Christmas 1976."

White Satin, 2½" diam.
250QX213-1, $2.50

Raggedy Ann™

Front — Raggedy Ann™ is hanging stockings on the decorated mantle of a glowing fireplace. Back — the stockings are filled, toys from Santa surround the fireplace, and "Merry Christmas 1976" is across the top.

White Satin, 2½" diam.
250QX212-1, $2.50

Currier and Ives Satin Ball, Currier and Ives Glass Ball

Norman Rockwell, Rudolph and Santa, Raggedy Ann™

Marty Links™ (set of two), Happy the Snowman, Charmers

Marty Links™

Front — smiling girl dressed in red places a gift under the tree. Back — red ball ornament with "Merry Christmas 1976." Front of second design — the "stockings are hung by the chimney with care" and mouse is admonished to be quiet. Back — a bow-topped holly wreath centered with "Noel 1976."

White glass, 2½" diam.
400QX207-1, 2 per box $4.00 ☐

Happy the Snowman

Front — on a dark green background the Happy Snowman enjoys the red birds and snowflakes around him. Back — two Happy Snowmen and "Happy Holidays." Front — companion piece shows three snowmen, snowflakes, and holly. Back — three Happy Snowmen one holding a ribbon banner bearing "Merry Christmas."

White Satin, 2½" diam.
350QX216-1, 2 per box $3.50 ☐

Charmers

Front of first design: — a boy watches his reflection in a pool. Front of second design: — little Charmer preparing holiday food over glowing campfire. Both are captioned "Christmas 1976."

White Satin, 2½" diam.
350QX215-1, 2 per box $3.50 ☐

Decorative Ball Ornaments

Chickadees

Front — two chickadees perch on a bough. Back — one bird perched on a bough. Caption: "Christmas 1976."

White Glass, 2⅝" diam.
225QX204-1, $2.25 ☐

Cardinals

Front — two nesting cardinals. Back — one cardinal on spray of evergreen. Caption: "Christmas 1976."

White Glass, 2⅝" diam.
225QX205-1, $2.25 ☐

Chickadees, Cardinals

Yesteryears Ornaments: Train, Santa, Partridge, Drummer Boy

Twirl-About Handcrafted Ornaments: Angel, Santa, Partridge, Soldier

Handcrafted Ornaments

Yesteryears

This collection of four, three-dimensional ornaments in "wood look" designs are intricately hand painted to enhance their "old world" character. Newly designed packaging included a gift tag with each ornament. Each ornament was year dated, and was priced at $5.00. Sizes vary from 2¾" to 4" tall.

500QX181-1	Train	☐
500QX182-1	Santa	☐
500QX183-1	Partridge	☐
500QX184-1	Drummer Boy	☐

Twirl-Abouts

Twirl-Abouts — three-dimensional ornaments centered with rotating figures on a brass pin — were introduced in 1976. Hand-painted, they are highly sought by collectors. Ranging from 3½" to 4" tall, all were priced at $4.50. Angel, partridge, and soldier bear year dates.

450QX171-1	Angel	☐
450QX172-1	Santa	☐
450QX173-1	Soldier	☐
450QX174-1	Partridge	☐

Tree Treats

Tree treats that look good enough to eat were new in 1976. Four ornaments of material resembling baker's dough are another choice for variety and spice in Christmas tree decorations. Tree Treats vary in size from 2¾" to 3⅝" tall and were priced at $3.00. Shepherd and Santa captions: "Season's Greetings 1976." Angel and Reindeer captions: "Merry Christmas 1976."

300QX175-1	Shepherd	☐
300QX176-1	Angel	☐
300QX177-1	Santa	☐
300QX178-1	Reindeer	☐

Tree Treats: Shepherd, Angel, Santa, Reindeer

Nostalgia Ornaments: Drummer Boy, Locomotive, Rocking Horse, Peace on Earth

Nostalgia Ornaments

The four reissues of the extremely popular Nostalgia Ornaments introduced the previous year had slight design modifications. Locomotive and Peace on Earth were captioned "Christmas 1976."

400QX128-1	Rocking Horse	☐
400QX130-1	Drummer Boy	☐
400QX222-1	Locomotive	☐
400QX223-1	Peace on Earth	☐

Yarn Ornaments

This merry group of six returned in 1976 with very minor changes. All are 4½" tall, individually packaged, and priced at $1.75. (See 1975 Annual Collection.)

175QX121-1	Raggedy Ann™
175QX122-1	Raggedy Andy™
175QX123-1	Drummer Boy
175QX124-1	Santa
175QX125-1	Mrs. Santa
175QX126-1	Caroler

THE 1977 COLLECTION

The year 1977 was one of tremendous expansion for the Hallmark Keepsake Ornament Collection. Three new ornament formats — sewn ornaments with silk-screened designs, acrylic ornaments, and ornaments with the look of stained glass — were introduced. A new decorative cap, with a design exclusive to Hallmark, appeared on glass ball ornaments, and two new colors — gold and chrome — appeared for the first time in the glass ball ornament line.

New commemorative ornaments were offered for Granddaughter, Grandmother, Mother, Love, Grandson, and New Home. And 1977 was the only year Hallmark offered ball ornaments with regional scenes and die cast metal snowflakes.

The Betsey Clark ball ornament (350QX264-2) for this year is especially hard to find. Initially, Hallmark had decided not to offer a Betsey Clark ornament in 1977. Consumer demand was high, however, and the ornament was quickly offered to retailers in August. Due to the delay in production, only a fraction of the normal quantity was distributed.

Commemoratives

Baby's First Christmas
Baby, surrounded by toys, hugs a stuffed bear. Caption: "Baby's First Christmas" and "1977."

White Satin, 3¼" diam.
350QX131-5, $3.50 ☐

Granddaughter
Little girl skates on a pond flanked by trees. Caption: "A Granddaughter is a gift whose worth cannot be measured except by the heart."

White Satin, 3¼" diam.
350QX208-2, $3.50 ☐

Grandson
Front — Santa and toys on a deep blue background. Caption: "A Grandson is…a joy bringer…a memory maker…a Grandson is love."

White Satin, 3½" diam.
350QX209-5, $3.50 ☐

Mother
A motif of pink roses and green holly circle the white glass globe. Caption: "In a Mother's heart, there is love…the very heart of Christmas."

White Glass, 3¼" diam.
350QX261-5, $3.50 ☐

Grandmother
Bordered band encloses a basket of Christmas flowers. Caption: "Grandmother is another word for love."

Gold Glass, 3¼" diam.
350QX260-2, $3.50 ☐

Baby's First Christmas, Granddaughter, Grandson

Mother, Grandmother

First Christmas Together, Love, New Home

First Christmas Together

Front — beautiful Christmas-red background with white circle inset showing two cardinals perched on bare branches. Back — date and caption printed in gold. Caption: "1977" and "Our First Christmas Together."

White Satin, 3¼" diam.
350QX132-2, $3.50

Love

Front — stained glass window look incorporating "Christmas 1977." Caption: "Love is a golden gift…cherished above all life's treasures."

Gold Glass, 3¼" diam.
350QX262-2, $3.50

For Your New Home

Front — holiday-decorated red house with 1977 "doormat," patchwork flowers, and checkered border. Back — patchwork flowers and large red heart enclosing caption. Caption: "Christmas fills a home with warmth and love…and memories that last forever.

Gold Glass, 3¼" diam.
350QX263-5, $3.50

Property Ornaments

Charmers

Flowers and greenery surround four little children caroling. Caption: "We wish you a Merry Christmas. 1977."

Gold Glass, 3¼" diam.
350QX153-5, $3.50

Currier & Ives

Shows the Currier & Ives paintings "The Old Grist Mill" and "Trotting Cracks on the Snow." Caption: "1977."

White Satin, 3¼" diam.
350QX130-2, $3.50

Norman Rockwell

Four favorite Rockwell designs of Christmas activities are reproduced in separate panels. Caption: "Christmas 1977."

White Glass, 3¼" diam.
350QX151-5, $3.50

Charmers, Currier and Ives, Norman Rockwell

Disney Satin Ball, Disney (set of two)

DISNEY
Mickey's head, framed by a wreath, is flanked by Donald Duck and Goofy. Caption: "Merry Christmas 1977."

White Satin, 3¼" diam.
350QX133-5, $3.50 ☐

DISNEY
Design 1: Mickey Mouse in a Santa suit gives Minnie Mouse her Christmas gift. Caption: "Merry Christmas." Design 2: Donald Duck pulls Huey, Luey, and Duey on a present-laden sled. Caption: "Happy Holidays."

White Satin, 2¼" diam.
400QX137-5, 2 per box $4.00 ☐

Betsey Clark—Fifth Edition
By popular demand the 1977 Betsey Clark ornament was added to the line at the last minute. This design is particularly scarce due to a limited production run. Front — three carolers around a songbook. Back — little girl feeding the birds. Caption: "The truest joys of Christmas come from deep inside" and "Christmas 1977."

White Glass, 3¼" diam.
350QX264-2, $3.50 ☐

Betsey Clark (Fifth Edition)

PEANUTS® Glass Ball, PEANUTS® Satin Ball, PEANUTS® (set of two)

PEANUTS® Collection

In 1977, the PEANUTS® gang from Charles Schulz's world-famous cartoon strip was introduced by Hallmark as exclusive additions to the Keepsake Ornament line. Glass and satin ornaments were cleverly packaged in SNOOPY'S Christmas-decorated doghouse.

PEANUTS®
Front — Charlie Brown and his sister Sally watch the empty stockings hanging from the fireplace. A decorated tree is in the background. Back — Schroeder plays the piano as Lucy presents him with a gift. Caption: "A watched stocking never fills" and "Merry Christmas."

White Glass, 2⅝" diam.
250QX162-2, $2.50 ☐

PEANUTS®
Charlie Brown and Lucy have built a snowman who holds a snow shovel. SNOOPY is tangled in Christmas tree lights while Woodstock dressed as Santa stands on a gift. Both are watching the Christmas tree. Caption: "1977."

White Satin, 3¼" diam.
350QX135-5, $3.50 ☐

PEANUTS®
Design 1: SNOOPY as Santa is being pulled in the sleigh by Woodstock and his flock. Design 2: Charlie Brown, Linus, Woodstock, SNOOPY, and Peppermint Patty are building a snowman, having a snowball fight, and ice skating.

White Glass, 2¼" diam.
400QX163-5, 2 per box $4.00 ☐

Grandma Moses
Two beautiful New England village snowscenes from the Grandma Moses paintings "Sugartime" and "Green Sleigh" are shown. A pamphlet giving the history of Grandma Moses and her beloved paintings was included with each gift packaged ornament.

White Glass, 3¼" diam.
350QX150-2, $3.50 ☐

Grandma Moses (Shown with enclosure card)

Christmas Expressions Collection: Bell, Ornaments, Mandolin, Wreath

The Beauty of America Collection: Mountains, Desert, Seashore, Wharf

Rabbit, Squirrel

Christmas Mouse, Stained Glass

Christmas Expressions Collection

Bell

Beautifully decorated bell blanketed with flowers and festooned with ribbons. Caption: "I heard the bells on Christmas Day/ Their old familiar carols play/ And wild and sweet, the words repeat/ Of peace on earth, good will to men. Henry Wadsworth Longfellow."

White Glass, 3¼" diam.
350QX154-2, $3.50 ☐

Ornaments

Banded ornament has beautiful array of Christmas ornaments with evergreens, ribbons and bows. Caption: "The spirit of Christmas is peace…the message of Christmas is love. Marjorie Frances Ames."

White Glass, 3¼" diam.
350QX155-5, $3.50 ☐

Mandolin

A mandolin and horns are nestled among Christmas greenery. Caption: "Sing a song of seasons; Something bright in all…Robert Louis Stevenson."

White Glass, 3¼" diam.
350QX157-5, $3.50 ☐

Wreath

A magnificent green wreath is bedecked with colorful ribbons and bows. Caption: "Christmas is a special time./ A season set apart — / A warm and glad remembering time,/ A season of the heart. Thomas Malloy."

White Glass, 3¼" diam.
350QX156-2, $3.50 ☐

The Beauty of America Collection

Mountains

Majestic snowcapped mountains with snow on the roofs of homes seen in the valley. Caption: "The spirit of Christmas is peace…the message of Christmas is love."

White Glass, 2⅝" diam.
250QX158-2, $2.50 ☐

Desert

A desert mission and a golden sunset. Caption: "Ring out Christmas Bells…and let all the world hear your joyful song."

White Glass, 2⅝" diam.
250QX159-5, $2.50 ☐

Seashore

Palm trees on a sandy shore, blue skies, and a sailboat regatta. Caption: "Christmas is — the company of good friends, the warmth of goodwill, and the memory of good times."

White Glass, 2⅝" diam.
250QX160-2, $2.50 ☐

Wharf

Front — tranquil winter scene of homes near the wharf. Back — oceanside view of lighthouse. Caption: "Christmas…when the world stands silent and the spirit of hope touches every heart."

White Glass, 2⅝" diam.
250QX161-5, $2.50 ☐

Decorative Ball Ornaments

Rabbit

A rabbit is engrossed with a little bird on a broken tree limb. Caption: "Nature's ever-changing beauty brings never-ending joy. Karl Lawrence."

White Satin, 2⅝" diam.
250QX139-5, $2.50 ☐

Squirrel

A little squirrel seems to be lucky — he has found food in the snow. A cardinal watches. Caption: "Each moment of the year has its own beauty…Emerson."

White Satin, 2⅝" diam.
250QX138-2, $2.50 ☐

Christmas Mouse

On soft blue background, Mr. and Mrs. Mouse put the finishing touches to their Christmas tree. Caption: "Tinsel and lights make the season so bright."

White Satin, 3¼" diam.
350QX134-2, $3.50 ☐

Stained Glass

The sleeve design is in the look of Art Deco stained glass. Caption: "Merry Christmas 1977."

Chrome Glass, 3¼" diam.
350QX152-2, $3.50 ☐

Colors of Christmas

Stained Glass Look

Four designs with the jeweled colors of
leaded stained glass were introduced to the
line in 1977. Made of acrylic, each
measures 3¼" in diameter, with price of
$3.50, each. All except the bell bear year
date, 1977.

350QX200-2   Bell
350QX201-5   Joy
350QX202-2   Wreath
350QX203-5   Candle

Holiday Highlights Collection

*A collection of four unbreakable clear
acrylic ornaments with the look of hand engraved
crystal featured scenes and messages
reflecting traditional Christmas sentiments.*

Joy

Large letters spelling "JOY," with the
center "O" filled with fruit. Background is
delicate scrolling. Caption: "JOY 1977."

Acrylic, 3¼" diam.
350QX310-2, $3.50

Peace on Earth

A snug village scene with snow-covered
houses, pine trees, and a church in the center
with its spire reaching for the moonlit sky.
Caption: "Peace on earth, good will toward
men. 1977."

Acrylic, 3¼" diam.
350QX311-5, $3.50

Drummer Boy

A drummer boy marches as he beats the
drum. Caption: "Rum-pa-pum-pum"
repeated four times around the border.

Acrylic, 3¼" diam.
350QX312-2, $3.50

Star

The star at the top casts etched beams of
light that radiate over the ornament's surface.
Caption: "Once for a shining hour heaven
touched earth."

Acrylic, 3¼" diam.
350QX313-5, $3.50

Colors of Christmas: Bell, Candle, Joy, Wreath

Holiday Highlights: Joy, Peace, Drummer Boy, Star

Snowflake Collection

Metal Ornaments

Snowflake Collection

A set of four 2⅛" snowflake die-cast in lightweight, chrome plated zinc were cleverly packaged in peek-through gift box which was accompanied by its own mailing box. This is the only year the snowflake set was offered.

Chrome Plated Zinc, 2⅛" diam.
500QX210-2, 4 per box $5.00 ☐

Twirl-About Collection

Snowman

Three-dimensional snowflake has snowman that rotates in circular center. The snowman wears a handpainted rakish hat, a red scarf around his neck, and a happy smile. Caption: "1977."

Handcrafted, 3¾" tall
450QX190-2, $4.50 ☐

Weather House

A timbered house with red-orange roof, double doorways, and shuttered window has hand-painted hearts and flowers trim. Swiss-clad boy and girl rotate in and out of the doorways. Caption: "1977."

Handcrafted, 3¹⁵/₁₆" tall
600QX191-5, $6.00 ☐

Bellringer

Little boy strikes a bell as he rotates inside an arched gate that is scrolled at the top and decorated on each side with large red bows. Sleigh full of toys and his dog are outside the gate.

Handcrafted, 3¹¹/₁₆" tall
600QX192-2, $6.00 ☐

Della Robia Wreath

Little girl, kneeling in prayer, twirls in center of traditional Della Robia wreath. Caption: "1977."

Handcrafted, 3⁹/₁₆" tall
450QX193-5, $4.50 ☐

Twirl-About Ornaments: Snowman, Weather House, Bellringer, Della Robia Wreath

Nostalgia Collection

The Nostalgia Collection is intricately molded and hand painted to create ring-shaped designs with a wooden, antique look. Individual packages included a gift tag.

Angel

Wide outer ring carries caption, flowers, and symbols with natural hand-carved look. In the center is a flying angel dressed in blue and blowing a horn. Caption: "Peace on earth" and "Good will toward men".

Handcrafted, 3¼" diam.
500QX182-2, $5.00 ☐

Toys

A stuffed bear with colorful, steaming locomotive and toy soldier occupy center of red and yellow ring. Caption: "1977."

Handcrafted, 3¼" diam.
500QX183-5, $5.00 ☐

Antique Car

Green antique car trimmed in red and yellow with its rumble seat filled with gift forms the center design. Caption: "Season's Greetings 1977."

Handcrafted, 3¼" diam.
500QX180-2, $5.00 ☐

Nativity

In the center of the ring is a star-topped stable sheltering the Holy Family and animals. A pine tree is on each side. Caption: "O come let us adore Him."

Handcrafted, 3¼" diam.
500QX181-5, $5.00 ☐

Nostalgia Collection: Angel, Toys, Antique Car, Nativity

Yesteryears Collection: Angel, Reindeer, Jack-in-the-Box, House

Yesteryears Collection

Angel
Smiling angel with arms outstretched is hand painted in gay, folk art style. Caption: "Joy to the world 1977."

Handcrafted, 3½" tall
600QX172-2, $6.00 ☐

Reindeer
Reindeer on wheels, with the nostalgic look of hand painted child's toy. Caption: "1977."

Handcrafted, 4¼" tall
600QX173-5, $6.00 ☐

Jack-in-the-Box
Jack, hand painted in green, blue and red has sprung up in the open red and pink box. Captures the look of antique, hand-carved wooden toy. Caption: "Merry Christmas 1977."

Handcrafted, 3¹³/₁₆" tall
600QX171-5, $6.00 ☐

House
Hand painted cottage features red roof and shuttered windows with painted designs on the red shutters. Fanlighted door is flanked by Christmas trees. Caption: "Happy Holidays 1977."

Handcrafted, 3¹¹/₁₆" tall
600QX170-2, $6.00 ☐

Cloth Doll Ornaments

These are the first two designs made from silk-screened cloth which is stuffed and then quilted.

Angel
A sweet angel with wings spread. Her wings are quilted and there is lace edging on the bottom of her dress.

Cloth, 4" tall
175QX220-2, $1.75 ☐

Santa
Plump jolly Santa is "Laying a finger beside his nose." A jingle bell is attached to his hat.

Cloth, 4" tall
175QX221-5, $1.75 ☐

Cloth Doll Ornaments: Angel, Santa

THE 1978 COLLECTION

The Hallmark Keepsake Collection continued to gain in popularity as collectibles when the 1978 line was introduced. This year, a design by Joan Walsh Anglund© joined the other exclusive properties held by Hallmark.

The popular Carrousel collectible series began in 1978 with a dated carrousel of children's toys. Chrome plated chimes were introduced in 1978 and Spencer Sparrow made his debut on ornaments. This also was the initial year of the 25th Christmas Together ornament, and the first year that ecru appeared as a color on soft-sheen satin ball ornaments. The smaller-sized ball ornaments made their last appearance in 1978.

Baby's First Christmas, Granddaughter, Grandson

First Christmas Together, Twenty-fifth Christmas Together, Love.

Grandmother, Mother, New Home

PEANUTS® Collection: Snoopy and Woodstock, Joy to the World, Snoopy as Santa, A Delightful Christmas

Commemoratives

Baby's First Christmas
Baby dressed in yellow is on a blanket playing with a kitten and a stuffed teddy bear. Caption: "Baby's First Christmas 1978."

White Satin, 3¼" diam.
350QX200-3, $3.50 ☐

Granddaughter
On a deep red background an adorable girl decorates her Christmas tree. Caption: "A Granddaughter...never far from thought, ever near in love."

White Satin, 3¼" diam.
350QX216-3, $3.50 ☐

Grandson
Raccoons are sledding, ice skating, and building a snowman. Caption: "A Grandson is loved in a special way for the special joy he brings."

White Satin, 3¼" diam.
350QX215-6, $3.50 ☐

First Christmas Together
Folk art design of red hearts, fruits, flowers, greenery, and a pair of red birds. Caption: "Sharing is the heart of loving" and "First Christmas Together 1978."

White Satin, 3¼" diam.
350QX218-3, $3.50 ☐

25th Christmas Together
Front — flower-entwined "25th Christmas Together," white doves, wedding bells, "1953" and "1978" year dates. Caption on back: "Time endears but cannot fade The memories that love has made."

White Glass, 3¼" diam.
350QX269-6, $3.50 ☐

Love
Birds hover over central heart motif enclosing year date, with poinsettias and berry laden boughs completing design. Caption: "Of life's many treasures, the most beautiful is love" and "1978."

Gold Glass, 3¼" diam.
350QX268-3, $3.50 ☐

Grandmother
Deep red American Beauty roses and holly leaves. Caption: "A Grandmother has a special way of bringing joy to every day."

White Satin, 3¼" diam.
350QX267-6, $3.50 ☐

Mother
Blue flowers and caption, white frosty snowflakes on a silvery white background. Caption: "The wonderful meaning of Christmas is found in a Mother's love" and "Christmas 1978."

White Glass, 3¼" diam.
350QX266-3, $3.50 ☐

For Your New Home
A brightly lighted window shows a beautiful wreath with a glowing candle. Caption: "Home...where the light of love shines brightest." and "Christmas 1978."

White Satin, 3¼" diam.
350QX217-6, $3.50 ☐

PEANUTS® Collection

PEANUTS®
SNOOPY and Woodstock bring their freshly cut tree home and decorate it. Caption: "1978."

White Satin, 2⅝" diam.
250QX204-3, $2.50 ☐

PEANUTS®
Linus holds a dated wreath while the rest of the PEANUTS® gang sing "Joy to the World." Caption: "Joy to the World 1978."

White Satin, 3¼" diam.
350QX205-6, $3.50 ☐

PEANUTS®
Front — SNOOPY, Woodstock, and his flock are playing in a toy store. Back — SNOOPY plays Santa as he hangs a filled stocking on the mantle. Caption: "1978."

White Satin, 3¼" diam.
350QX206-3, $3.50 ☐

PEANUTS®
Charlie Brown is all wrapped up in the Christmas tree lights by Woodstock as SNOOPY decorates his doghouse. Caption: "Have a delightful Christmas."

White Satin, 2⅝" diam.
250QX203-6, $2.50 ☐

Property Ornaments

Betsey Clark — Sixth Edition

A little girl is at home wrapping a gift…then she is all dressed up and has delivered the present to a friend. This is the first ornament to use the new ecru soft-sheen satin. Caption: "The Christmas spirit seems to bring a cheerful glow to everything" and "1978."

Ecru Soft-Sheen Satin, 3¼" diam.
350QX201-6, $3.50   ☐

Joan Walsh Anglund©

Front — Anglund children are caroling in the snow. Back — they are decorating a snow-covered tree. Caption: "As long as we have love and friends, Christmas never really ends 1978."

White Satin, 3¼" daim.
350QX221-6, $3.50   ☐

Spencer Sparrow

Front — Spencer sits in a wreath. Back — Spencer is pulling a sled loaded with gifts. Caption: "Holly days are jolly days" and "Christmas 1978."

Ecru Soft-Sheen Satin, 3¼" diam.
350QX219-6, $3.50   ☐

DISNEY

Disney characters ride on a wooden train with bell ringing Mickey Mouse dressed as Santa. Dated 1978.

White Satin, 3¼" daim.
350QX207-6, $3.50   ☐

Decorative Ball Ornaments

Merry Christmas (Santa)

Front — Santa and his reindeer soar over rooftops on Christmas Eve. Back — a jolly Santa shoulders his pack. Caption: "Merry Christmas" and "1978."

White Satin, 3¼" diam.
350QX202-3, $3.50   ☐

Hallmark's Antique Card Collection Design

Bells, holly, and ornate lettering are reproduced from an antique card in Hallmark's Collection. Caption: "Christmas is a special time, a season set apart — a warm and glad remembering time, a season of the heart."

Ecru Soft-Sheen Satin, 3¼" diam.
350QX220-3, $3.50   ☐

Betsey Clark-Sixth Edition, Joan Walsh Anglund, Spencer Sparrow, DISNEY

Merry Christmas, Antique Card, Yesterday's Toys, Nativity

The Quail, Drummer Boy, Joy

Holiday Highlights: Snowflake, Santa, Dove, Nativity

Yesterday's Toys

Toys of yesterday circle the band of the ornament. Caption: "Every joy of yesterday is a memory for tomorrow. 1978."

Gold Glass, 3¼″ diam.
350QX250-3, $3.50 ☐

Nativity

A beautiful Old World Nativity scene is displayed on a rich blue background. Caption: "The joy of heaven is come to earth."

White Glass, 3¼″ diam.
350QX253-6, $3.50 ☐

The Quail

A magnificent quail is depicted in his own habitat. Caption: "Nature has a wonderful way of making a wonder-filled world. 1978."

Gold Glass, 3¼″ diam.
350QX251-6, $3.50 ☐

Drummer Boy

A little drummer boy, followed by sheep and geese, marches to the beat of his own drum to where the Christ Child lies in a manger. Caption: "1978."

Gold Glass, 3¼″ diam.
350QX252-3, $3.50 ☐

Joy

Front — the word, "Joy," sprigged with holly, is incorporated in a leaded stained-glass-effect oval. Back — Christmas message is enclosed in matching oval. Caption: "Joy" and "The beauty of Christmas shines all around us."

White Glass, 3¼″ diam.
350QX254-3, $3.50 ☐

Holiday Highlights

In 1978, the elegant Holiday Highlights group featured four designs with the look of hand-cut crystal. Of unbreakable acrylic, they ranged from 2¹¹/₁₆″ to 3⅝″ tall and were priced at $3.50, each. The snowflake motif was dated.

350QX307-6   Santa ☐
350QX308-3   Snowflake ☐
350QX309-6   Nativity ☐
350QX310-3   Dove ☐

Reindeer Chimes

Holiday Chimes

Reindeer Chimes

Three prancing reindeer suspended from a large snowflake are a glistening Christmas mobile. A new format for 1978.

Chrome-plated brass, 5½" tall
450QX320-3, $4.50 ☐

Little Trimmers

Thimble Series (Mouse) — First Edition

Little white mouse wearing a red cap is peeking out of a silver colored thimble. This ornament was the first edition in the Thimble Series.

Handcrafted, 1¾" tall
250QX133-6, $2.50

Santa

Waving Santa holds a gift wrapped in blue and tied in red ribbon.

Handcrafted, 2¼" tall
250QX135-6, $2.50 ☐

Praying Angel

Angel in pink gown is kneeling in prayer.

Handcrafted, 2" tall
250QX134-3, $2.50 ☐

Drummer Boy

Drummer boy dressed in red, green, and blue is beating his drum.

Handcrafted, 2¹/₁₆" tall
250QX136-3, $2.50 ☐

Little Trimmer Collection

Miniature versions of Thimble Mouse, Praying Angel, Drummer Boy, and Santa were offered as a boxed set. (Not shown)

Handcrafted, 4 per box
900QX132-3, $9.00 ☐

Colors of Christmas

Merry Christmas

A luscious oval Christmas ornament in red, green, yellow, and white. Caption: "Merry Christmas 1978."

Acrylic, 4⅛" tall
350QX355-6, $3.50 ☐

Locomotive

Red train framed in blue, green, and yellow. Caption: "1978."

Acrylic, 3¼" diam.
350QX356-3, $3.50 ☐

Angel

An angel wearing red dress and halo with golden hair and wings.

Acrylic, 3⅝" tall
350QX354-3, $3.50 ☐

Candle

Lovely red candle with glowing flame is banked with holly and berries.

Acrylic, 3⅝" tall
350QX357-6, $3.50 ☐

☐ Handcrafted Ornaments

Dove

Majestic white dove twirls in the center of the white lacy snowflake. Caption: "1978."

Handcrafted, 3⁹/₁₆" tall
450QX190-3, $4.50 ☐

Holly and Poinsettia Ball

Large ball with the look of intricate hand carving is circled with large poinsettias and holiday greenery.

Handcrafted, 3½" diam.
600QX147-6, $6.00 ☐

Schneeberg Bell

An elegant reproduction of an intricate Schneeberg wood carving collage. This design used eighty-two decorating processes to achieve the natural wood look. Caption: "Merry Christmas 1978."

Handcrafted, 4" tall
800QX152-3, $8.00 ☐

Angels

Angels twirl about decorating a Christmas tree. Caption: "1978."

Handcrafted, 3⅞" tall
800QX150-3, $8.00 ☐

Thimble Series - First Edition, Santa, Praying Angel, Drummer Boy

Colors of Christmas: Merry Christmas, Train, Angel, Candle

Dove, Holly and Poinsettia Ball, Schneeberg Bell, Angels

Carrousel Series - First Edition

Carrousel Series — First Edition

Hand painted in red, yellow, blue, and green, carrousel has toys that spin around. Made in the look of hand-carved wood, this is the first model in the Carrousel series. Caption: "Christmas 1978" is painted around the top.

Handcrafted, 3″ tall
600QX146-3, $6.00 ☐

Joy

Little elfin boy dressed in blue is popping through the center letter "O" of the word "Joy." Hand-painted "bread dough" letters are red trimmed with white.

Handcrafted, 4³/₁₆″ tall
450QX138-3, $4.50 ☐

Angel

Handcrafted, bread-dough look barefoot angel is dressed in blue and holds a star.

Handcrafted, 2¹⁵/₁₆″ tall
450QX139-6, $4.50 ☐

Joy, Angel, Calico Mouse, Red Cardinal

Panorama Ball, Skating Raccoon, Rocking Horse, Animal Home

Calico Mouse

Smiling red calico mouse with green ears and nose holds sprig of green holly.

Handcrafted, 3⁷/₁₆″ tall
450QX137-6, $4.50 ☐

Red Cardinal

This clip-on Cardinal perches realistically on the branches of the Christmas tree.

Handcrafted, 4″ tall
450QX144-3, $4.50 ☐

Panorama Ball

Little boy dressed in red has fallen on the ice after he skated a holiday greeting. In the snow-covered background are a fence and trees. Scene is viewed through the peek-through window of this white ornament. Caption: "Merry Christmas 1978," is skate-written on the pond.

Handcrafted, 3⁵/₈″ diam.
600QX145-6, $6.00 ☐

Skating Raccoon

Ice-skating raccoon wears red mittens and scarf and real metal skates.

Handcrafted, 2¾″ tall
600QX142-3, $6.00 ☐

Rocking Horse

Hand painted polka-dot horse with flying white yarn mane and red rockers has the look of hand-carved wood. Caption: "1978."

Handcrafted, 3⁹/₁₆″ tall
600QX148-3, $6.00 ☐

Animal Home

A family of mice has taken residence in a precious little mushroom with red shuttered windows, garlanded doorway, and stone steps. Mr. Mouse is in the doorway and Mrs. Mouse is inside.

Handcrafted, 2⁹/₁₆″ tall
600QX149-6, $6.00 ☐

Yarn Collection

The collection of four Yarn ornaments for 1978 were all 4½″ tall, individually packaged, and priced at $2.00

200QX123-1	Green Boy	☐
200QX125-1	Mrs. Claus	☐
200QX126-1	Green Girl	☐
200QX340-3	Mr. Claus	☐

Yarn Collection: Mrs. Santa, Santa, Green Boy, Green Girl

THE 1979 COLLECTION

Two new commemorative ball ornaments for Teacher and Special Friend joined the greatly enlarged Hallmark Keepsake Ornament Collection in 1979.

By then, Baby's First Christmas satin ball ornaments had become solid sellers. In response to consumer demand, Hallmark expanded the Baby's First Christmas offering to include a handcrafted design which was in the form of a green-and-white knitted stocking filled to overflowing with baby toys.

Three new collectible series were inaugurated this year — the dated ceramic bell ornaments, Santa-in-a-vehicle ornaments, and SNOOPY panorama ball ornaments.

Ball ornaments were given new packages in 1979, and nearly 60 percent of the ornaments were dated.

Commemoratives

Baby's First Christmas

Front — toys and gifts for Baby ride a sleigh pulled by animal friends. Back — Baby's toys surround Christmas tree being trimmed by birds. Caption: "Baby's First Christmas 1979."

White Satin, 3¼" diam.
350QX208-7, $3.50 ☐

Baby's First Christmas

A real green-and-white knitted stocking is filled with toys for baby. The first time Baby's First Christmas commemorative was offered in the handcrafted ornaments. Caption: "Baby's First Christmas 1979."

Handcrafted, 4" tall
800QX154-7, $8.00 ☐

Grandson

Stocking-capped SNOOPY and Woodstock are sledding in the snow. Caption: "A Grandson…a special someone whose merry ways bring extra joy to the holidays. Christmas 1979."

White Satin, 3¼" diam.
350QX210-7, $3.50 ☐

Granddaughter

A little girl, warmly dressed for the weather, is feeding red birds, rabbits, and squirrels in the snow. Caption: "A Granddaughter fills each day with joy by filling hearts with love. 1979."

White Satin, 3¼" diam.
350QX211-9, $3.50 ☐

Mother

An abundance of white poinsettias and small blossoms band the ornament and form the message. Caption: "It's love that makes Christmas so special — and Mother who makes us feel loved."

White Glass, 3¼" diam.
350QX251-9, $3.50 ☐

Baby's First Christmas: Satin Ball, Handcrafted

Grandson, Granddaughter, Mother, Grandmother

First Christmas Together, Twenty-Fifth Anniversary, Love

Friendship, Teacher, New Home

Grandmother

Little birds enjoy the nectar from a basket of flowers. Caption: "Grandmothers bring happy times — time and time again" and "1979."

White Glass, 3¼" diam.
350QX252-7, $3.50 ☐

Our First Christmas Together

Golden wedding bells with ribbon bows and poinsettias with greenery are shown against a dark green background. Caption: "Our First Christmas Together 1979" and "Christmas and Love are for sharing."

Gold Glass, 3¼" diam.
350QX209-9, $3.50 ☐

Our Twenty-Fifth Anniversary

White satin ribbon entwines wedding bells, wedding rings, and garland of Christmas greenery. Caption: "Year of our Twenty-Fifth Anniversary 1979. Those warm times shared in past Decembers…The mind still sees, the heart remembers."

White Glass, 3¼" diam.
350QX250-7, $3.50 ☐

Love

Light scrolling, white snowflakes, red Gothic printing, and green holly and white background. Caption: "Love…warm as candleglow, wondrous as snowfall, welcome as Christmas" and "Christmas 1979."

White Glass, 3¼" diam.
350QX258-7, $3.50 ☐

Friendship

Front — friends are skating on a large frozen pond beside an old mill. Back — a sleighride along a country road. Caption: "There is no time quite like Christmas for remembering friendships we cherish" and "Christmas 1979."

White Glass, 3¼" diam.
350QX203-9, $3.50 ☐

Teacher

Front — a raccoon writes message to teacher on a holiday-decorated blackboard. Back — a sleigh with a gift is being drawn toward a Christmas tree with white doves. Caption: "To a Special Teacher" and "Merry Christmas 1979."

White Satin, 3¼" diam.
350QX213-9, $3.50 ☐

New Home

A quaint painting of a snow-covered village, covered bridge, and ice skaters. Caption: "Christmas…when love fills the heart, when hearts look to home" and "1979."

Ecru Soft Sheen Satin, 3¼" diam.
350QX212-7, $3.50 ☐

Betsey Clark-Seventh Edition, PEANUTS, Spencer Sparrow

Joan Walsh Anglund, Winnie-the-Pooh™, Mary Hamilton

Night Before Christmas, Christmas Chickadees, Behold the Star

Property Ornaments

Betsey Clark — Seventh Edition

Front — Miss Clark's little children are sitting at home reading. Back — they are returning home from shopping with their tree-laden sled. This is the seventh ornament in the series. Caption: "Holiday fun times make memories to treasure. 1979."

White Satin, 3¼″ diam.
350QX201-9, $3.50

PEANUTS® (Time to Trim)

Woodstock and his merry, green-capped flock are decorating the tree with the candy canes that SNOOPY is passing out to them. Caption: "Merry Christmas 1979."

White Satin, 3¼″ diam.
350QX202-7, $3.50

Spencer Sparrow

Spencer swinging on a popcorn and cranberry garland, jauntily tips his hat. Caption: "Christmas time means decorating, spreading cheer and celebrating!" and "1979."

Ecru Soft-Sheen Satin, 3¼″ diam.
350QX200-7, $3.50

Joan Walsh Anglund©

Front — the Anglund children are hanging their stockings on the fireplace. Back — little girl is opening her gift under the candlelit tree, while the little boy rides his new hobby horse. Caption: "The smallest pleasure is big enough to share. 1979."

White Satin, 3¼″ diam.
350QX205-9, $3.50

Winnie-the-Pooh

Pooh's friends gather and deliver "Hunny" to a very happy bear. This is a Walt Disney design. Caption: "Merry Christmas 1979."

White Satin, 3¼″ diam.
350QX206-7, $3.50

Mary Hamilton

An angelic choir sings to an audience of forest friends. Caption: "…and heaven and nature sing" and "1979."

Ecru Soft-Sheen Satin, 3¼″ diam.
350QX254-7, $3.50

Decorative Ball Ornaments

Night Before Christmas

Front — this favorite Christmas poem is illustrated with Santa preparing to fill the "stockings hung by the chimney with care." Back — pictures Santa continuing on his journey and concluding lines of poem. Caption: "…I heard him exclaim, ere he drove out of sight, Happy Christmas to all, and to all a good night—C.C. Moore" and "1979."

White Satin, 3¼" diam.
350QX214-7, $3.50

Christmas Chickadees

A pair of chickadees enjoy the red berries of a holly branch. Two others frolic in the snow on a pine bough. Caption: "Beauty is a gift nature gives every day" and "Christmas 1979."

Gold Glass, 3¼" diam.
350QX204-7, $3.50

Behold the Star

The three wise men and shepherds with their flock follow the star to Bethlehem where the Child lies in a manger. Caption: "And the light was for all time"; "And the love was for all men."

White Satin, 3¼" diam.
350QX255-9, $3.50

Christmas Traditions

Homey Christmas traditions are exemplified in jar of candy, basket of fresh fruit, lantern with glowing candle, kitchen scales, wooden carved toy, and old mantle clock shown against a wood paneled wall. Caption: "The old may be replaced with new, traditions rearranged, but the wonder that is Christmas will never ever change. 1979."

Gold Glass, 3¼" diam.
350QX253-9, $3.50

Christmas Collage

Old-fashioned toys and the caption are highlighted on a dark brown and blue profusely decorated band reproduced from a photograph of a Schneeberg collage. Caption: "Season's Greetings" and "1979."

Gold Glass, 3¼" diam.
350QX257-9, $3.50

Christmas Traditions, Christmas Collage, Black Angel, Light of Christmas

Black Angel

Young adult angel wearing a red and white robe is shown in two scenes which utilized contemporary photographic effects to illustrate the radiance of the Christmas season. Caption: "Merry Christmas 1979."

Gold Glass, 3¼" diam.
350QX207-9, $3.50

The Light of Christmas

Reminiscent of Art Deco designs in stained glass, this red, orange, and green design encircles the caption on one side and, on the other, frames three lighted candles. Caption: "There's no light as bright as Christmas to adorn and warm the night. 1979."

Chrome Glass, 3¼" diam.
350QX256-7, $3.50

Holiday Highlights: Christmas Angel, Snowflake, Christmas Tree

Colors of Christmas: Words of Christmas, Wreath, Partridge, Star over Bethlehem

Holiday Highlights: Christmas Cheer, Love

Holiday Highlights

Christmas Angel

Flying angel with elegantly "etched," long floral dress, feathery wings, and halo holds nosegay of flowers. A ribbon worn over the shoulder and falling to her side carries the caption: "Christmas 1979."

Acrylic, 4¼" wide
350QX300-7, $3.50

Snowflake

Exquisitely shaped snowflake has date "etched" in center hexagon. Caption: "1979."

Acrylic, 3½" diam.
350QX301-9, $3.50

Christmas Tree

A perfectly shaped, "etched" tree of leaves and flowers highlights a lone dove near the top. On the top in a halo effect is "1979." The date is stamped in silver foil. Caption: "1979."

Acrylic, 4½" tall
350QX302-7, $3.50

Christmas Cheer

A plump little bird with berries in its beak perches on a holly bough. Caption: "1979."

Acrylic, 3½" diam.
350QX303-9, $3.50

Love

Beribboned flowers border a heart containing a message stamped in silver foil flowing script. Caption: "Time of memories and dreams...Time of love. Christmas 1979."

Acrylic, 3½" tall
350QX304-7, $3.50

Colors of Christmas

Words of Christmas

Message forms a design in stained-glass look. The colors are red, green, and gold. Caption: "The message of Christmas is love."

Acrylic, 3¾" tall
350QX350-7, $3.50

Holiday Wreath

Wreath decorated with colorfully designed ornaments and topped with a red bow frames red year date. Caption: "1979."

Acrylic, 3½" tall
350QX353-9, $3.50

Partridge in a Pear Tree

A richly colored partridge surrounded by golden pears and green leaves is the center focus of this design. Caption: "1979."

Acrylic, 3¼" diam.
350QX351-9, $3.50

Star Over Bethlehem

Three shepherds and their flock behold the city of Bethlehem in the distance brilliantly illuminated by the "Star."

Acrylic, 3½" diam.
350QX352-7, $3.50

Little Trimmer Collection

Thimble Series — Mouse

First in the Thimble Series introduced in 1978, the popular Thimble Mouse was reissued in 1979. (See 1978 Collection for photograph and description.)

Handcrafted, 1¾" tall
300QX133-6, $3.00

Santa

Santa, introduced in 1978, was reissued in 1979. (See 1978 Collection.)

Handcrafted, 2¼" tall
300QX135-6, $3.00

A Matchless Christmas

A small white mouse has made a comfy bed in a half-opened matchbox. Wearing a red nightcap and lying on a white pillow with red stripes, he sleeps snugly under a blue-and-white checked blanket. This ornament clips onto the tree branch.

Handcrafted, 2½" long
400QX132-7, $4.00

Note: *The Angel, Matchless Christmas, and Santa also were packaged together as a trio of "Little Trimmers."*

Angel Delight

Little angel with white wings, golden halo, and light blue gown sails along in her walnut shell.

Handcrafted, 1¾" tall
300QX130-7, $3.00

A Matchless Christmas, Angel Delight

Handcrafted Ornaments

Holiday Scrimshaw

Ivory angel wtih widespread wings and clasped hands has the look of scrimshaw carving. Caption: "Peace-Love-Joy 1979."

Handcrafted, 3½" tall
400QX152-7, $4.00 ☐

Christmas Heart

Two doves rotate through the center of this heart-shaped ornament. Design has the look of hand-carved wood, with raised floral motif highlighted by hand painting. Caption: "1979."

Handcrafted, 3½" tall
650QX140-7, $6.50 ☐

Christmas Eve Surprise

A wood-look shadow box reveals a three-dimensional scene of toy-laden Santa who is about to go down the chimney. Caption: "1979."

Handcrafted, 4¼" tall
650QX157-9, $6.50 ☐

Santa's Here

Santa is the center of attention as he twirls inside this snowflake. Caption: "1979."

Handcrafted, 4" diam.
500QX138-7, $5.00 ☐

Holiday Scrimshaw, Christmas Heart, Christmas Eve Surprise, Santa's Here

Downhill Run, The Drummer Boy, Outdoor Fun

Raccoon

Mr. Raccoon on skates of real metal skated out of 1978 and into the 1979 Hallmark Keepsake Collection. This is a reissue. (See 1978 Annual Collection.)

Handcrafted; 2" tall
650QX142-3, $6.50

The Downhill Run

Red capped squirrel and rabbit wearing blue scarf are having fun on a red toboggan making a fast downhill run.

Handcrafted, 3" tall
650QX145-9, $6.50 ☐

The Drummer Boy

Standing in the snow near a fence and a tree is a drummer boy playing for a lamb and a duck.

Handcrafted, 3¼" diam.
800QX143-9, $8.00 ☐

Outdoor Fun

Young girl on swing gently glides between two Christmas trees in snow scene.

Handcrafted, 3" tall
800QX150-7, $8.00 ☐

A Christmas Treat

A teddy bear wearing red cap and jacket trimmed in white tries climbing a large candy cane which is designed to hook over a tree branch.

Handcrafted, 4¾" tall
500QX134-7, $5.00 ☐

The Skating Snowman

Wearing a green-and-white, real cloth scarf, ice skates of real metal, and black top hat, this snowman cuts a fancy figure.

Handcrafted, 4¼" tall
500QX139-9, $5.00 ☐

Christmas is for Children

Green bonneted little girl dressed in a red dress and red-and-white stockings holds a white kitten as she swings. All made in the look of hand carved wood.

Handcrafted, 4¼" tall
500QX135-9, $5.00 ☐

Ready for Christmas

White birdhouse with a sparkling, snow-covered roof and green garland with a red bow over the door makes a cozy home for "Mr. and Mrs. Redbird."

Handcrafted, 3" tall
650QX133-9, $6.50 ☐

A Christmas Treat, Skating Snowman, Christmas is for Children, Ready for Christmas

Collectible Series

Carrousel — Second Edition

Second issue in the popular Carrousel Series has four angel musicians dressed in red, blue, deep rose, and green revolving on a red, blue, and green carrousel. Caption: "Christmas 1979" twice around the carrousel's top.

Handcrafted, 3½" tall
650QX146-7, $6.50 ☐

Thimble — Second Edition
A Christmas Salute

Soldier, with epaulets on the shoulders of his red jacket, wears blue trousers and thimble "hat." He salutes left-handed.

Handcrafted, 2¼" tall
300QX131-9, $3.00 ☐

SNOOPY and Friends -
First Edition
Ice Hockey Holiday

SNOOPY and Woodstock play ice hockey on a frozen pond. Caption: "1979."

Handcrafted, 3¼" diam.
800QX141-9, $8.00 ☐

Here Comes Santa — First Edition
Santa's Motorcar

Santa is waving his hand as he drives into the holidays in a vintage motorcar. The car has the look of real cast metal and the wheels actually turn. The car is red trimmed in green, and the tires are black with golden spokes in the wheels. Santa's toy-filled bag is painted green and rests on the back of the car. Caption: "1979."

Handcrafted, 3½" tall
900QX155-9, $9.00 ☐

Bellringer — First Edition

Merry elf swings on the clapper of white porcelain bell decorated with fired on wreath decal. Rim of bell is hand painted in gold. Caption: "1979" in center of wreath.

Porcelain & Handcrafted, 4" tall
10QX147-9, $10.00 ☐

Collectible Series: Carrousel-Second Edition, Thimble-Second Edition

Collectible Series First Editions: Snoopy and Friends, Here Comes Santa, The Bellringer

Holiday Chimes

Reindeer Chimes
A reissue from 1978. (See 1978 Annual Collection.)

Chrome plate, 5½″ tall
450QX320-3, $4.50

Star Chimes
Stars within stars twirl to create dancing reflections. Solid center star carries impressed year date. Caption: "1979."

Chrome Plate, 4″ tall
450QX137-9, $4.50 ☐

Yarn and Fabric Ornaments

Sewn Trimmers
Four new sewn designs are added that feature quilting and stitched edges. Ranging from 4″ to 5″ tall, they were $2.00 each.

200QX340-7	*The Rocking Horse*	☐
200QX342-7	*Merry Santa*	☐
200QX341-9	*Stuffed Full Stocking*	☐
200QX343-9	*Angel Music*	☐

Yarn Ornaments
The four designs available in 1978 were offered again in 1979. (See 1978 Annual Collection for photograph and description.)

Holiday Chimes: Reindeer Chime, Star Chime

Sewn Ornaments: Rocking Horse, Merry Santa, Stuffed Full Stocking, Angel Music

THE 1980 COLLECTION

In 1980, Hallmark introduced seventy-six new ornament designs, eighteen more than the fifty-eight offered in 1979. Seven commemorative ball ornaments were inaugurated — Son, Daughter, Grandparents, Dad, Mother and Dad, Grandfather, and Baby's First Christmas for a black child. New properties included Jim Henson's MUPPETS™ and the drawing of Marty Links.™

Friendship, Mother, and First Christmas Together captioned ornaments were added to the acrylic line. Pastel colored, unbreakable "cameo" designs were introduced. Made of acrylic, they feature delicate, milk-white "cameo" reliefs on soft pastel backgrounds. The rims are chrome with a loop for hanging. Other new designs and formats in 1980 included frosted images (with the look of softly etched crystal), a flocked ornament, and a pressed tin ornament.

Two new collectible series were issued: Frosty Friends (an Eskimo and a polar bear on a dated icecube) and the first Norman Rockwell cameo ornament. Two special edition ornaments also made their first appearance: Checking It Twice (a very detailed Santa checking his list) and Heavenly Minstrel (a beautiful blue angel).

By 1980, marketing surveys indicated that 55 percent of all Hallmark ornament purchases were made by collectors adding to their collections.

Baby's First Christmas: Satin Ball, Satin Ball (Black Baby), Handcrafted

Commemoratives

Baby's First Christmas
Santa with his bag on his back is talking to a baby who is in a brass baby bed. Caption: "Baby's First Christmas, 1980."

White Satin, 3¼" diam.
400QX200-1, $4.00 ☐

Black Baby's First Christmas
Another Hallmark first, a black baby dressed in a nightie sits by a decorated Christmas tree that holds nested birds in its branches. Toys surround the tree. Caption: "Baby's First Christmas, 1980."

White Satin, 3¼" diam.
400QX229-4, $4.00 ☐

Baby's First Christmas
A wood-look shadow box in the shape of a Christmas tree has five compartments. The compartments hold a silver cup with "Baby" on it, a rubber duck, alphabet blocks, a white ball with a blue star on it, four wood-look rings in red, yellow, and green, and a teddy bear. Caption: "Baby's First Christmas" and "1980."

Handcrafted, 3⁵⁷/₆₄" tall
12QX156-1, $12.00 ☐

Grandson
Front — a jolly snowman rides a sled pulled by raccoons. Back — the snowman adds a candy cane to a decorated tree. Caption: "Grandsons and Christmas are joys that go together. Christmas 1980."

White Satin, 3¼" diam.
400QX201-4, $4.00 ☐

Granddaughter
Little girl, nestled under a patchwork quilt in a brass bed, dreams of sweets and toys. Caption: "A Granddaughter is a dream fulfilled, a treasure to hold dear, a joy to warmly cherish, a comfort through the year. Christmas 1980."

Ecru Soft-Sheen Satin, 3¼" diam.
400QX202-1, $4.00 ☐

Son
Nostalgic scene of favorite boys' toys. Caption: "A son is...a maker of memories, a source of pride...A son is love. Christmas 1980."

Gold Glass, 3¼" diam.
400QX211-4, $4.00 ☐

Daughter
This is the first year of the Daughter ornament. Front — white kitten naps next to potted flowers and plants. Back — kitten plays with ornaments hanging on a potted plant. Caption: "A Daughter is the sweetest gift a lifetime can provide. Christmas 1980."

White Glass, 3¼" diam.
400QX212-1, $4.00 ☐

Grandson, Granddaughter, Son, Daughter

Dad

Front — the word "DAD" is printed on red plaid background. Back — red oval containing caption. Caption: "A Dad is always caring, always sharing, always giving of his love. Christmas 1980."

Gold Glass, 3¼" diam.
400QX214-1, $4.00 ☐

Mother

Large poinsettias and other Christmas flowers ring ornament and frame caption. Caption: "A Mother has the special gift of giving of herself. Christmas 1980."

White Satin, 3¼" diam.
400QX203-4, $4.00 ☐

Mother and Dad

Against a light green background, darker green script printing and sprays of holly and red berries circle the ornament. Caption: "When homes are decked with holly and hearts are feeling glad, it's a wonderful time to remember a wonderful Mother and Dad. Christmas 1980."

White Glass, 3¼" diam.
400QX230-1, $4.00 ☐

Grandmother

Flowers, birds, and animals frame the caption and date. Caption: "Love and joy and comfort and cheer are gifts a Grandmother gives all year. Christmas 1980."

White Glass, 3¼" diam.
400QX204-1, $4.00 ☐

Grandfather

Two snow scenes, one of an old covered bridge, and the other of an idle wagon in a barnyard are pictured. Caption: "A Grandfather is…strong in his wisdom, gentle in his love. Christmas 1980."

White Glass, 3¼" diam.
400QX231-4, $4.00 ☐

Grandparents

Large home by wooded pond reproduced from Currier & Ives print, "Early Winter." Caption: "Grandparents have beautiful ways of giving, of helping, of teaching…especially of loving. 1980."

Gold Glass, 3¼" diam.
400QX213-4, $4.00 ☐

Dad, Mother, Mother and Dad

Grandmother, Grandfather, Grandparents

25th Christmas Together, First Christmas Together, Christmas Love

Friendship, Christmas at Home, Teacher

Love, Beauty of Friendship, First Christmas Together, Mother

25th Christmas Together

Applique-style garlands, bells, and ribbons frame the captions. Caption: "The good times of the present blend with memories of the past to make each Christmas season even dearer than the last. 25th Christmas Together. 1980."

White Glass, 3¼" diam.
400QX206-1, $4.00 □

First Christmas Together

A couple takes a moonlight sleighride in the snow. Caption: "First Christmas Together. Christmas is a love story written in our hearts. 1980."

White Glass, 3¼" diam.
400QX205-4, $4.00 □

Christmas Love

This ornament is a reproduction of a Bob Schneeberg collage. Motif in delicate, soft pastels is of hearts trimmed in beads and pearls, a large snowflake, and "LOVE" in ornate lettering. Caption: "Love at Christmas...happy moments spent together, memories to be shared forever. Christmas 1980."

White Glass, 3¼" diam.
400QX207-4, $4.00 □

Friendship

White lace, red ribbons, and flowers on a muted green background. Caption: "Hold Christmas ever in your heart — For its meaning never ends; Its spirit is the warmth and joy of remembering friends. Christmas 1980."

White Glass, 3¼" diam.
400QX208-1, $4.00 □

Christmas at Home

Yule decorated hearth and brightly burning logs personify the comfort and warmth of home. Caption: "A Home that's filled with Christmas Glows with the joyful light Of the special warmth and happiness That makes the season bright. Christmas 1980."

Gold Glass, 3¼" diam.
400QX210-1, $4.00 □

Teacher

Front — warmly dressed kitten bearing a gift is walking to school. Back — he is placing the gift on the teacher's desk. A blackboard has a special message for teacher. Caption: "Merry Christmas, Teacher. Christmas 1980."

White Satin, 3¼" diam.
400QX209-4, $4.00 □

□ *Betsey Clark-Eighth Edition, Betsey Clark, Betsey Clark's Christmas*

Love

Lettering of caption appears cut and etched, with the word "LOVE" enhanced by silver foil stamping. Large snowflake in the center of the "O" is the focal point of the ornament. Caption: "Where there is love, there is the spirit of Christmas. 1980."

Acrylic, 4" tall
400QX302-1, $4.00 □

Beauty of Friendship

Clear, disk-shaped ornament has floral garland border and center caption and date stamped in silver foil. Caption: "Friendship brings beauty to our days, joy to our world. Christmas 1980."

Acrylic, 3¼" diam.
400QX303-4, $4.00 □

First Christmas Together

Heart-shaped, with floral and ribbon border, has caption and date stamped in silver foil. Caption: "First Christmas Together 1980."

Acrylic, 3½" tall
400QX305-4, $4.00 □

Mother

Heart with ribbon-tied floral border has silver foil stamped caption and date. Caption: "Mother is another word for Love. Christmas 1980."

Acrylic, 3½" tall
400QX304-1, $4.00 □

Property Ornaments

Betsey Clark — Eighth Edition

Betsey Clark's charming children are sledding past a sign in the snow announcing "Christmas 1980." This is the eighth dated design in the Betsey Clark Series. Caption: "It's joy-in-the-air time, love everywhere time, good-fun-to-share time, it's Christmas. Christmas 1980."

White Glass, 3¼" diam.
400QX215-4, $4.00 □

Betsey Clark

On a soft blue background, a Betsey Clark angel is kneeling in prayer with clasped hands. A banner beneath her carries the date. The angel is surrounded by embossed stars and a holly border, as is the caption on the back of the ornament. Caption: "Love came down at Christmas, Love all lovely, Love divine; Love was born at Christmas, Star and Angels gave the sign" and "Christmas 1980."

Light Blue Cameo, 3⅜" diam.
650QX307-4, $6.50 □

Betsey Clark's Christmas

A red shadow box trimmed in white band with red ribbon features Betsey Clark girl in a three-dimensional snowscene. Caption: "1980."

Handcrafted, 4" tall
750QX149-4, $7.50 □

PEANUTS®

SNOOPY sings as Woodstock and his friends reenact verses from traditional Christmas carol. Caption: "Four colly birds…three French hens…and a partridge in a pear tree. Christmas 1980."

White Satin, 3¼″ diam.
400QX216-1, $4.00 ☐

Joan Walsh Anglund©

The Anglund children are having an ice skating holiday. Caption: "Each and every bright December brings the best times to remember. Christmas 1980."

White Satin, 3¼″ diam.
400QX217-4, $4.00 ☐

DISNEY

Front — Mickey and Minnie Mouse are ice skating. Back — Mickey plays Santa as he approaches a house to make a delivery. Caption: "Merry Christmas 1980."

White Satin, 3¼″ diam.
400QX218-1, $4.00 ☐

Mary Hamilton

Two charming children are reflected in the glow of an old-fashioned candlelit Christmas tree. Caption: "Christmas — the warmest, brightest season of all. Christmas 1980."

Gold Glass, 3¼″ diam.
400QX219-4, $4.00 ☐

MUPPETS™

Front — KERMIT™ waves a greeting. Back — MUPPETS™ are merrily caroling. This design is the first appearance of Jim Hensen's MUPPETS™ as a Hallmark Keepsake Ornament. Caption: "Merry Christmas 1980."

White Satin, 3¼″ diam.
400QX220-1, $4.00 ☐

Marty Links™

Little girl directs as a little boy and animals carol in the snow. Caption: "We wish you a Merry Christmas and a Happy New Year. Christmas 1980."

White Satin, 3¼″ diam.
400QX221-4, $4.00 ☐

Decorative Ball Ornaments

Christmas Choir

Front — snowscene of country church. Back — three darling black children dressed in choir robes are singing the message of Christmas. One is so small she stands on a stool. Caption: "Go tell it on the mountain…Jesus Christ is born! Christmas 1980."

Gold Glass, 3¼″ diam.
400QX228-1, $4.00 ☐

PEANUTS®, Joan Walsh Anglund,©DISNEY

Mary Hamilton, Muppets™, Marty Links™

Christmas Choir, Nativity, Christmas Time

Nativity

Animals and birds gather beside small children kneeling in prayer at the manger of the Christ Child. Caption: "Silent night…holy night…Christmas 1980."

Gold Glass, 3¼″ diam.
400QX225-4, $4.00 ☐

Christmas Time

Front — a stagecoach rolling along in the snow toward timbered inn. Back — holly-sprigged top hat and steaming mug of coffee. Caption: "These are the days of merry-making, get-togethers, journey-taking, moments of delight and love that last in memory. Christmas 1980."

Ecru Soft-Sheen Satin, 3¼″ diam.
400QX226-1, $4.00 ☐

Santa's Workshop

Front — merry Santa has added a warm scarf to his traditional costume. Back — Santa checking his list at his North Pole workshop. Caption: "What merriment is all around when dear old Santa comes to town. Christmas 1980."

White Satin, 3¼″ diam.
400QX223-4, $4.00 ☐

Happy Christmas

Front — a Koala bear waters a potted tree. Back — tree has magically grown into "pear tree" of Christmas song with small bird perched at top. Caption: "Tis the season when hearts are glowing, love is growing, and happiness rounds out the year! Christmas 1980."

Ecru Soft-Sheen Satin, 3¼″ diam.
400QX222-1, $4.00 ☐

Jolly Santa

Ice skating Santa and reindeer spell out the season's greetings. Caption: "Merry Christmas. Christmas 1980."

White Glass, 3¼″ diam.
400QX227-4, $4.00 ☐

Christmas Cardinals

Two cardinals perch on berry-laden branches of holly. Caption: "Nature at Christmas…a wonderland of wintry art. Christmas 1980."

White Glass, 3¼″ diam.
400QX224-1, $4.00 ☐

Santa's Workshop, Happy Christmas, Jolly Santa, Christmas Cardinals

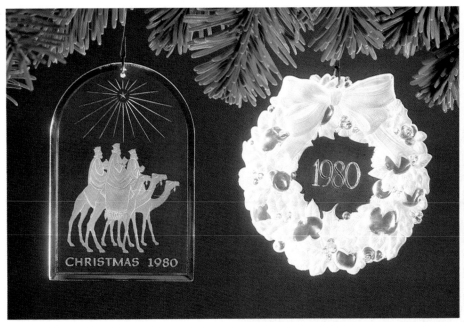

Holiday Highlights: Three Wisemen, Wreath

Colors of Christmas: Joy

Holiday Highlights

Three Wise Men

Three Wise Men follow the star to Bethlehem. Intricate detail shows their regal attire and the gifts they are bearing. Created with the look of hand-cut, etched crystal. Caption: "Christmas 1980."

Acrylic, 4" tall
400QX300-1, $4.00　☐

Wreath

Wreath topped with luxurious bow features leaves and holly in etched effect. Clear fruit and berries form pleasing contrast. Date is stamped in silver foil on clear center. Caption: "1980."

Acrylic, 3¼" diam.
400QX301-4, $4.00　☐

Colors of Christmas

Joy

Fashioned in rich colors with the look of leaded stained glass, the ornament is molded to spell "JOY," with year date on ribbon scroll over the "O". Caption: "Joy 1980."

Acrylic, 4" tall
400QX350-1, $4.00　☐

Frosted Images: Santa, Drummer Boy, Dove

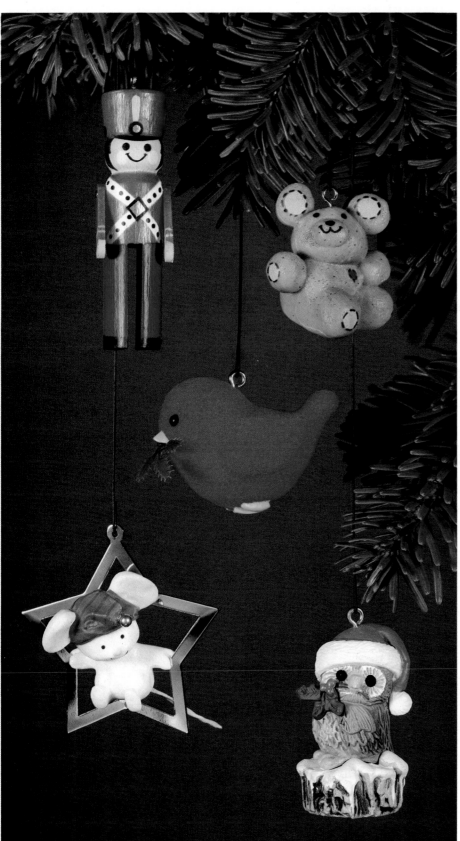

Frosted Images

Three new frosted images were new introductions in the 1980 collection of Hallmark Keepsake Ornaments. The naturalistically shaped acrylic ornaments have the appearance of delicate, frosted crystal. They range in size from 1⅞″ to 2¼″ tall and were $4.00 each.

400QX309-4   Drummer Boy ☐
400QX310-1   Santa ☐
400QX308-1   Dove ☐

Little Trimmers

Clothespin Soldier
Proud little soldier in the style of a clothespin is dressed in hand-painted blue trousers, red jacket with white trim, and a red hat.

Handcrafted, 2¹⁵/₁₆″ tall
350QX134-1, $3.50 ☐

Christmas Teddy
Small brown teddy bear has a smile painted on his face, black painted outline around the ears and paws, and a red heart painted on his chest. He is made from dough-look material.

Handcrafted, 1¼″ tall
250QX135-4, $2.50 ☐

Merry Redbird
In a new format, merry redbird wears softly flocked "feathers" and carries a sprig of holly in his yellow bill.

Handcrafted-Flocked, 1²⁷/₃₂″ long
350QX160-1, $3.50 ☐

Swingin' on a Star
Tiny white mouse in a red-and-green striped cap with a brass bell is swinging on a brass star.

Handcrafted, 2⁵/₃₂″ tall
400QX130-1, $4.00 ☐

Christmas Owl
A Christmas owl cutie wearing a "Santa" cap clutches holly and berries in his beak as he perches on a snow-covered tree stump.

Handcrafted, 1²⁷/₃₂″ tall
400QX131-4, $4.00 ☐

Thimble Series — A Christmas Salute
This is a reissue of the second design in the Thimble Series; it was introduced in 1979. (See 1979 Annual Collection.)

Handcrafted, 2¼″ tall
400QX131-9, $4.00

Little Trimmers: Clothespin Soldier, Christmas Teddy, Merry Redbird, Swinging on a Star, Christmas Owl

Handcrafted Ornaments

The Snowflake Swing

An angel clad in green swings merrily from a dainty star molded of clear acrylic.

Handcrafted, 3" tall
400QX133-4, $4.00 ☐

Santa 1980

Snow-capped chimney represents the "1" in 1980, and Santa is seen making an entrance to mouse's house, below. Small mouse with empty stocking awaits Santa's visit. Ornament is fashioned in "dough-look" material.

Handcrafted, 4⁵/₃₂" tall
550QX146-1, $5.50 ☐

Drummer Boy

The drummer boy in bread-dough design has textured hair and is dressed in green with brown sandals and stocking cap. His red drum is accented in gold. Caption: "1980."

Handcrafted, 3³/₆₄" tall
550QX147-4, $5.50 ☐

Christmas Is for Children

This little girl in swing with real motion is reissue of popular model introduced in 1979. (See 1979 Annual Collection.)

Handcrafted, 4¼" tall
550QX135-9, $5.50 ☐

A Christmas Treat

The teddy climbing a large candy cane is reissue of a favorite in the 1979 line. (See 1979 Annual Collection.)

Handcrafted, 4¾" tall
550QX134-7, $5.50 ☐

Skating Snowman

Wearing a top hat, a real cloth scarf, and metal skates, appealing snowman is a 1979 reissue. (See 1979 Annual Collection.)

Handcrafted, 4¼" tall
550QX139-9, $5.50 ☐

A Heavenly Nap

An angel dressed in blue is taking a nap on a crescent-shaped moon. There must be a man in the moon, for this frosted acrylic moon seems to be fast asleep in a nightcap with a gold star tassel.

Handcrafted, 3½" tall
650QX139-4, $6.50 ☐

Snowflake Swing, Santa 1980, Drummer Boy

A Heavenly Nap, Heavenly Sounds, Caroling Bear, Santa's Flight

The Animal's Christmas, A Spot of Christmas Cheer, Elfin Antics, A Christmas Vigil

Heavenly Sounds

Angels dressed in pink and blue produce "heavenly sounds" by ringing a gold metal bell. They twirl about in the center of a wood-look pink ring decorated with green scrolls. Caption: "1980."

Handcrafted, 3³⁰/₆₄" tall
750QX152-1, $7.50

Caroling Bear

A happy brown bear wearing a green-and-red striped scarf is singing a duet with a red bird perched on his arm. His green songbook carries the caption and date. Caption: "Carols 1980."

Handcrafted, 3⁷/₃₃" tall
750QX140-1, $7.50

Santa's Flight

Santa gives up the sleigh and reindeer to make Christmas deliveries in a dirigible of pressed tin. The white dirigible, decorated in blue and gold, is festooned with a green garland tied in red ribbon. Santa rides in the strawlike tin basket. The propeller actually twirls around! Caption: "Merry Christmas 1980."

Pressed Tin, 4" tall
550QX138-1, $5.50

The Animals' Christmas

A brown rabbit and a brown bird are decorating a snow-sprinkled Christmas tree.

Handcrafted, 2³⁷/₆₄" tall
800QX150-1, $8.00

A Spot of Christmas Cheer

Inside a plump teapot, a chipmunk busily trims a Christmas tree. On the outside there is a window with shutters and windowed door with a golden doorknob and 1980 "house number." Green garland with perky red bow gracefully decorates this small "home." Caption: "1980."

Handcrafted, 2⁴⁷/₆₄" tall
800QX153-4, $8.00

Elfin Antics

Dressed in holiday colors, acrobatic elves are tumbling down from the Christmas tree branch and right into Christmas. The bottom elf is ringing a gold metal bell.

Handcrafted, 4⁹/₁₆" tall
900QX142-1, $9.00

A Christmas Vigil

Pajama-clad little boy and his dog peek out the bedroom window just in time to glimpse Santa and his reindeer flying through the sky on Christmas Eve.

Handcrafted, 3¹³/₁₆" tall
900QX144-1, $9.00

Special Editions: A Heavenly Minstrel, Checking It Twice

Special Editions

Heavenly Minstrel

A beautiful old world angel with widespread wings is wearing a softly flowing blue dress, beige stole trimmed in gold, and turquoise ribbon in her hair. She is playing a celestial lute. Intricate details of this design make it exceptionally appealing.

Handcrafted, 6¼" tall
15QX156-7, $15.00

Checking It Twice

An elfin Santa with pointed ears is "checking his list" with real names printed on it. He is wearing spectacles of real metal, green elf-type shoes, red-and-white striped stockings, and suspendered red pants that end just below the knee. A ring of keys is caught in his belt loop.

Handcrafted, 5¹⁵/₁₆" tall
20QX158-4, $20.00

Holiday Chimes

Snowflake Chimes

Three stamped snowflakes revolve sparkling and chiming as they hang suspended from a fourth snowflake.

Chrome Plate, 1 59/64" diam.
550QX165-4, $5.50 □

Reindeer Chimes

Three reindeer "prance" from snowflake creating soft chimes and twinkling reflections. (Reissue from 1978 Annual Collection.)

Chrome Plate, 5½" tall
550QX320-3, $5.50

Santa Mobile

Santa with his sleigh and reindeer soar over three homes with smoking chimneys.

Chrome Plate, 3 57/64" tall
550QX136-1, $5.50 □

Collectible Series

Norman Rockwell — First Edition "Santa's Visitors"

Norman Rockwell's famous "Santa's Visitors" is reproduced in delicate white relief on a soft green background. This lovely collectible is sought by collectors of Norman Rockwell items as well as Christmas ornament collectors. Caption: "Santa's Visitors. The Norman Rockwell Collection, Christmas 1980."

Light Green Cameo, 3⅜" diam.
650QX306-1, $6.50 □

Frosty Friends — First Edition A Cool Yule

Sweet little Eskimo and polar bear friend are reading books with snowflakes on the covers while sitting on an icecube made of clear acrylic. The icecube is etched with the caption. This is the first issue in the Eskimo and Friend Series. Caption: "Merry Christmas 1980."

Handcrafted, 2 63/64" tall
650QX137-4, $6.50 □

SNOOPY and Friends — Second Edition SNOOPY Ski Holiday

The second design in this series reveals SNOOPY and Woodstock on a ski holiday. SNOOPY, wearing a red-and-green stocking cap, executes a dashing slalom, while just ahead of him Woodstock rides the slopes in SNOOPY's feeding bowl. Caption: "1980." and "SNOOPY."

Handcrafted, 3¼" diam.
900QX154-1, $9.00 □

Holiday Chimes: Santa Mobile, Snowflake Chime

New Collectible Series: Norman Rockwell-First Edition, Frosty Friends-First Edition

Collectible Series: Snoopy and Friends, Carrousel, Thimble

Collectible Series: Here Comes Santa, The Bellringer

Yarn Ornaments: Angel, Santa, Snowman, Soldier

Carrousel — Third Edition
Merry Carrousel

Santa and his reindeer are making their "rounds" on the carrousel design for 1980. The carrousel has bands of dots, circles, and flowers in red, white, green, and gold. The caption is on the top. This is the third in a very pretty and popular series. Caption: "Christmas 1980."

Handcrafted, 3⅛" tall
750QX141-4, $7.50 ☐

Thimble — Third Edition
Thimble Elf

Playful elf dressed in red and green swings on a thimble "bell" that hangs from a golden rope. This is third design in the Thimble Series.

Handcrafted, 2³¹/₃₂" tall
400QX132-1, $4.00 ☐

Here Comes Santa —
Second Edition
Santa's Express

Santa steams into Christmas 1980 in an old-fashioned locomotive. In the look of iron, the locomotive is red and black trimmed in gold. The wheels actually turn. Santa the engineer waves from the cab. This is the second design in this collectible series. Caption: "1980."

Handcrafted, 3" tall
12QX143-4, $12.00 ☐

The Bellringers — Second Edition

Two blue gowned angels, suspended from red ribbon streamers at the top of the bell, circle and ring the white porcelain with star "clappers" they are holding. This is number two in the Bellringer series. Caption: "1980" in center of gold, red, and green garland.

Porcelain & Handcrafted, 2⁷/₆₄" tall
15QX157-4, $15.00 ☐

Yarn and Fabric Ornaments

Yarn Ornaments

Four exquisitely detailed yarn ornaments with accents of lace and felt were introduced in 1980. These new offerings were all 5" tall and priced at $3.00.

300QX161-4	Santa	☐
300QX162-1	Angel	☐
300QX163-4	Snowman	☐
300QX164-1	Soldier	☐

Sewn Trimmers

The four versatile family favorites in the 1979 line were reissued in 1980. (See 1979 Annual Collection for photograph and description.)

THE 1981 COLLECTION

Two commemorative ball ornaments were introduced in 1981 for Godchild and 50 Years Together. In addition, new Baby's First Christmas ball ornaments designed specifically for a boy and a girl were added to the line.

Photo holder ornaments were also introduced this year, and a wooden ornament (Drummer Boy) with movable arms and legs was a distinctive addition to the line. Plush, "stuffed animal" ornaments were first seen this year, and the first edition of the instantly popular handcrafted Rocking Horse series made its debut.

Commemoratives

Baby's First Christmas — Girl

Design in pink and white pictures a baby girl holding a teddy bear. They are centered in a delicate floral ring. Floral border circles ornament to frame caption and scene of toys and gifts. Caption: "Baby's First Christmas 1981" and "There's nothing like a baby girl to cheer and brighten all the world at Christmas."

White Satin, 3¼" diam.
450QX600-2, $4.50   ☐

Baby's First Christmas — Boy

A baby boy holding a stuffed animal is in a circled frame of snowflakes that continue around the ornament. Toys and gifts border the soft blue ornament. Caption: "Baby's First Christmas 1981" and "There's nothing like a baby boy to bring a world of special joy at Christmas."

White Satin, 3¼" diam.
450QX601-5, $4.50   ☐

Baby's First Christmas — Black

Front — a happy black baby rests on green gingham cushions with his teddy bear and other toys. Back — the baby plays peekaboo under his comforter. Caption: "Baby's First Christmas 1981" and "A baby is a gift of joy, a gift of love at Christmas."

Ecru Soft-Sheen Satin, 3¼" diam.
450QX602-2, $4.50   ☐

Baby's First Christmas

A green wreath decorated with a red bow, baby shoes, rattle, bells, blocks that spell "BABY," frames photograph opening. Back — design repeat and caption in gold and white. Caption: "A Baby is the nicest gift of all" and "Baby's First Christmas 1981."

Acrylic, 4" diam.
550QX516-2, $5.50   ☐

Baby's First Christmas

Front — cameo design on soft green background is of a large, gift-wrapped box, a rocking horse on wheels, blocks, stuffed animal, and toys. Back — caption circled with raised design of ribbon and lace. Caption: "Baby's First Christmas 1981" and "A baby adds a special joy to all the joys of Christmas."

Light Green Cameo, 3⅜" diam.
850QX513-5, $8.50   ☐

Baby's First Christmas

Baby is tucked under captioned, fabric blanket in an old-fashioned baby carriage designed in the look of wicker. The wheels actually roll and the top of the carriage is festooned with red ribbon and bow. Caption: "Baby's First Christmas, 1981" printed on fabric blanket.

Handcrafted, 3¾" long
1300QX440-2, $13.00   ☐

Godchild

An angel and his puppy, floating on a cloud, are gathering stars from the sky and placing them in a bag. Background is blue. This is the first issue of this commemorative. Caption: "For a special Godchild" and "Christmas 1981."

White Satin, 3¼" diam.
450QX603-5, $4.50   ☐

Grandson

Santa and a reindeer are busy making and painting toys in his workshop. Caption: "A Grandson makes the 'Holly Days' extra bright and jolly days" and "Christmas 1981."

White Satin, 3¼" diam.
450QX604-2, $4.50   ☐

Granddaughter

Front — a plump white rocking horse with red, white, and blue ruffled and ribboned saddle is on a yellow background framed in a narrow red border design with blue nosegays at each side. Back — toys and the caption framed in border motif. Caption: "A Granddaughter adds a magical touch to the beauty and joy of Christmas" and "1981."

White Satin, 3¼" diam.
450QX605-5, $4.50   ☐

Daughter

Geometric design of "wallpaper" centered with pink flowers forms background of Christmas scene showing a kitten napping in a wicker chair, a doll, gifts, candy-filled jars, basket of flowers, and lighted candles. Caption: "A Daughter fills each day with joy by filling hearts with love" and "Christmas 1981."

Ecru Soft-Sheen Satin, 3¼" diam.
450QX607-5, $4.50   ☐

Son

Christmas tree, Santa, and a variety of toys are shown in multicolored squares. Caption: "A son puts the merry in Christmas" and "Christmas 1981."

White Satin, 3¼" diam.
450QX606-2, $4.50   ☐

Mother

Red roses and Christmas greenery surround the caption and date. Caption: "In a Mother's heart there is love…the very heart of Christmas." and "Christmas 1981."

White Satin, 3¼" diam.
450QX608-2, $4.50   ☐

Father

A beautiful male deer pausing briefly in a blue frozen forest. Caption: "Life changes season to season, year to year…but a Father's love is for always" and "Christmas 1981."

White Satin, 3¼" diam.
450QX609-5, $4.50   ☐

Mother and Dad

Front — white heart and red-lettered caption against background of holly and poinsettias on dark green. Back — Christmas message framed in holly and poinsettias. Caption: "For Mother and Dad, Christmas 1981" and "The wonderful meaning of Christmas is found in the circle of family love."

Ecru Soft-Sheen Satin, 3¼" diam.
450QX700-2, $4.50   ☐

Baby's First Christmas: For Girls, Boys and for Black Babies

Baby's First Christmas: Photoholder, Cameo, Handcrafted

Godchild, Grandson, Granddaughter, Daughter, Son

Mother, Father, Mother and Dad

Friendship

The caption is bordered by a harvest of fruit and flowers in shades of red and green. Caption: "The beauty of friendship never ends" and "Christmas 1981."

White Satin, 3¼" diam.
450QX704-2, $4.50

The Gift of Love

On a rich, deep blue background, red roses and holly leaves outlined in gold frame the gold-printed date and caption. Caption: "Love is a precious gift, priceless and perfect, cherished above all life's treasures" and "Christmas 1981."

Gold Glass, 3¼" diam.
450QX705-5, $4.50

Home

A lovely Victorian village scene with Christmas trees, gabled homes, and snow. Caption: "Christmas 1981" and "Love in the home puts joy in the heart."

White Satin, 3¼" diam.
450QX709-5, $4.50

Teacher

Red background and a red, green, blue, and white stocking filled with red apples for teacher. Caption: "For a special teacher, Christmas 1981."

White Satin, 3¼" diam.
450QX800-2, $4.50

Grandfather

The caption in red and gold is bordered by sprays of holly on a deep brown background. Caption: "Grandfather holds a special place in the heart" and "Christmas 1981."

Gold Glass, 3¼" diam.
450QX701-5, $4.50

Grandmother

Beige background with lacy border and poinsettias. Caption: "A Grandmother is so loving and dear at Christmas and throughout the year" and "Christmas 1981."

Ecru Soft-Sheen Satin, 3¼" diam.
450QX702-2, $4.50

Grandparents

A holly-sprigged basket filled with fruit, a jar of candy canes, Christmas ball ornaments, poinsettias, and a gift. Caption: "Grandparents give the gift of love at Christmas and all year 'round" and "1981."

White Glass, 3¼" diam.
450QX703-5, $4.50

Friendship, Gift of Love, Home, Teacher

Grandfather, Grandmother, Grandparents

First Christmas Together

Couple dressed in the style of the 1800s are ice skating against a red background sprinkled with golden snow-flakes. Hearts, poinsettias, blossoms, and holly in red, blue, and white band the ornament and frame heart shape enclosing caption on the back. Caption: "First Christmas Together 1981" and "Christmas…the season for sharing the spirit of Love."

Chrome Glass, 3¼" diam.
450QX706-2, $4.50 ☐

25th Christmas Together

White heart, white wedding bell, and white doves on green leaved and red floral background with red ribbons and bows. Caption: "25 Years Together, Christmas 1981" and "Christmas season of the heart, time of sweet remembrance."

White Glass, 3¼" diam.
450QX707-5, $4.50 ☐

50th Christmas

Brilliant red poinsettias, holly, and berries surround the captions on the front and back panels of this design. Caption: "Fifty Years Together, Christmas 1981" and "A treasure of memories is a very special happiness."

Gold Glass, 3¼" diam.
450QX708-2, $4.50 ☐

Love

A heart with the caption in its center has a wide border of etched holly and poinsettias. Caption is stamped with silver foil. Caption: "Love…the nicest gift of all. Christmas 1981."

Clear Acrylic, 3½" tall
550QX502-2, $5.50 ☐

Friendship

Perky squirrel holding a songbook sings a Christmas duet with his feathered friend. The caption curves across the top and is stamped with silver foil. Caption: "Friends put the "Merry" in Christmas" and "1981."

Clear Acrylic, 3¼" diam.
550QX503-5, $5.50 ☐

First Christmas Together

Quatrefoil ornament has the caption etched on the face and stamped with gold foil. Caption: "First Christmas Together 1981."

Clear Acrylic, 3" tall
550QX505-5, $5.50 ☐

First Christmas, Twenty-Fifth Christmas, Fiftieth Christmas

Love, Friendship, First Christmas, Twenty-Fifth Christmas

25th Christmas Together

Two molded wedding bells with frosted border designs are caught and tied with large ribbon bow and holly. The caption is etched on the forward bell and stamped in silver foil. Caption: "25 Years Together, Christmas 1981."

Clear Acrylic, 4½" tall
550QX504-2, $5.50 ☐

Property Ornaments

Betsey Clark

The background in soft blue is edged with raised border of ribbons and flowers. The cameo is of a little girl petting a small fawn. Caption: "Christmas, when hearts reach out to give and receive the gentle gifts of love" and "1981."

Soft Blue Cameo, 3⅜″ diam.
850QX512-2, $8.50 ☐

Betsey Clark

A Betsey Clark girl dressed in red and white and an inquisitive fawn are standing in the snow looking at a snow-covered tree topped with a yellow star.

Handcrafted, 3⁹/₃₂″ tall
900QX423-5, $9.00 ☐

Betsey Clark — Ninth Edition

Front — lace-bordered circle around scene of a little girl leaving a gift for her small friend who is standing in the doorway of her home. Back — the little girl pulls a gift-filled sleigh as she continues on her way delivering gifts. Background is in red, white, and blue patchwork. Ninth design in this collectible series. Caption: "Christmas 1981" and "The greatest joy of Christmas day comes from the joy we give away."

White Glass, 3¼″ diam.
450QX802-2, $4.50 ☐

MUPPETS™

Front — KERMIT™, dressed as Santa with a bag of toys, is on his way down the chimney. Back — MISS PIGGY™, elegantly gowned, lounges in front of fireplace awaiting Santa's visit. Her empty "stocking" is a high-heeled, fur-trimmed red boot. Caption: "Let's hear it for Christmas" and "Let's hear it for Santa" and "1981."

White Satin, 3¼″ diam.
450QX807-5, $4.50 ☐

KERMIT the FROG™

KERMIT™ dons a red-and-white cap for a coasting adventure on his realistic sled.

Handcrafted, 3¹¹/₃₂″ long
900QX424-2, $9.00 ☐

THE DIVINE MISS PIGGY™

MISS PIGGY™ poses as an angel with a brass halo and white wings. She is dressed in an aqua evening gown, lavender shoes, long gloves, and her trademark "diamond" ring is on her pinkie.

Handcrafted, 4″ long
1200QX425-5, $12.00 ☐

Betsey Clark Cameo, Handcrafted, Betsey Clark - Ninth Edition

MUPPETS™, KERMIT the FROG™, THE DIVINE MISS PIGGY™

Mary Hamilton, Marty Links

Mary Hamilton

Little angels are decorating, reading, napping, and playing musical instruments on a heavenly blue background. Caption: "Christmas 1981" and "Christmas decorates the world with wonder."

Gold Glass, 3¼" diam.
450QX806-2, $4.50 □

Marty Links

Front — two Marty Links children carrying a very large candy cane are followed by their hungry puppy. Back — laughing little girl holds mistletoe over her head. Caption: "Christmas 1981" and "Happy hearts and good times go hand in hand at Christmas."

White Satin, 3¼" diam.
450QX808-2, $4.50 □

PEANUTS™

SNOOPY, Woodstock, and his flock sing merrily as they deck the halls. Each bird adds a "la" to the chorus. Caption: "Deck the halls with boughs of holly…Christmas 1981."

White Satin, 3¼" diam.
450QX803-5, $4.50 □

Joan Walsh Anglund©

Front — three Anglund children are decorating the stair rail. Back — the three are seated on a green couch reading from a book. The couch is on a braided rug with a decorated tree at one side and a table with lighted candle at the other. Caption: " 'Tis the time of dreams come true. 'Tis the time for merrymaking" and "Christmas 1981."

White Satin, 3¼" diam.
450QX804-2, $4.50 □

DISNEY

Sorcerer's apprentice Mickey Mouse creates the magic of a decorated, candlelit tree filled with presents and toys against deep blue of star-sprinkled nighttime sky. Caption: "Christmas 1981" and "Christmas is a time of magic, it's the season of surprise, everything begins to sparkle right before your very eyes."

White Satin, 3¼" diam.
450QX805-5, $4.50 □

PEANUTS™, Joan Walsh Anglund,© DISNEY

Christmas 1981 - Schneeberg, Christmas Magic, Traditional (Black Santa), Let Us Adore Him

Decorative Ball Ornaments

Christmas 1981 — Schneeberg

Design reproduced from a photograph of a Schneeberg collage has birds, beads, musical instruments, and candy on a white background. A Christmas tree decorated with birds, animals, beads, and candy is central motif. Santa is pictured leaving array of toys under it. Back — beautiful sunburst made of beads and colored glass ball ornaments is centered with dated banner. Caption: "1981."

White Satin, 3¼" diam.
450QX809-5, $4.50 ☐

Christmas Magic

A gnomelike Santa and animals are ice skating. Caption: "Christmas 1981" and "It's here, there, everywhere…Christmas magic's in the air."

White Satin, 3¼" diam.
450QX810-2, $4.50 ☐

Traditional (Black Santa)

Front — Santa feeds his animal friends in a snowy forest. Back — wreath-framed Santa gives a merry wave. Caption: "It's Christmas. It's time for sharing…and dreaming, and caring and merry gift bearing…" and "1981."

White Satin, 3¼" diam.
450QX801-5, $4.50 ☐

Let Us Adore Him

A beautiful, radiant scene of the Nativity with cherubim adoring the Christ Child in the manger. The background is dark brown. Caption: "Christmas 1981" and "O come let us adore him."

Gold Glass, 3¼" diam.
450QX811-5, $4.50 ☐

Santa's Coming

Front — Santa holds the reins of his toy-filled sleigh while Mrs. Santa makes sure his scarf is wrapped snugly around his neck. The reindeers are poised and ready. Back — Santa and his reindeers are flying through the air on a moonlit night. Caption: "Christmas 1981" and "Hustle, bustle, hurry, scurry, Santa's coming…never worry."

White Satin, 3¼" diam.
450QX812-2, $4.50 ☐

Christmas in the Forest

On a snowy Christmas night the animals and birds admire the white blossoms peeking through the snow. Caption: "Christmas 1981" and "Softly…gently…joyfully… Christmas arrives in the heart."

Gold Glass, 3¼" diam.
450QX813-5, $4.50 ☐

Santa's Coming, Christmas in the Forest, Merry Christmas, Santa's Surprise

Crown Classics: Angel, Tree Photoholder, Unicorn

Frosted Images: Angel, Mouse, Snowman

Merry Christmas

Front — gold-accented burgundy diamonds with tiny red flowers on green background centered with "1981." Back — same design with colors reversed. Caption: "Merry Christmas 1981."

Gold Glass, 3¼" diam.
450QX814-2, $4.50   ☐

Santa's Surprise

On a wintry night Santa plucks the stars from the deep blue sky and uses them to decorate a small evergreen tree in the snow. Caption: "Twinkle, glimmer, sparkle, shimmer…let the Christmas season shine" and "Christmas 1981."

White Satin, 3¼" diam.
450QX815-5, $4.50   ☐

Crown Classics

Angel

Golden-haired angel with white wings is wearing long robe in shades of red which is tied with a green sash. Designed with the look of leaded stained glass.

Acrylic, 3¾" tall
450QX507-5, $4.50   ☐

Tree Photoholder

Front — green Christmas tree decorated with multicolored ornaments has a round opening to hold a photograph. Back — design repeat and captions in gold. Caption: "Christmas 1981."

Acrylic, 3²⁷/₃₂" tall
550QX515-5, $5.50   ☐

Unicorn

Front — graceful unicorn in white cameo is shown on a soft green background. Back — raised floral medallions frame white lettered caption. Caption: "A time of magical moments, dreams come true…Christmas 1981."

Light Green Cameo, 3⅜" diam.
850QX516-5, $8.50   ☐

Frosted Images

Three frosted, three-dimensional ornaments with the look of etched crystal. Ranging in size from 1¹⁵/₃₂" to 1¹⁹/₃₂" tall, they were priced at $4.00

400QX508-2	Mouse	☐
400QX509-5	Angel	☐
400QX510-2	Snowman	☐

Holiday Highlights: Shepherd Scene, Christmas Star

Holiday Highlights

Shepherd Scene
A shepherd with his sheep see the distant city of Bethlehem glowing by the light of the star. Caption is stamped with silver foil. Caption: "Christmas 1981."

Clear Acrylic, 4" tall
550QX500-2, $5.50 □

Christmas Star
Star with a raised, faceted border has emerald shapes tucked between the points. Silver foil stamping accents the caption. Caption: "Christmas 1981."

Clear Acrylic, 3½" tall
550QX501-5, $5.50 □

Little Trimmers

Puppy Love
A bread-dough look tan puppy with a red heart on his chest and a cord of real red ribbon around his neck.

Handcrafted, 1⁵⁄₃₂" tall
350QX406-2, $3.50 □

Jolly Snowman
Smiling snowman wears a black top hat and a real fabric scarf.

Handcrafted, 2⁷⁄₃₂" tall
350QX407-5, $3.50 □

Perky Penguin
Tiny penguin wears a red cap and red and green striped scarf.

Handcrafted, 1⁵⁄₁₆" tall
350QX409-5, $3.50 □

Clothespin Drummer Boy
Drummer boy dressed in a black and brown uniform and a red hat beats his red drum.

Handcrafted, 2¹³⁄₁₆" tall
450QX408-2, $4.50 □

The Stocking Mouse
A white mouse wearing a blue-and-white polka dot nightcap peeks out of the top of a green and red real knit stocking.

Handcrafted, 2¼" tall
450QX412-2, $4.50 □

Handcrafted Ornaments

Space Santa
Space-helmeted Santa is flying in a silver suit carrying a dated silver star. Caption: "1981."

Handcrafted, 3" tall
650QX430-2, $6.50 □

Little Trimmers: Puppy Love, Jolly Snowman, Perky Penguin, Clothespin Drummer Boy, The Stocking Mouse

Candyville Express

A locomotive designed with the look of sugar-coated gumdrops has wheels of "cookies" and "licorice candy."

Handcrafted, 3″ long
750QX418-2, $7.50 □

Ice Fairy

A lovely white ice fairy with frosted acrylic wings holds a clear acrylic snowflake.

Handcrafted & Acrylic, 4⅛″ tall
650QX431-5, $6.50 □

Star Swing

Little girl dressed in red, blue, and green swings from a chrome-plated brass star with the date on it.

Brass & Handcrafted, 3⅝″ tall
550QX421-5, $5.50 □

A Heavenly Nap

Design is reissued from 1980. (See 1980 Annual Collection.)

Handcrafted, 3¼″ tall
650QX139-4, $6.50 □

Dough Angel

In the style of bread-dough, a little angel wearing a blue-and-white dress holds a star. A reissue from 1978. (See 1978 Annual Collection.)

Handcrafted, 2¹⁵/₁₆″ tall
550QX139-6, $5.50 □

Topsy-Turvy Tunes

An opossom hangs by his tail from a tree branch, while a little red bird perches on the songbook that the opossom is holding. Caption: "Carols" on the green book cover.

Handcrafted, 3″ tall
750QX429-5, $7.50 □

A Well-Stocked Stocking

Real knit red-and-white stocking is filled to capacity with a doll, jack-in-the-box, candy cane, and other toys.

Handcrafted, 4½″ tall
900QX154-7, $9.00 □

The Friendly Fiddler

A rabbit wearing a green and red scarf plays a Christmas tune on a fiddle tucked under his chin.

Handcrafted, 3⁵/₃₂″ tall
800QX434-2, $8.00 □

The Ice Sculptor

Bear "artist" in red smock and green tam is busily sculpting a self portrait in ice (clear acrylic).

Handcrafted, 3¹/₃₂″ tall
800QX432-2, $8.00 □

Space Santa, Candyville Express, Ice Fairy, Star Swing

Topsy-Turvy Tunes, A Well-Stocked Stocking, The Friendly Fiddler, The Ice Sculptor

Christmas Dreams

Front — this peek-through design shows a little boy dressed in a blue snowsuit, white scarf, and brown knit cap admiring a teddy bear displayed in a toy shop window. Back — peek-through view from inside the toy store. Caption: "Toy Shop 1981."

Handcrafted, 3¼" diam.
1200QX437-5, $12.00 ☐

Christmas Fantasy

A graceful white goose with a real brass ribbon caught in his bill gives a ride to an elf astride his back. The elf is dressed in red and green.

Handcrafted, 3¾" long
1300QX155-4, $13.00 ☐

Sailing Santa

Santa is sailing in the basket of a red hot air balloon. Green-and-red Christmas stockings are used for weights on the basket. The balloon has gold painted trim and white caption and date. Caption: "Merry Christmas 1981."

Handcrafted, 5" tall
1300QX439-5, $13.00 ☐

Love and Joy (Porcelain Chimes)

White bisque chimes are comprised of three white doves suspended from a white heart bearing impressed caption and date. Chimes have red fabric ribbon. Caption: "1981."

Porcelain, 3¾" tall
900QX425-2, $9.00 ☐

Drummer Boy

This hand-painted drummer boy is made of real wood and has movable arms and legs.

Wood, 3½" tall
250QX148-1, $2.50 ☐

St. Nicholas

Traditional European St. Nicholas wearing a long coat holds a lantern to light his way as he makes his rounds delivering presents from his pack.

Pressed Tin, 4⅜" tall
550QX446-2, $5.50 ☐

Mr. & Mrs. Claus

Mr. & Mrs. Claus are reissued from their introductory year, 1975. Santa has a kitten on his shoulder and Mrs. Claus, wearing a red dress, white bonnet and apron, holds two kittens in her arms. (See 1975 Annual Collection.)

Handcrafted, 3¾" tall
1200QX448-5, 2 in box $12.00 ☐

Christmas Dreams front and back

Christmas Fantasy, Sailing Santa

Love and Joy, Drummer Boy, St. Nicholas

Holiday Chimes: Snowman Chime

Checking It Twice

This popular Santa is a reissue from 1980.
(See 1980 Annual Collection.)

Handcrafted, 5¹⁵/₁₆″ tall
2250QX158-4, $22.50

Holiday Chimes

Snowman Chimes

New in the chimes collection is the
Snowman and his family. Mr. Snowman
wears a top hat and holds a straw broom.
Mrs. Snowman has a design on her dress, and
the Snowchild wearing a knit-type hat
holds a cane and gift. They are suspended
from a large snowflake.

Chrome Plate, 4″ tall
550QX445-5, $5.50   □

Santa Mobile

550QX136-1, Reissue from 1980, $5.50

Snowflake Chimes

550QX165-4, Reissue from 1980, $5.50

(See 1980 Annual Collection for
photographs and descriptions of these
reissues.)

Collectible Series

Rocking Horse — First Edition

A brown and white palomino horse with
tail of real brown yarn is rocking along on
dated red rockers. Saddle is red and the
blanket under the saddle is blue. Caption:
"1981."

Handcrafted, 2″ tall
900QX422-2, $9.00   □

New Collectible Series: Rocking Horse - First Edition

Collectible Series

Bellringer — Third Edition
Swingin' Bellringer

The clapper of this gold-rimmed porcelain bell is a candy cane with a mouse wearing a green cap sitting in its curve. Third design in this series. Caption: "1981" in the center of fired-on wreath decal.

Ceramic & Handcrafted, 4" tall
1500QX441-5, $15.00

Norman Rockwell —
Second Edition
"Carolers"

Front — delicate white cameo representation of Rockwell's "Carolers." Back — caption in white letters. Caption: "Carolers, second in a series, the Norman Rockwell Collection Christmas 1981."

Dark Blue Cameo, 3 ⅜" diam.
850QX511-5, $8.50

Here Comes Santa —
Third Edition
Rooftop Deliveries

Santa changed his mode of transportation this year. He "drives" over roofs in a vehicle that resembles an old milk truck. The roof of the truck is green. The sign on the side is ornately printed in red, deep yellow, and green. The black tired wheels have golden spokes. Third design in this series. Caption: "S. Claus & Co. Rooftop Deliveries 1981."

Handcrafted, 4¹⁄₁₆" tall
1300QX438-2, $13.00

Carrousel — Fourth Edition
Skaters Carrousel

Fourth design in this series features a family of four ice-skating around a green pole in the center of the carrousel. Carrousel top has hand-painted bands of green, red, and blue with white snowflakes. The date is stamped on the top edge of the carrousel roof. Caption: "1981."

Handcrafted, 2¹⁵⁄₃₂" tall
900QX427-5, $9.00

SNOOPY and Friends —
Third Edition

A "birdsled" team of Woodstock and friends is pulling SNOOPY past a SNOOPY snowman. The snowman is wearing a black top hat and green scarf. A sign in the snow is dated. This is third design in this series. Caption: "1981."

Handcrafted, 3¼" diam.
1200QX436-2, $12.00

Collectible Series: The Bellringer - Third Edition; Norman Rockwell - Second Edition; Here Comes Santa - Third Edition; Carrousel - Fourth Edition

Collectible Series: Snoopy and Friends - Third Edition; Thimble - Fourth Edition; Frosty Friends - Second Edition

Sewn Ornaments: Peppermint Mouse, Gingham Dog, Calico Kitty, Cardinal Cutie

Thimble — Fourth Edition

A flying angel with white wings and brass halo is holding a diminutive Christmas tree that is potted in a thimble. Her pink robe is edged in gold.

Handcrafted, 1½" diam.
450QX413-5, $4.50 ☐

Frosty Friends — Second Edition

An Eskimo and a Husky puppy are sheltered snugly in an igloo. Date over the entrance is framed with green holly and red berries. This is the second design in this series. Caption: "1981."

Handcrafted, 2" tall
800QX433-5, $8.00 ☐

Yarn and Fabric Ornaments

Sewn Ornaments

New for 1981, these darling fabric animals feature ribbon trims and quilting details. All are 3" tall and priced at $3.00

300QX400-2	*Cardinal Cutie*	☐
300QX401-5	*Peppermint Mouse*	☐
300QX402-2	*Gingham Dog*	☐
300QX403-5	*Calico Kitty*	☐

Yarn Ornaments

The four designs in this series were reissued from 1980 by popular demand. (See 1980 Annual Collection for photograph and description.)

Plush Animals

Two charming plush animals were new introductions in 1981 and were individually packaged in gift boxes.

Christmas Teddy

Teddy wears a red knitted stocking cap and perky plaid ribbon bow.

Plush, 4" tall
550QX404-2, $5.50 ☐

Raccoon Tunes

Merry raccoon caroler is clad in felt vest and holds a felt songbook.

Plush, 4" tall
550QX405-5, $5.50 ☐

Plush Ornaments: Christmas Teddy, Raccoon Tunes

THE 1982 COLLECTION

In 1982 Hallmark's Keepsake Ornament Collection celebrated its tenth issue year by introducing three new series of collectible ornaments. Making their first appearances were the Holiday Wildlife series, the Tin Locomotive series, and the Clothespin series.

Six decorative glass ball ornaments were introduced in a special "Designer Keepsakes" offering which included a clear glass ball ornament featuring a permanent, fired-on decal. Four new ornament formats were added to the line: cloisonné, hand-embroidered fabric, sculptured acrylic, and dimensional brass ornaments.

The end of the first decade also marked the adoption of a new procedure specially created to assist Keepsake collectors. Beginning in 1982, all of the ornaments in the Collector's Series were stamped with an identifying Christmas Tree symbol or the words "—— in a series" (which permanently documents which issue the item is in the series). An edition number was also printed in the tree symbol to mark the ornament's issue date. The new identifying symbols made collecting easier and more exciting for the Hallmark Keepsake collectors — a group which represented 65 percent of all Hallmark Keepsake Ornament purchasers in 1982.

Commemoratives

Baby's First Christmas - Photoholder

Red-and-white Christmas stocking filled with toys, candy, and gifts. Caption appears on the back. Caption: "Baby's First Christmas 1982" and "Oh what joy and sweet surprise Christmas brings to little eyes."

Acrylic, 4¼" tall
650QX312-6, $6.50 □

Baby's First Christmas

A baby's white rattle with a peek-in window showing baby taking a nap in a crib beside a window. Gold handle topped with red ring is tied in green ribbon. All hand painted. Caption: "Baby's First Christmas 1982."

Handcrafted, 3" tall
1300QX455-3, $13.00 □

Baby's First Christmas (Boy)

Most uniquely, this design was actually hand embroidered by an artist and then photographed for this ornament. The baby girl ornament was also created in the same manner. Caption: "Baby's First Christmas 1982" and "A baby boy is a precious gift — a blessing from above."

Light Blue Satin, 3¼" diam.
450QX216-3, $4.50 □

Baby's First Christmas (Girl)

Embroidered toys for a baby girl form a quilt motif. Caption: "Baby's First Christmas 1982" and "A baby girl is the sweetest gift a lifetime can provide."

Light Pink Satin, 3¼" diam.
450QX207-3, $4.50 □

Baby's First Christmas - Photoholder, Handcrafted, For Boy, For Girl

Godchild

A little angel stands on a holly bough to reach an elusive snowflake. Caption: "Merry Christmas to a Special Godchild. 1982."

White Glass, 3¼" diam.
450QX222-6, $4.50

Grandson

Bunnies sledding in the snow. Caption: "A Grandson...makes days bright, hearts light and Christmas time a real delight. Christmas 1982."

White Satin, 3¼" diam.
450QX224-6, $4.50

Granddaughter

Puppies, teddy bears, and bunnies hold a rope of green garland which encircles the ornament. This design was reproduced from a three-dimensional soft sculpture. Caption: "A Granddaughter has a special gift for giving special joy" and "Christmas 1982."

White Satin, 3¼" diam.
450QX224-3, $4.50

Son

Marching band dressed in red and teal blue uniforms keeps perfect step on a caramel-colored background. Caption: "A Son is the pride of your heart, the joy of your life" and "Christmas 1982."

Caramel Soft-Sheen Satin, 3¼" diam.
450QX204-3, $4.50

Daughter

Colors of peppermint pink, candy cane red, and soft pastels are used to illustrate tempting array of Christmas goodies. Caption: "A Daughter's love makes Christmas special. 1982."

Ecru Soft-Sheen Satin, 3¼" diam.
450QX204-6, $4.50

Father

Framed, hand colored, woodcut-style artwork bands this ornament. Caption: "A Father's love brightens the season" and "Christmas 1982."

Ecru Soft-Sheen Satin, 3¼" diam.
450QX205-6, $4.50

Mother

Front — poinsettia bouquet tied in pink ribbons. Back — holly and pine garland around caption. Caption: "The spirit of Christmas lives in a Mother's loving heart. Christmas 1982."

White Glass, 3¼" diam.
450QX205-3, $4.50

Godchild, Grandson, Granddaughter, Son, Daughter

Father, Mother, Mother and Dad, Sister

Mother and Dad

Sprays of holly leaves, berries, and evergreens caught with red ribbons form beautiful contrast against the white porcelain glass. Caption: "A Mother and Dad know so many ways to warm a heart with love" and "Christmas 1982."

White Porcelain Glass, 3¼" diam.
450QX222-3, $4.50

Sister

Front — small girl ice skating on a pond with three houses in the background. Back — the girl petting a white bunny. All in soft pastels. This is a new introduction of an ornament commemorating Sister. Caption: "A Sister brings the beauty of memories and the warmth of love to Christmas 1982."

White Glass, 3¼" diam.
450QX208-3, $4.50

Grandmother, Grandfather, Grandparents

First Christmas Together: Cameo, Glass Ball, Brass Locket

Grandparents

Homes on snow covered hillsides, an ice skating outing, and an old covered bridge. Caption: "With thoughts of Grandparents come thoughts of days the heart will always treasure" and "Christmas 1982."

White Glass, 3¼" diam.
450QX214-6, $4.50 ☐

First Christmas Together

Dressed in style of Charles Dickens' characters, a couple ice skate together. Caption: "Christmas is for sharing with the special one you love." and "First Christmas Together 1982."

Turquoise Cameo, 3⅜" diam.
850QX306-6, $8.50 ☐

First Christmas Together

Delicate frosty background gives lacy, silvered effect to stark bare trees. A pair of redbirds soaring in the snowy mist symbolize the caption. Caption: "Quiet moments together...love that lasts forever" and "First Christmas Together 1982."

Silver Chrome Glass, 3¼" diam.
450QX211-3, $4.50 ☐

First Christmas Together — Locket

Dimensional, hinged, heart-shaped brass locket opens to become two hearts, each with insert for a photo. Includes brass hanger. Caption: "First Christmas Together 1982."

Polished Brass, 2⅝" tall
1500QX456-3, $15.00 ☐

Christmas Memories

Square white frame is trimmed in red ribbon and green holly leaves. Outline of red bow shapes the top which has tab for hanging on the tree. The caption is stamped in raised letters on the back of the design. Caption: "How bright the joys of Christmas, how warm the memories" and "1982."

Acrylic, 4⅛" tall
650QX311-6, $6.50 ☐

Teacher

Elves in their antics cast shadows that spell "CHRISTMAS 1982." The last elf holds up an apple with the caption on the gift tag. Caption: "To a Special Teacher" and "Christmas 1982."

White Glass, 3¼" diam.
450QX214-3, $4.50 ☐

Grandmother

Patchwork quilt effect of lace, ribbon, fabric, and embroidery. Caption: "A Grandmother is love. Christmas 1982."

Dark Pink Satin, 3¼" diam.
450QX200-3, $4.50 ☐

Grandfather

A graceful deer amid feathery scrolls. Caption: "Grandfather...in his strength he teaches, in his gentleness he loves. Christmas 1982."

Dark Blue Satin, 3¼" diam.
450QX207-6, $4.50 ☐

New Home

Nighttime scene of colorful village homes and snow-covered hillsides. Caption: "Christmas time fills hearts with love and homes with warmth and joy. 1982."

Dark Blue Satin, 3¼" diam.
450QX212-6, $4.50 ☐

Teacher

Snow-covered red schoolhouse has a belltower and Christmas tree at the side. Caption: "Merry Christmas to my Teacher" and "1982."

Acrylic, 3¹⁵/₁₆" tall
650QX312-3, $6.50 ☐

25th Christmas Together

Pictures the warm, welcoming glow of lighted windows on a frosty, snow-covered night. Caption: "Christmas…as timeless as snowfall, as forever as candleglow, as always as love" and "Twenty-fifth Christmas together 1982."

White Porcelain Glass, 3¼" diam.
450QX211-6, $4.50 ☐

50th Christmas Together

Gold-on-gold background has design of scrolled borders and ornate lettering in burgundy highlighted with white. Caption: "We measure our time, not by years alone, but by the love and joy we've known" and "50th Christmas Together 1982."

Gold Glass, 3¼" diam.
450QX212-3, $4.50 ☐

Moments of Love

Stagecoach with galloping team is silhouetted in white against deep blue sky sprinkled with snowflakes. Caption: "Each moment of love lives forever in memory" and "Christmas 1982."

Blue Soft-Sheen Satin, 3¼" diam.
450QX209-3, $4.50 ☐

Love

Wreaths of Christmas flowers and greenery frame the caption and date. Caption: "Christmas…season bright with love" and "Christmas 1982."

Ecru Soft-Sheen Satin, 3¼" diam.
450QX209-6, $4.50 ☐

Friendship

Happy animals ice skating merrily. Caption: "Hearts are happy when friends are together" and "Christmas 1982."

White Satin, 3¼" diam.
450QX208-6, $4.50 ☐

Christmas Memories Photoholder, Teacher: Glass Ball, New Home, Teacher Photoholder

Twenty-Fifth Christmas Together, Fiftieth Christmas Together, Moments of Love, Love, Friendship

Teacher, Baby's 1st Christmas, First Christmas Together, Love, Friendship

Teacher — Apple

A clear acrylic apple with green foil stamped leaves, red foil-stamped caption, and etched scrolls. Caption: "To a Special Teacher. 1982."

Acrylic, 3½" tall
550QX301-6, $5.50

Baby's First Christmas

Cuddly teddy bear in frosted acrylic holds clear acrylic block that contains caption which is stamped in silver foil. Caption: "Baby's First Christmas 1982."

Acrylic, 3¹⁷/₃₂" tall
550QX302-3, $5.50

First Christmas Together

A contemporary, tailored tree with caption and date stamped in silver foil. Caption: "1982" and "First Christmas Together."

Acrylic, 4¼" tall
550QX302-6, $5.50

Love

Heart-shaped with etched leaves and scrolls, and caption stamped in gold foil. Caption: "Love is forever between two hearts that share it. 1982."

Acrylic, 4⅛" tall
550QX304-3, $5.50

Friendship

Kitten in a stocking is held by a puppy wearing knitted Santa cap. Caption is stamped with silver foil. Caption: "Christmas is for friends 1982."

Acrylic, 3¼" tall
550QX304-6, $5.50

Property Ornaments

MISS PIGGY and KERMIT™

Front — MISS PIGGY™ lounges among gifts with a beautiful tree in the background. Back — KERMIT™ hangs Christmas balls on a garland. Caption: "Have yourself a lavish little Christmas" and "Season's greenings 1982."

White Satin, 3¼" diam.
450QX218-3, $4.50

MUPPETS™ Party

The whole MUPPETS™ gang is gathered for a Christmas party. There are musicians, carolers, gifts, and MISS PIGGY™ in her finery seated on the piano next to a tall candelabra. Caption: "Merry Christmas 1982."

White Satin, 3¼" diam.
450QX218-6, $4.50

KERMIT the FROG™

KERMIT™ is a real sport skiing down the slopes of the Christmas tree wearing red cap trimmed in white and red skiis and poles.

Handcrafted, 3³/₁₆" tall
1100QX495-6, $11.00

THE DIVINE MISS PIGGY™

Reissue from 1981. (See 1981 Annual Collection.)

Handcrafted, 4" long
1200QX425-5, $12.00

Betsey Clark

Little angel is decorating a Christmas tree while floating on a cloud. Caption: " 'Tis the season for trimming trees and making merry memories" and "Christmas 1982."

Blue Cameo, 3⅜" diam.
850QX305-6, $8.50

MISS PIGGY and KERMIT™, MUPPET™ Party, KERMIT the FROG™

Betsey Clark Cameo, Norman Rockwell - Third Edition, Betsey Clark - 10th Edition, Norman Rockwell Satin Ball

PEANUTS®, DISNEY, Mary Hamilton, Joan Walsh Anglund©

Norman Rockwell — Third Edition

Design in white on red of Christmas mantel and Santa laughing at a very tiny stocking he is supposed to fill. Caption and date stamped in silver foil are on the back. Caption: "Filling the Stockings. Third in a Series. The Norman Rockwell Collection. Christmas 1982."

Red Cameo, 3⅜″ diam.
850QX305-3, $8.50 ☐

Betsey Clark — Tenth Edition

Three children in their nighties share a bedtime story beside a tiny decorated Christmas tree and wrapped gifts. Caption: "The joys of Christmas are multiplied when shared with those we love" and "Christmas 1982."

White Satin, 3¼″ diam.
450QX215-6, $4.50 ☐

Norman Rockwell

A young boy pictured in three panels is putting on a Santa suit and stuffing a pillow in the front of the pants; carolling enthusiastically in church; and dressed in robe and pajamas holding a candle. Caption: "From the Norman Rockwell Collection 1982. Hearts are light, smiles are bright, child's delight, it's Christmas."

Red Soft-Sheen Satin, 3¼″ diam.
450QX202-3, $4.50 ☐

PEANUTS®

SNOOPY cycles his way into the holidays riding a tandem bicycle with Woodstock and the flock. Caption: "Christmas 1982."

Light Blue Satin, 3¼″ diam.
450QX200-6, $4.50 ☐

DISNEY

The Seven Dwarfs are carrying candy canes, toys, gifts, wreath, and the tree as they prepare for Christmas. Caption: "Christmas…time for surprises — in all shapes and sizes" and "1982."

White Satin, 3½″ diam.
450QX217-3, $4.50 ☐

Mary Hamilton

Tiny angels are ringing bells, floating on clouds, and perched on musical notes as they sing and play Christmas carols. Caption: "Joy to the world. 1982."

Blue Soft-Sheen Satin, 3¼″ diam.
450QX217-6, $4.50 ☐

Joan Walsh Anglund©

Joan Walsh Anglund's children admire a snow-laden tree with a gold star on top. Caption: "Friends make Christmas memories. 1982."

White Satin, 3¼″ diam.
450QX219-3, $4.50 ☐

Designer Keepsakes: Old World Angels, Patterns of Christmas, Old Fashioned Christmas

Designer Keepsakes: Stained Glass, Merry Christmas, Twelve Day of Christmas

Designer Keepsakes

Old World Angels
Old-world angels holding lighted candles float amid stars and streamers.

White Porcelain Glass, 3¼″ diam.
450QX226-3, $4.50 □

Patterns of Christmas
Oriental designs of poinsettias and holly are highlighted in gold. The use of gold inks adds extra richness to this elegant design.

Gold Glass, 3¼″ diam.
450QX226-6, $4.50 □

Old Fashioned Christmas
Reproduction of antique English greeting cards from the late 1800s depicts children decorating for Christmas. Caption "Merry Christmas" and "Happy New Year."

White Porcelain Glass, 3¼″ diam.
450QX227-6, $4.50 □

Stained Glass
Created in the style of a leaded, stained glass window, design of holly and poinsettias forms pleasing contrast with panels of lavender, blue, and green. The use of pearlized inks makes this design shimmer.

White Glass, 3¼″ diam.
450QX228-3, $4.50 □

Merry Christmas
This design is the first to use fired-on decal application to a clear glass ball. Caption: "Merry Christmas" and "Happy Holidays."

Clear Glass, 3¼″ diam.
450QX225-6, $4.50 □

Twelve Days of Christmas
Attractive painting illustrates the verses of favorite old Christmas carol. White pebbled glass captures the look of a snowscape realistically. Caption: "The Twelve Days of Christmas 1982."

White Pebbled Glass, 3¼″ diam.
450QX203-6, $4.50 □

Decorative Ball Ornaments

Christmas Angel
Beautiful angel on a deep blue background shelters the flame of a glowing candle. Caption: "From Heaven above the light of love shines into our hearts at Christmas" and "1982."

Gold Glass, 3¼″ diam.
450QX220-6, $4.50 □

Christmas Angel, Santa, Currier and Ives, A Season for Caring

Santa

Front — a close-up of Santa. Back — Santa smoking his pipe. Caption: "His eyes, how they twinkled, his dimples, how merry" and "Christmas 1982."

White Porcelain Glass, 3¼" diam.
450QX221-6, $4.50 ☐

Currier & Ives

This reproduction of "The Road — Winter" is from an original Currier and Ives print "registered according to an Act of Congress in 1853." A couple takes an afternoon sleigh ride on a country road. Caption: "Christmas 1982" and "The Road — Winter"; "Currier and Ives."

White Porcelain Glass, 3¼" diam.
450QX201-3, $4.50 ☐

Season for Caring

A beautiful soft blue night scene of the star shining over Bethlehem. A little shepherd with his sheep are following the star. Caption: "Christmas...Season for caring" and "1982."

Light Blue Soft-Sheen Satin, 3¼" diam.
450QX221-3, $4.50 ☐

Colors of Christmas

Nativity

Traditional portrayal of the Holy Family is shown in the look of a leaded, stained glass window.

Acrylic, 4" tall
450QX308-3, $4.50 ☐

Santa's Flight

Santa aboard a hot air balloon is created in stained glass style. Caption "Christmas 1982."

Acrylic, 4¼" tall
450QX308-6, $4.50 ☐

Colors of Christmas: Nativity, Santa's Flight

Ice Sculptures

Snowy Seal

A happy, smiling seal is sculptured in clear acrylic.

Clear Acrylic, 1¹⁹/₃₂" tall
400QX300-6, $4.00 ☐

Arctic Penguin

A penguin molded in clear acrylic.

Clear Acrylic, 1½" tall
400QX300-3, $4.00 ☐

Ice Sculptures: Snowy Seal, Artic Penguin

Holiday Highlights

Christmas Sleigh

A sleigh bearing gifts and a Christmas tree has runners and caption that are stamped in silver foil. Caption: "Christmas 1982."

Acrylic, 3²³/₃₂" tall
550QX309-3, $5.50 ☐

Angel

Angel wearing flowing gown plays a heavenly harp. Caption is stamped in gold foil. Caption: "Rejoice."

Acrylic, 3½" tall
550QX309-6, $5.50 ☐

Christmas Magic

Etched design is of a little rabbit admiring an ornament hanging from a bough. This Crown Classic is in the shape of an oval Christmas ornament with scrolling that outlines the cap at the top. The caption is stamped with silver foil. Caption: "Christmas…season of magical moments."

Acrylic, 3¹³/₁₆" tall
550QX311-3, $5.50 ☐

Holiday Highlights: Christmas Sleigh, Angel, Christmas Magic

Handcrafted Ornaments

Three Kings

On a dark blue background the Three Kings are traveling to the city of Bethlehem shown in the distance. Caption: "By a star shining brightly, Three Kings set their course and followed the heavenly light to its source" and "1982."

Blue Cameo, 3⅜" diam.
850QX307-3, $8.50 ☐

Baroque Angel

A beautiful cherubim wearing a regal lavender ribbon is holding a pole with a stamped brass banner as he flies into Christmas. Caption: "Joyeux Noel."

Brass and Handcrafted, 4⁷/₁₆" tall
1500QX456-6, $15.00 ☐

Cloisonné Angel

An open heart with blue enameled leaf border is centered with an angel herald enameled in blue, white, and red. On the reverse of the angel are the words "Peace, Love, Joy" in raised letters.

Cloisonné, 2²¹/₃₂" tall
1200QX145-4, $12.00 ☐

Three Kings, Baroque Angel, Cloisonne Angel

Brass Ornaments: Santa and Reindeer, Brass Bell, Santa's Sleigh

Brass Ornaments

Unique ornaments crafted of highly polished brass are lacquer-coated to prevent tarnishing. These distinctive ornaments were introduced in 1982.

Santa and Reindeer

Santa flies through the night in a brass runnered sleigh drawn by four stamped-brass reindeer.

Brass and Handcrafted, 2⁹/₃₂″ tall
900QX467-6, $9.00 ☐

Brass Bell

Stamped design of holly leaves and berries decorates top and rim of handsomely paneled bell. Topped with red bow and ribbon for hanging.

Polished Brass, 2¹¹/₃₂″ tall
1200QX460-6, $12.00 ☐

Santa's Sleigh

Stamped design of Santa in a sleigh filled with toys.

Polished Brass, 2⅝″ tall
900QX478-6, $9.00 ☐

Handcrafted Ornaments

The Spirit of Christmas

Santa flies around the tree waving at onlookers in a silver colored, red trimmed, old-fashioned biplane. Caption: "The Spirit of Christmas 1982."

Handcrafted, 1²⁹/₃₂″ tall
1000QX452-6, $10.00 ☐

Jogging Santa

A sporty Santa in red-and-white jogging suit, green jogging shoes, and a brass jingle bell on the end of his cap is practicing for the great "All Christmas Marathon." His sweater is dated "82."

Handcrafted, 2²⁷/₃₂″ tall
800QX457-6, $8.00 ☐

Santa Bell

Realistic Santa dressed in red and white wears black boots which ring the bell.

Hand-decorated Porcelain, 3¹¹/₁₆″ tall
1500QX148-7, $15.00 ☐

Spirit of Christmas, Jogging Santa, Santa Bell, Santa's Workshop, Cycling Santa

Santa's Workshop

Santa is busy painting a dollhouse in his snow-covered cottage that is all decorated for Christmas. Cottage is open so one can peek in from three sides.

Handcrafted, 3″ tall
1000QX450-3, $10.00 ☐

Cycling Santa

Santa pedals an old "velocipede" with wheels that actually turn. The handlebar basket holds a special present, and his toy-filled pack is safely stowed behind. Three brass bells attached to his pack jingle merrily.

Handcrafted, 4⅜″ tall
2000QX435-5, $20.00 ☐

Cowboy Snowman, Pinecone Home, Raccoon Surprises, Elfin Artist

Christmas Fantasy

Reissue from 1981. (See 1981 Annual Collection.)

Brass and Handcrafted, 3¾″ long
1300QX155-4, $13.00

Cowboy Snowman

Dressed in the latest Western fashion, snowman is ready for the "Christmas Rodeo." He is wearing a red cowboy hat with a green band, red handkerchief around his neck, rope on his shoulder, green gloves, a cowboy belt, and red cowboy boots. He holds a candy cane. Mr. Snowman, rodeo time is a bit warm for you!

Handcrafted, 2²⁷/₃₂″ tall
800QX480-6, $8.00 ☐

Pinecone Home

Little white mouse in red pajamas and nightcap peeks out of the shuttered window of his cozy pinecone home and sees his filled stocking. A red fabric ribbon bow adorns the top.

Handcrafted, 2²³/₃₂″ tall
800QX461-3, $8.00 ☐

Raccoon Surprises

A roguish little raccoon is standing on a tree branch while raiding a red, green, and white argyle Christmas stocking. His redbird friend watches from his shoulder.

Handcrafted, 3″ tall
900QX479-3, $9.00 ☐

Elfin Artist

Little bearded elf hangs onto his bucket of red paint as he swings from a bosun's chair while painting the stripes on a piece of ribbon candy.

Handcrafted, 3″ tall
900QX457-3, $9.00 ☐

Ice Sculptor

Reissue from 1981. (See 1981 Annual Collection.)

Handcrafted, 3¹/₃₂″ tall
800QX432-2, $8.00

Tin Soldier

A proper British soldier stands at stiff attention, holding a rifle in his right hand and saluting left-handed. Uniform is gray, red, and white. Tall hat is black.

Pressed Tin, 4⅞″ tall
650QX483-6, $6.50 ☐

Peeking Elf

Little elf peeks over the top of a silver ball ornament which is diagonally tied in red ribbon.

Handcrafted, 3³/₃₂″ tall
650QX419-5, $6.50 ☐

Jolly Christmas Tree

A smiling Christmas tree, dressed in Christmas finery and a gumdrop "topper," waves a star as he "flies" into Christmas.

Handcrafted, 2¹³/₁₆″ tall
650QX465-3, $6.50 ☐

Embroidered Tree

Dark green fabric tree is decorated with hand-embroidered red, yellow, blue, orange, and pink flowers. The base and tree are trimmed in red braided cord.

Fabric, 4⁹/₁₆″ tall
650QX494-6, $6.50 ☐

Little Trimmers

Cookie Mouse

A star-shaped cookie, outlined in green icing with a dated center in red, has lost one of its points to the cute little white mouse who sits on top happily munching the tasty morsel. Caption: "1982."

Handcrafted, 2¹/₁₆″ tall
450QX454-6, $4.50 ☐

Musical Angel

Tiny angel with a brass halo and dressed in blue plays a lyre while floating on a cloud.

Handcrafted, 1¹⁵/₁₆″ tall
550QX459-6, $5.50 ☐

Merry Moose

Lovable young moose, caught up in his middle with red leather strappings, has lost his balance while ice skating.

Handcrafted, 1¾″ tall
550QX415-5, $5.50 ☐

Christmas Owl

Reissue from 1980. (See 1980 Annual Collection)

Handcrafted, 1⅞″ tall
450QX131-4, $4.50

Dove Love

A white dove swings in the center of a clear red heart in contemporary style.

Acrylic, 2¹/₁₆″ tall
450QX462-3, $4.50 ☐

Perky Penguin

Reissue from 1981. (See 1981 Annual Collection.)

Handcrafted, 1⁵/₁₆″ tall
400QX409-5, $4.00

Christmas Kitten

Brown and white kitten wears a red fabric ribbon collar with brass bell attached.

Handcrafted, 1¼″ tall
400QX454-3, $4.00 ☐

Jingling Teddy

Brown flocked teddy bear wearing a red fabric ribbon collar holds a brass bell.

Flocked, Brass, 2⅛″ tall
400QX477-6, $4.00 ☐

Tin Soldier, Peeking Elf, Jolly Christmas Tree, Embroidered Tree

Cookie Mouse, Musical Angel, Merry Moose

Dove Love, Christmas Kitten, Jiggling Teddy

Collectible Series

Holiday Wildlife — First Edition
Round wooden plaque with white decoform inset (looks like porcelain). Inset has two red cardinals on a pine tree bough. First in a Collectible Series. Caption: "Cardinalis, Cardinalis. First in a series, Wildlife Collection Christmas 1982."

Wood and Decoform, 4" diam.
700QX313-3, $7.00 ☐

Tin Locomotive — First Edition
The first in the Tin Locomotive Series is reminiscent of the "Iron Horse" of early railroad days. Decorated in muted red, blue, and silver, it has a brass bell which hangs in front of the engineer's cab. Caption: "1982."

Pressed Tin, 3⅝" tall
1300QX460-3, $13.00 ☐

Clothespin Soldier — First Edition
In a red, white, and blue uniform and wearing a tall black hat, mustachioed clothespin soldier holds a black baton as if he were leading the future soldiers of this series who will fall in line behind him year by year.

Handcrafted, 3⁵/32" tall
500QX458-3, $5.00 ☐

The Bellringer — Fourth Edition
The clapper is a handcrafted red-and-green wreath with a playful angel in its center. Caption: "1982" on a red banner trimmed in gold enclosing sprays of holly.

Ceramic & Handcrafted, 2²⁷/32" tall
1500QX455-6, $15.00 ☐

Carrousel Series — Fifth Edition
Snowmen holding hockey stock, broom, etc., are skating around in holiday frolic, wearing caps and a top hat. Caption: "Merry Christmas 1982" on the snow-covered top.

Handcrafted, 3" tall
1000QX478-3, $10.00 ☐

SNOOPY and Friends — Fourth Edition
SNOOPY plays Santa on Christmas Eve. He is seen leaving a snow-covered rooftop in a sleigh pulled by Woodstock and friends. Caption: "1982" on the red brick chimney.

Handcrafted, 3¼" diam.
1300QX480-3, $13.00 ☐

Collectible Series First Editions: Holiday Wildlife, Tin Locomotive, Clothespin Soldier

Collectible Series: The Bellringer-Fourth Edition; Carrousel-Fifth Edition; Snoopy and Friends-Fourth Edition; Here Comes Santa-Fourth Edition

Collectible Series: Rocking Horse-Second Edition; Thimble-Fifth Edition; Frosty Friends-Third Edition

Here Comes Santa — Fourth Edition
Jolly Trolley

Santa wearing conductor's cap is seated in the driver's seat of this lovely old trolley car. The colors are red, green, and tan. The rolled-up awnings are green and tan. Santa has a passenger. Caption: "1982 Jolly Trolley" in gold banner across the front.

Handcrafted, 3⅜" tall
1500QX464-3, $15.00 ☐

Rocking Horse — Second Edition

This year's rocking horse is in the same style and size as the first rocking horse issued in 1981, except for color. The second issue is a black stallion with a tail of black yarn, a maroon saddle with blue blanket, and a maroon rocker bordered in gold.

Handcrafted, 2" tall
1000QX502-3, $10.00 ☐

Thimble — Fifth Edition

Cute little white mouse "soldier" with big ears is standing at attention. He is wearing a red jacket, blue shirt, green necktie, and a silver colored thimble for a hat.

Handcrafted, 2¹¹/₃₂" tall
500QX451-3, $5.00 ☐

Frosty Friends — Third Edition

The little Eskimo scales an icicle "mountain." His little Husky friend sits at the top next to the dated flag.

Handcrafted, 4⅛" tall
800QX452-3, $8.00 ☐

Holiday Chimes

Tree Chimes

Lacy, stamped brass tree has five bells and two doves incorporated into its leaf-filled branches.

Stamped Brass, 4⁷/₁₆" tall
550QX484-6, $5.50 ☐

Bell Chimes

Three stamped bells, each with a different snowflake cutout, hang from a large snowflake.

Chrome-Plated Brass, 3" tall
550QX494-3, $5.50 ☐

Holiday Chimes: Bell Chime, Tree Chime

THE 1983 COLLECTION

The Hallmark Keepsake Ornament Collection entered its second decade with a tremendous new look. Commemorative ornaments were introduced in a new ceramic bell format, while Hallmark continued to expand its use of colors on ball ornaments. A variety of new shapes were introduced to supplement the traditional ball-shaped ornaments.

Porcelain ornaments were offered in several original designs, including a new Collectible Series which featured a porcelain teddy bear.

Satin ball ornaments received distinctive new caps in 1983 making them instantly recognizable by their Hallmark "crowns." New commemorative titles included Grandchild's First Christmas, Baby's Second Christmas, Child's Third Christmas, and Tenth Christmas Together.

Two Collectible Series ended in 1983 — the Carrousel ornaments (total of six editions) and the SNOOPY and Friends Panoramic Ball ornaments (total of five issues).

Commemoratives

Baby's First Christmas

In the new oval shape, an old-fashioned rocking horse is modeled in ivory on a red background. Caption is accented with silver foil stamping. Caption: "Baby's First Christmas 1983" and "A Baby fills each day with joy by filling hearts with love."

Red Cameo, 3¾″ wide
750QX301-9, $7.50   ☐

Baby's First Christmas

Baby is in a cradle painted in a Folk Art-style Christmas motif. The fabric blanket and pillow are trimmed in lace and accented with a real ribbon bow. Cradle is captioned "Baby's First Christmas" and "1983."

Handcrafted, 3⁵/₃₂″ tall
1400QX402-7, $14.00   ☐

Baby's First Christmas — Girl

Design is a reproduction of original stitchery of a red dress with white polka dots, a white apron pinafore, and a matching red bonnet. The pinafore pockets are filled with candy canes. The background is white bordered in green ribbon with flowers, ABC blocks, baby's rattle, and diaper pins. Caption: "A Baby Girl is a special gift of love." and "Baby's First Christmas 1983."

White Soft Sheen Satin, 3¼″ diam.
450QX200-7, $4.50   ☐

Baby's First Christmas: Cameo, Handcrafted, Girl, Boy, Photoholder

Baby's First Christmas — Boy

Design features six tumbling teddy bears wearing blue sweaters and red scarfs. Caption: "A baby boy is love and joy…and pride that lasts a lifetime" and "Baby's First Christmas 1983."

Light Blue Soft Sheen Satin, 3¼″ diam.
450QX200-9, $4.50

Baby's First Christmas

An open baby book with area for inserting photograph. Caption: "A Baby is a dream fulfilled, a treasure to hold dear — a Baby is a love that grows more precious every year. Baby's First Christmas 1983."

Acrylic, 3⅞″ tall
700QX302-9, $7.00

Grandchild's First Christmas

This is the first offering of this commemorative in any form. Baby rides in a white, wicker-look buggy with red wheels and green trim. Red, real cloth blanket with white dots carries caption. Caption: "Grandchild's First Christmas 1983."

Handcrafted, 3¾″ long
1400QX430-9, $14.00

Child's Third Christmas

Front — Santa with "1983." Back — "To Celebrate a Child's Third Christmas. How merry the season, how happy the day When Santa brings Christmas surprises your way." The ball is double wrapped in matt-textured and glossy satin to create a piqué effect — a new texture complimenting a new commemorative in the line.

White Satin Piqué, 3¼″ diam.
450QX226-9, $4.50

Grandchild's First Christmas

This commemorative ornament was specifically designed to fit the Classic shape introduced in 1983. Front — a baby with "A Grandchild is a special reason why Christmas is such a merry season." Back — toys and "Grandchild's First Christmas 1983."

Classic Shape, 3¼″ diam.
600QX312-9, $6.00

Baby's Second Christmas

Front — snowman, tree, and caption, "Baby's Second Christmas 1983." Back — snowpeople and caption, "A child knows such special ways to jolly up the holidays!"

White Soft Sheen Satin, 3¼″ diam.
450QX226-7, $4.50

Grandchild's First Christmas Handcrafted, Child's Third Christmas, Grandchild's First Christmas Classic Shape, Baby's Second Christmas

Granddaughter

Three vignettes of artwork from the Hallmark Historical Collection, each picturing a young girl. A fourth vignette carries the caption and date. Caption: "A Granddaughter brings beautiful moments and memories to treasure" and "Christmas 1983."

White Porcelain Glass, 3¼" diam.
450QX202-7, $4.50 ☐

Grandson

A kitten plays with a red ornament as a puppy looks on. Caption: "Christmas 1983" and "A Grandson, like Christmas, brings joy to the heart."

Ecru Soft Sheen Satin, 3¼" diam.
450QX201-9, $4.50 ☐

Son

Little boy, house, Christmas trees, and snowman riding a snowhorse are depicted. Caption: "A Son brings a bit of Christmas cheer to every day throughout the year" and "1983."

Deep Blue Satin, 3¼" diam.
450QX202-9, $4.50 ☐

Daughter

In a reproduction based on original stitchery, rows of ruffled lace and velvet, and green and deep red ribbons are intermingled with pearls. The caption is on a card which is circled with pink flowers. Caption: "A Daughter's love makes Christmas beautiful 1983."

Pink Glass, 3¼" diam.
450QX203-7, $4.50 ☐

Godchild

Design features an angel and a tiny bird singing a holiday duet. Caption: "To wish a special Godchild a very merry Christmas 1983."

White Classical Glass, 3¼" diam.
450QX201-7, $4.50 ☐

Grandmother

A snowscene of a fenced-in farmhouse and barn shows a family approaching in a horse drawn sleigh. Caption: "Over the river and through the woods to Grandmother's house we go...Christmas 1983."

White Porcelain Glass, 3¼" diam.
450QX205-7, $4.50 ☐

Granddaughter, Grandson, Son, Daughter, Godchild

Grandmother, Mother and Dad, Sister, Grandparents

Mom and Dad

White ceramic bell with a red fabric ribbon has fired-on decals of poinsettias and holly framing the captions. Caption: "Mom and Dad" and "Christmas 1983."

Ceramic, 3" tall
650QX429-7, $6.50 ☐

Sister

Candies, cookies, nuts, and a gingerbread man are pictured with flowers, ribbons, bows, basket, jars, and a wreath. Caption: "A Sister is a forever friend" and "1983."

White Classical Glass, 3¼" diam.
450QX206-9, $4.50 ☐

Grandparents

White ceramic bell with red fabric ribbon has fired on decals. Wreath on the front encircles "Christmas 1983." Caption on back: "Grandparents are love."

Ceramic, 3" tall
650QX429-9, $6.50 ☐

First Christmas Together

Candy canes form three hearts which surround the caption and the date. The design is printed directly on the surface of the ball. This is a new process for Hallmark. Caption: "First Christmas Together" and "1983."

White Glass, 3¼" diam.
450QX208-9, $4.50 ☐

First Christmas Together

A winter forest scene is shown in the newly introduced Classic shape. Caption: "First Christmas Together 1983" and "All the world is beautiful when seen through eyes of love."

Classic Shape, 3¼" diam.
600QX310-7, $6.00 ☐

First Christmas Together

In a new oval shape, an ivory relief of a couple in a horse-drawn sleigh is set against deep blue background. Caption is accented with silver foil stamping. Caption: "First Christmas Together 1983" and "Love is beauty shared, dreams come true...special memories made by two."

Dark Blue Cameo, 3¾" wide
750QX301-7, $7.50 ☐

First Christmas Together — Brass Locket

This polished brass locket opens to reveal space for two photos. Caption: "First Christmas Together 1983."

Polished Brass, 2⅝" tall
1500QX432-9, $15.00 ☐

First Christmas Together: Ball, Classic Shape, Cameo, Brass Heart.

Love is A Song, Love Handcrafted, Love Classic Shape, Love Glass Ball

Love Is a Song

Silhouettes of Dickens' characters are pictured in red, green, and white on a silver glass bell. Caption: "Christmas is a song of love for every heart to sing" and "1983."

Silver Glass Bell, 2½" tall
450QX223-9, $4.50 ☐

Love

White porcelain heart with embossed design of holly and berries frames a plump red heart hanging in its center which carries caption lettered in gold. A red satin ribbon is attached for hanging. Caption: "Love 1983."

Porcelain, 3⅛" tall
1300QX422-7, $13.00 ☐

Love

Hearts and greenery are reproduced from original needlepoint worked in sampler style. This design is also in the new Classic shape. Caption: "Love, the spirit which enhances all the seasons of our lives" and "Christmas 1983."

Classic Shape, 3¼" diam.
600QX310-9, $6.00 ☐

Love

Woodland snowscene pictures holiday travelers in a horse-driven sled. Caption: "Love makes each day a joy, each moment a memory" and "Christmas 1983."

Light Green Glass, 3¼" diam.
450QX207-9, $4.50 ☐

Teacher, First Christmas Together, Friendship, Love, Mother

Twenty-Fifth Christmas Together, Teacher, Friendship, New Home, Tenth Christmas Together

Teacher

A smiling raccoon writes "Merry Christmas, Merry Christmas, Merry Christmas, Teacher 1983" in silver foil stamping.

Acrylic, 3¾" tall
600QX304-9, $6.00

First Christmas Together

Bell-shaped design has caption stamped in silver foil. Caption: "First Christmas Together 1983."

Acrylic, 4¼" tall
600QX306-9, $6.00

Friendship

Caption: "Friendship grows more beautiful with each passing season. Christmas 1983." Caption is applied with silver foil stamping.

Acrylic, 5" tall
600QX305-9, $6.00

Love

Skaters form the words of the caption in the clear "ice" of the ornament. Caption: "Love" and "Christmas 1983" stamped in silver foil.

Acrylic, 4" tall
600QX305-7, $6.00

Mother

Heart-shaped design has caption stamped in silver foil. Caption: "Mother...always caring, always sharing, always there to love. 1983."

Acrylic, 4" tall
600QX306-7, $6.00

25th Christmas Together

White lacy snowflakes create a delicate winter wonderland effect on a silver glass bell. Caption: "25th Christmas Together" and "1983."

Silver Glass Bell, 2½" tall
450QX224-7, $4.50

Teacher

Schoolhouse and green-and-white lettering are bordered with green bands. Caption: "1983" and "For a Special Teacher at Christmas."

Silver Glass Bell, 2½" tall
450QX224-9, $4.50

Friendship

Santa's neighbor, a cute little Eskimo, is shown in Christmas scenes. Caption: "Friendship is a special gift that gives your heart a happy lift" and "Christmas 1983."

White Classic Glass, 3¼" diam.
450QX207-7, $4.50

Betsey Clark Handcrafted, Porcelain, Betsey Clark-Eleventh Edition

New Home

Snowy scene of homes and merry carolers on Christmas Eve. Caption: "Christmas is the perfect way of rounding out each year, for every heart and home's aglow with love and warmth and cheer. 1983."

White Soft Sheen Satin, 3¼" diam.
450QX210-7, $4.50

Tenth Christmas Together

A new commemorative is introduced in the form of a white ceramic bell. Front is decorated with a golden French horn. Caption on back: "Tenth Christmas Together 1983." The bell is hung from a red fabric ribbon.

Ceramic, 3" tall
650QX430-7, $6.50

Property Ornaments

Betsey Clark

A Betsey Clark child clad in white-dotted blue sleepers is napping peacefully on a yellow flocked moon.

Handcrafted, 3" tall
650QX404-7, $6.50

Betsey Clark

Betsey Clark angel dressed in blue sits on a cloud and catches a star with her fishing pole.

Porcelain, 3½" tall
900QX440-1, $9.00

Betsey Clark — Eleventh Edition

Two boys and two girls dressed for the winter holiday season are riding on a Christmas carrousel with their little feathered friends. Caption: "Christmas happiness is found...wherever good friends gather round. 1983."

White Glass, 3¼" diam.
450QX211-9, $4.50

PEANUTS®, DISNEY, SHIRT TALES™, *Mary Hamilton*

MISS PIGGY™, MUPPETS™

*Norman Rockwell-Fourth edition, Norman
Rockwell Glass Ball*

Currier and Ives, Christmas Joy, Here Comes Santa

PEANUTS®

Comic strip panels show SNOOPY bringing Woodstock and his nest in out of the cold. Caption: "May the joy of the season warm every heart" and "Christmas 1983."

White Soft Sheen Satin, 3¼" diam.
450QX212-7, $4.50 □

DISNEY

Design shows Mickey Mouse's beaming face framed by a wreath., Caption: "1983."

Chrome Glass, 3¼" diam.
450QX212-9, $4.50 □

SHIRT TALES™

SHIRT TALES™ make their first appearance in the Keepsake line. They are animals whose shirts bear special messages. This design shows a walrus, a penguin, and a polar bear, each wearing green, red, and yellow shirts. Fronts of shirts read, "Deck The Halls." "Tis the season to be jolly" and on the back, shirts read, "Fa La-La La-La." Caption: "Christmas 1983."

White Classical Glass, 3½" tall
450QX214-9, $4.50 □

Mary Hamilton

The forest creatures gather and pray with their friend, a little girl. Caption: "A wee little, warm little Christmas time prayer — may God bless us always with friendships to share. 1983."

White Classical Glass, 3½" tall
450QX213-7, $4.50 □

MISS PIGGY™

Ever the fashion plate, MISS PIGGY™ cuts a graceful figure on her silver skates. Her skating costume, in soft shades of lavender, is complete with long gloves, pearl choker, and silver tiara.

Handcrafted, 4⁹/₁₆" tall
1300QX405-7, $13.00 □

The MUPPETS™

KERMIT™ and MISS PIGGY™ are skywriting in a biplane; FOZZIE™ floats behind in a hot air balloon. Caption: "1983" and "Merry Christmas" in skywriting.

Light Blue Satin, 3¼" diam.
450QX214-7, $4.50 □

KERMIT THE FROG™

Reissue. (See 1982 Annual collection.)

Handcrafted, 3⁹/₁₆" tall
1100QX495-6, $11.00

Oriental Butterflies, Angels

Norman Rockwell — Fourth Edition

Circular ornament has relief of Rockwell painting in ivory against a deep blue background. Silver foil stamping highlights the caption. Caption: "Dress Rehearsal. Fourth in a series. Christmas 1983. The Norman Rockwell Collection."

Dark Blue Cameo, 3" diam.
750QX300-7, $7.50 □

Norman Rockwell

In three famous Rockwell scenes mother and dad decorate the tree; dad gets fitted by mom in his Santa suit; and young son catches Santa (dad) kissing mom. Caption: "Things are humming, Santa's coming, hearts are full of cheer. Lights are gleaming, kids are dreaming…Christmas time is here. From the Norman Rockwell Collection 1983."

Light Green Glass, 3¼" diam.
450QX215-7, $4.50 □

Decorative Ball Ornaments

Currier & Ives

Favorite old print from Currier & Ives is faithfully reproduced on this dated ornament. Caption: "Christmas 1983, Central Park Winter, The Skating Pond, Currier and Ives."

White Porcelain Glass, 3¼" diam.
450QX215-9, $4.50 □

Christmas Joy

Muffin, a new Hallmark property, is dressed in a green outfit and a red knitted hat. On the front she is feeding a carrot to a rabbit. Muffin and her dog are pictured on the back. Caption: "May all the joy you give away…return to you on Christmas Day 1983."

Ecru Soft Sheen Satin, 3¼" diam.
450QX216-9, $4.50 □

Here Comes Santa

Four views of Santa's face form the design. Caption "Merry Christmas 1983."

Red Glass, 3¼" diam.
450QX217-7, $4.50 □

Oriental Butterflies

An array of eight colorful butterflies is reproduced from original stitchery.

Turquoise Glass, 3¼" diam.
450QX218-7, $4.50 □

Angels

Gold tinsel starburst sparkles from the inside of this clear glass ball. On the outside are old world angels in soft pastels accented in rich gold. One angel is holding a tambourine.

Clear Glass, 3¼" diam.
500QX219-7, $5.00 □

Seasons Greetings, 1983, The Wisemen

Christmas Wonderland, Old Fashioned Christmas, The Annunciation

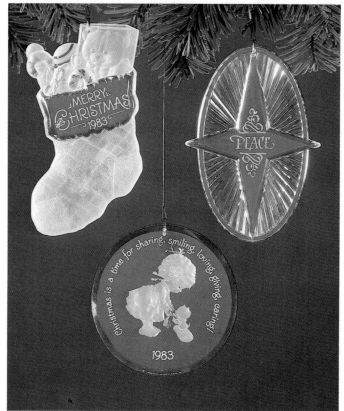

Holiday Highlights: Christmas Stocking, Star of Peace,
A Time for Sharing

Crown Classics: Memories to Treasure Photoholder, Christmas Wreath,
Mother and Child

Season's Greetings

The caption, "Season's Greetings" formed by "neon" lettering, makes a striking, contemporary ornament in chrome glass.

Chrome Glass, 3¼″ diam.
450QX219-9, $4.50 ☐

1983

Contemporary design has date in gold on a narrow band around its center. This raspberry glass ornament is trimmed with platinum colored stripes. Caption: "1983."

Raspberry Glass, 3¼″ diam.
450QX220-9, $4.50 ☐

The Wise Men

Three magnificent kings raise their precious gifts to the star that is leading them to Bethlehem. Two camels and a horse are shown on the back.

Gold Glass, 3¼″ diam.
450QX220-7, $4.50 ☐

Christmas Wonderland

Animals are busy celebrating Christmas in the forest. A "peek through" section shows another scene inside the clear glass ball."

Clear Glass, 3¼″ diam.
450QX221-9, $4.50 ☐

An Old Fashioned Christmas

Views of Santa's face, roses, Christmas flowers, and children dressed in fashions of yesteryear are printed on a green glass ball. Design is reminiscent of the greeting cards of long ago.

Green Porcelain Glass, 3¼″ diam.
450QX217-9, $4.50 ☐

The Annunciation

Design is a beautiful reproduction of "The Annunciation" by Fra Filippo Filippi from the National Gallery of Art, Washington, D.C.; Samuel H. Kress Collection. Caption: "And the Angel said to her, 'The Holy Spirit will come upon you, and the power of the Most High will overshadow you: Therefore the Child to be born will be called Holy, the Son of God…' Luke 1:35 (RSVB)."

White Porcelain Glass, 3¼″ diam.
450QX216-7, $4.50 ☐

Holiday Highlights

Christmas Stocking

An "etched" argyle Christmas stocking is filled to the brim with gifts, animals, toys, and candy. Caption: "Merry Christmas 1983" stamped in silver foil.

Acrylic, 4″ tall
600QX303-9, $6.00 ☐

Star of Peace

Oval shape is centered with caption and a four-pointed star with reflective facets. Caption: "Peace" in gold foil stamping.

Acrylic, 4″ tall
600QX304-7, $6.00 ☐

Time for Sharing

Mary Hamilton creates a scene of a kitten sitting on a log as a little girl stoops to tie a scarf around its neck. Caption: "Christmas is a time for sharing, smiling, loving, giving, caring 1983," stamped in silver foil.

Acrylic, 4″ tall
600QX307-7, $6.00 ☐

Crown Classics

Enameled Christmas Wreath

Colorfully enameled patchwork wreath has a bezel of solid brass. Caption: "Each moment of the season has beauty all its own. Christmas 1983."

Enameled, 2¾″ tall
900QX311-9, $9.00 ☐

Memories to Treasure

Santa profile with area for inserting photograph. Caption: "Holiday fun times make memories to treasure. 1983."

Acrylic, 4¼″ tall
700QX303-7, $7.00 ☐

Mother and Child

Oval shaped, blue-with-ivory Madonna and Child design is the first Cameo Keepsake with a translucent appearance. Caption is accented with silver foil stamping. Caption: "Come let us celebrate His love for this is the season of rejoicing."

Dark Blue Cameo, 3¾″ tall
750QX302-7, $7.50 ☐

Holiday Sculpture

Santa

New three-dimensional Santa, molded in translucent red acrylic.

Acrylic, 2″ tall
400QX308-7, $4.00 ☐

Heart

Red, three-dimensional heart, molded in translucent acrylic.

Acrylic, 2″ tall
400QX307-9, $4.00 ☐

Holiday Sculpture: Santa, Christmas Heart

Handcrafted Ornaments

Embroidered Stocking

A quilted red stocking accented with hand embroidery is lace trimmed and filled with toys.

Fabric, 3¼″ tall
650QX479-6, $6.50 ☐

Embroidered Heart

Red fabric edged in green cording is hand-embroidered with brightly colored Christmas flowers and greenery.

Fabric, 4¹³⁄₁₆″ tall
650QX421-7, $6.50 ☐

Scrimshaw Reindeer

Created with the look of handcarved ivory scrimshaw accented in brown, a reindeer leaps gracefully into the air.

Handcrafted, 3¾″ tall
800QX424-9, $8.00 ☐

Jack Frost

Jack Frost "paints" beautiful imagery from his pail of frost on windowpanes that can be viewed from "inside" and "outside."

Handcrafted, 3¾″ tall
900QX407-9, $9.00 ☐

Unicorn

Beautiful prancing unicorn made of porcelain has hand applied gold trim.

Porcelain, 4″ tall
1000QX426-7, $10.00 ☐

Porcelain Doll, Diana

Diana's fine porcelain features are hand painted in the exquisite style of an antique doll. Her burgundy costume is banded and edged in ivory lace, and the matching bonnet is faced in contrasting ivory material.

Porcelain and Fabric, 4¼″ tall
900QX423-7, $9.00 ☐

Brass Santa

Front and back views of the head of Santa are in polished stamped brass that is protectively coated.

Brass, 4″ tall
900QX423-9, $9.00 ☐

Santa's on His Way

Four vignettes show Santa "making gifts," "packing his sleigh," "climbing down the chimney," and "by the fireplace and Christmas tree" in three-dimensional, hand-painted scenes.

Handcrafted, 3″ tall
1000QX426-9, $10.00 ☐

Hand-Embroidered Ornaments: Stocking, Heart

Scrimshaw Reindeer, Jack Frost, Unicorn, Diana

Brass Santa, Santa's On His Way, Old Fashioned Santa

Ski Lift Santa, Hitchhiking Santa, Mountain Climbing Santa, Jolly Santa, Santa's Many Faces

Old-Fashioned Santa

Jointed, realistic interpretation of an old-fashioned Santa wears knee-length red suit and red-and-white striped hose. His balding head is bare, and he carries a brass bell in one hand. Santa's arms and legs are movable.

Handcrafted, 5⁹/₆₄″ tall
1100QX409-9, $11.00   ☐

Cycling Santa

Very popular Cycling Santa Special Edition is a reissue. (See 1982 Annual Collection.)

Handcrafted, 4⅜″ tall
2000QX435-5, $20.00

Santa's Workshop

This miniature version of Santa in his workshop is a reissue. (See 1982 Annual Collection.)

Handcrafted, 3″ tall
1000QX450-3, $10.00

Ski Lift Santa

Santa waves as he rides a ski lift to the mountain top. A brass bell is the pompom for his hat. Caption: "1983" on his ski lift ticket.

Handcrafted-Brass, 3⅞″ tall
800QX418-7, $8.00   ☐

Hitchhiking Santa

Santa, ready for a vacation from winter, dons sunglasses and summer clothes. He is seated on his suitcase holding a sign that reads "Goin' South," with his right hand making the gesture of hopeful hitchhikers everywhere.

Handcrafted, 2²¹/₃₂″ tall
800QX424-7, $8.00   ☐

Mountain Climbing Santa

Santa the sportsman is climbing a mountain with a real rope; his backpack is a bag of toys, of course.

Handcrafted, 2¹³/₃₂″ tall
650QX407-7, $6.50   ☐

Jolly Santa

Merry Santa poses with his pack of toys.

Handcrafted, 1¹⁵/₁₆″ tall
350QX425-9, $3.50   ☐

Santa's Many Faces

Six scenes of Santa circle the center of Classic-shaped ornament. Caption: "Merry Christmas 1983."

Red Classic Shape, 3¼″ diam.
600QX311-7, $6.00   ☐

Baroque Angels, Madonna and Child

Mouse on the Cheese, Peppermint Penguin, Skating Rabbit, Skiing Fox, Mouse in a Bell

Baroque Angels

Two beautifully rendered angels with white wings are entwined in gilt trimmed, rose banners.

Handcrafted, 2½" tall
1300QX422-9, $13.00   ☐

Madonna and Child

White robed Madonna wearing blue and white mantle is holding the Christ Child. The Infant is wrapped in gold and white swaddling clothes.

Porcelain, 3¹/₁₆" tall
1200QX428-7, $12.00   ☐

Mouse on Cheese

A mischievous mouse enjoys a large morsel taken from the gift-wrapped cheese on which he is seated.

Handcrafted, 2³⁷/₆₄" tall
650QX413-7, $6.50   ☐

Peppermint Penguin

Penguin attired in red bow tie and red-and-white cap pedals a "peppermint candy" unicycle.

Handcrafted, 2¾" tall
650QX408-9, $6.50   ☐

Skating Rabbit

This skating rabbit has a tail of real cotton and a cleverly designed stocking cap that covers each ear separately.

Handcrafted, 3¼" tall
800QX409-7, $8.00   ☐

Skiing Fox

A fox is skiing downhill with his green muffler flying in the wind.

Handcrafted, 2⁵/₃₂" tall
800QX420-7, $8.00   ☐

Mouse in Bell

The clapper of this clear glass bell is a handcrafted mouse with a real leather tail. A brass ring secures his stocking cap by the pompom.

Handcrafted-Glass, 4" tall
1000QX419-7, $10.00   ☐

Mailbox Kitten

A fluffy kitten with a stack of letters in his paws is peeking out of a pressed tin, red-and-white mailbox. Caption: "1983 Peppermint Lane" on the mailbox.

Handcrafted, 1⁹/₁₆" tall
650QX415-7, $6.50   ☐

Mailbox Kitten, Tin Rocking Horse, Bell Wreath, Angel Messenger

Holiday Puppy, Rainbow Angel, Sneaker Mouse, Christmas Koala, Caroling Owl

Tin Rocking Horse

Made of lithographed tin, this colorful, three-dimensional rocking horse is a dappled gray. He has been carefully crafted to resemble an Early American nursery toy.

Pressed Tin, 3¹¹/₆₄″ tall
650QX414-9, $6.50 ☐

Bell Wreath

Bow-topped holly wreath of solid brass has seven tinkling bells.

Brass, 3¹³/₁₆″ tall
650QX420-9, $6.50 ☐

Angel Messenger

A beautiful angel wearing a blue robe carries furling banner of real brass. Caption: "1983."

Handcrafted, 2″ tall
650QX408-7, $6.50 ☐

Holiday Puppy

Cute little puppy has red fabric ribbon around his neck.

Handcrafted, 1¹⁹/₃₂″ tall
350QX412-7, $3.50 ☐

Rainbow Angel

Playful, brass-haloed angel is depicted sliding down a rainbow. A fleecy cloud guarantees a soft landing.

Handcrafted, 2¹⁵/₁₆″ tall
550QX416-7, $5.50 ☐

Sneaker Mouse

White mouse with pink ears has adapted a red and white sneaker with laces of yarn for a bed. His blanket is blue with white polka dots.

Handcrafted, 1¹¹/₁₆″ tall
450QX400-9, $4.50 ☐

Christmas Koala

A flocked koala bear holds holly berries and a sprig of evergreen.

Handcrafted, 2³/₁₆″ tall
400QX419-9, $4.00 ☐

Caroling Owl

Small white owl, wearing real cloth muffler, is perched on a brass ring and holds a Christmas carol book.

Handcrafted, 2⁹/₃₂″ tall
450QX411-7, $4.50 ☐

Christmas Kitten

Reissue. (See 1982 Annual Collection.)

Handcrafted, 1¼″ tall
400QX454-3, $4.00

Collectible Series

The Bellringer — Fifth Edition

White porcelain bell with decal of holly branch and berries and star is dated "1983." A brown teddy bear holding a gold star rings the bell. This is the fifth design in the Bellringer series.

Porcelain & Handcrafted, 2²⁷/₃₂" tall
1500QX403-9, $15.00 ☐

Holiday Wildlife — Second Edition

Porcelain-look insert showing chickadees perched on a berried branch is framed in natural wood. Caption: "Black-capped Chickadees, Parus Atricapillus" and "Second in a series, Wildlife Collection — Christmas 1983."

Decoform and Wood, 3" diam.
700QX309-9, $7.00 ☐

Here Comes Santa — Fifth Edition

Santa pumps a railroad handcar which is carrying gifts of a teddy bear, a wrapped present, and a ball. Handcar features the look of aged wood with green-painted accents. The red wheels actually turn.

Handcrafted, 3⁷/₁₆" tall
1300QX403-7, $13.00 ☐

SNOOPY and Friends — Fifth Edition

SNOOPY dressed as Santa has delivered a bag of gifts to Woodstock who is flying in the air with pure delight! This is the last design in this series. Dated 1983.

Handcrafted, 3¼" diam.
1300QX416-9, $13.00 ☐

Carrousel — Sixth Edition

Santa leads a marching band of horn-blowing children around the red, white, and green carrousel which is titled "Santa and Friends." This is the last design in this series. Caption: "Christmas 1983" circling carrousel top.

Handcrafted, 3³/₃₂" tall
1100QX401-9, $11.00 ☐

Porcelain Bear — First Edition

First in a new series is this bear named Cinnamon made of fine porcelain and hand painted.

Porcelain, 2¹⁵/₆₄" tall
700QX428-9, $7.00 ☐

Collectible Series: The Bellringer-Fifth Edition, Holiday Wildlife-Second Edition, Here Comes Santa-Fifth Edition

Final Collectible Series Editions: Snoopy and Friends-Fifth Edition, Carrousel Series-Sixth Edition

Clothespin Soldier — Second Edition

American Revolutionary clothespin soldier is beating his bass drum with arms that actually move.

Handcrafted, 2⁷/₁₆″ tall
500QX402-9, $5.00 ☐

Rocking Horse — Third Edition

The third "trusty steed" in the series is russet in color, has blue saddle and bridle, tail of real ecru yarn, and green rocker dated "1983."

Handcrafted, 2⅞″ tall
1000QX417-7, $10.00 ☐

Frosty Friends — Fourth Edition

An Eskimo child and white baby seal covered with flocking are playing on a clear, freeform block of ice. Caption: "Merry Christmas 1983."

Handcrafted, 1⁵⁹/₆₄″ tall
800QX400-7, $8.00 ☐

Thimble — Sixth Edition

A merry elf is enjoying a cherry-topped ice cream treat served in a thimble.

Handcrafted, 1¹⁵/₁₆″ tall
500QX401-7, $5.00 ☐

Tin Locomotive — Second Edition

An early locomotive lithographed in red and green and trimmed in gold features wheels that actually turn. Dated 1983.

Pressed Tin, 3″ tall
1300QX404-9, $13.00 ☐

Collectible Series: Clothespin Soldier-Second Edition; Rocking Horse-Third Edition; Frosty Friends-Fourth Edition; Thimble Elf-Sixth Edition; Tin Locomotive-Second Edition

New Collectible Series: Porcelain Teddy Bear-First Edition

THE 1984 COLLECTION

The 1984 Hallmark Keepsake Collection offered tremendous excitement and expansion that included four new Collectible Series (Twelve Days of Christmas, Art Masterpiece, Wooden Toy and Nostalgic Houses and Shops); two new Friendship captions (Gratitude and Baby-sitter); timely designs inspired by the '84 Olympics (Marathon Santa) and the national elections (Uncle Sam); and a new property, Katybeth. Smaller sized ball ornaments were introduced, new handcrafted juvenile caps appeared on selected satin ornaments, and a new decorating process that included printing directly on the glass ball ornaments.

    The 1984 Christmas season saw the last of The Bellringer series with Elfin Artist, and the first musical ornaments in the Keepsake line. "Holiday Magic Lighted Ornaments," a unique Hallmark innovation, debuted as did the first announced limited edition ornament, Classical Angel. Produced in an edition size of only 24,700, it was one of the most sought after items of the year.

Commemoratives

Baby's First Christmas
A holiday parade of animals, led by a baby in a sled, circles the ornament. Caption: "A Baby is...happiness, pleasure, a gift from above...a wonderful, magical treasure of love. Baby's First Christmas 1984."
Melody: "Babes in Toyland"

Musical, Classic Shape, 4¼" tall
1600QX904-1, $16.00 ☐

Baby's First Christmas
A finely detailed teddy bear races downhill on an old-fashioned wooden-look sled bearing gifts. Caption: "1984 Baby's First Christmas."

Handcrafted, 3½" wide
1400QX438-1. $14.00 ☐

Baby's First Christmas
A snowy white fabric photoholder with dainty, embroidered holly sprigs at the top. Borders are fashioned of delicate, ruffled eyelet laced with pale green ribbon. Caption: "Baby's First Christmas. A Baby is a special dream come true. 1984."

Fabric, 3¼" diam.
700QX300-1, $7.00 ☐

Baby's First Christmas
Etched teddy bear holds a stocking filled with toys. Caption is accented with gold foil stamping: "1984 Baby's First Christmas."

Acyrlic, 3¾" tall
600QX340-1, $6.00 ☐

Baby's First Christmas: Musical, Handcrafted

Baby's First Christmas: Photoholder

Baby's First Christmas: Acrylic

Baby's First Christmas—Boy

A bear drives a train filled with Christmas toys while a handcrafted mouse stands on top of the ornament. Caption: "A Baby Boy is a bundle of pleasure to fill every day with love beyond measure. Baby's First Christmas 1984."

White Satin, 2⅞" diam.
450QX240-4, $4.50 ☐

Baby's First Christmas—Girl

A handcrafted mouse appears atop a festive parade of happy little girls and Christmas toys. Caption: "A Baby Girl is love that grows in the warmth of caring hearts. Baby's First Christmas 1984."

Cream Satin, 2⅞" diam
450QX240-1, $4.50 ☐

Baby's Second Christmas

A golden crown caps the scene of Pooh Bear sharing Christmas with his friends. Caption: "Children and Christmas are joys that go together. Baby's Second Christmas 1984."

White Satin, 2⅞" diam.
450QX241-1. $4.50 ☐

Child's Third Christmas

A group of teddy bears decorate for Christmas on this satin ball topped with a handcrafted mouse. Caption: "A Child's Third Christmas. Christmas is a time for fun and wonderful surprises! 1984."

Ecru Satin, 2⅞" diam.
450QX261-1, $4.50 ☐

Grandchild's First Christmas

Flocked white lamb with red fabric ribbon around its neck balances on a colorful pull toy. At the lamb's feet are a baby rattle and a ball dated "1984." Caption: "Grandchild's First Christmas."

Handcrafted, 3⅜" tall
1100QX460-1, $11.00 ☐

Grandchild's First Christmas

A spring green satin ball provides the background for a unique "torn paper" scene of Santa loading toys into his bag. Ornament is capped with a handcrafted mouse. Caption: "A Baby makes Christmas delightfully bright. Grandchild's First Christms 1984."

Green Satin, 2⅞" diam.
450QX257-4, $4.50 ☐

Godchild

Elf-like children paint the holly berries red for the holidays. Caption: "Merry Christmas, Godchild 1984."

Gold Glass, 3" diam.
450QX242-1, $4.50 ☐

Baby's First Christmas: Boy, Girl; Baby's Second Christmas, Child's Third Christmas

Grandchild's First Christmas: Handcrafted, Satin Ball; Godchild

Grandson, Granddaughter, Grandparents, Grandmother

Father, Mother

Mother and Dad, Sister, Daughter, Son

The Miracle of Love, First Christmas Together

Grandson

A polar bear family shares Christmas fun. Caption: "A Grandson has a wonderful way of adding love to every day. Christmas 1984."

Blue Glass, 3" diam.
450QX242-4, $4.50 ☐

Granddaughter

A festive holiday sampler is reproduced from original stitchery. Caption: "A Granddaughter is warmth, hope and promise. Christmas 1984."

Green Glass, 2⅞" diam.
450QX243-1, $4.50 ☐

Grandparents

A contemporary snow scene, reproduced from original stitchery, provides the perfect setting for the caption: "Grandparents ... wherever they are, there is love. Christmas 1984."

French Blue Glass, 2⅞" diam.
450QX256-1, $4.50 ☐

Grandmother

Lovely, muted pastel flowers frame a holiday tribute to Grandmother. Caption: "There's a special kind of beauty in a Grandmother's special love. Christmas 1984."

Light Blue Glass, 2⅞" diam.
450QX244-1, $4.50 ☐

Father

The wonderful sounds of Christmas are symbolized by holly and musical instruments etched across the top. Stamped in gold foil, the caption reads, "A Father has a special gift of giving of himself. Christmas 1984."

Acrylic, 3¼" wide
600QX257-1, $6.00 ☐

Mother

Etched fir branches tied with a ribbon are accented by the silver foil-stamped caption: "A Mother has a beautiful way of adding love to every day. 1984."

Acrylic, 3¼" wide
600QX343-4, $6.00 ☐

Mother and Dad

Gold highlights the classic Christmas design motifs that adorn this delicate bone china bell tied with red ribbon. Caption: "Mother and Dad. Christmas 1984."

Bone China, 3" tall
650QX258-1, $6.50 ☐

Sister

A bright basket of poinsettias rests against a dark blue background, framed in red on a delicate bone china bell. Caption: "For a wonderful Sister. Christmas 1984."

Bone China, 3" tall
650QX259-4, $6.50 ☐

First Christmas Together: Musical, Brushed Brass, Cameo, Silver Glass

Daughter

Bright holiday flowers and the striking contrast of green and gold complement the loving caption: "A Daughter is joy that grows deeper, pride that grows stronger, love that touches your heart every day. Christmas 1984."

Gold Glass, 3" diam.
450QX244-4, $4.50 ☐

Son

Whimsical Christmas designs form letters that spell "Merry Christmas." Caption: "For a wonderful Son. Christmas 1984."

White Glass, 3" diam.
450QX243-4, $4.50 ☐

The Miracle of Love

Romantic acrylic heart etched with festive ribbon and holly design. Caption is gold foil stamped: "Love...a miracle of the heart. Christmas 1984."

Acrylic, 4" tall
600QX342-4, $6.00 ☐

First Christmas Together

A delicately etched design shows two doves perched on a holly branch. The caption, stamped with silver foil, says, "First Christmas Together 1984."

Acrylic, 3⅝" diam
600QX342-1, $6.00 ☐

First Christmas Together

The love of a first Christmas together is captured in the melody of "Lara's Theme" while reindeer prance across the deep blue background. Caption: "First Christmas Together 1984." Melody: "Lara's Theme"

Musical, Classic Shape, 4" tall
1600QX904-4, $16.00 ☐

First Christmas Together

Brushed brass oval locket opens to hold two photos and comes with its own felt pouch. Hanger allows open or closed display on your tree. The caption is engraved on the cover and framed by embossed hearts. Caption: "First Christmas Together 1984."

Brushed Brass, 2½" tall
1500QX436-4, $15.00 ☐

First Christmas Together

An elegant couple, carved in ivory relief, waltz across a dark blue background. Caption: "Each moment spent together is a special celebration. First Christmas Together 1984."

Cameo, 3¼" diam.
750QX340-4, $7.50 ☐

First Christmas Together

Silver ball is surrounded by a contemporary pattern of holiday birds, flowers and greenery. Caption: "Love...a joy for all seasons. First Christmas Together 1984."

Silver Glass, 3" diam.
450QX245-1, $4.50 ☐

Heartful of Love

A bone china puffed heart is decorated with a romantic design of pink, red and yellow roses. The date "1984" appears on one side and a banner across the other bears the caption: "Love...the most beautiful treasure of Christmas."

Bone China, 3¾" wide
1000QX443-4, $10.00 ☐

Love...the Spirit of Christmas

The shiny black band and the bright Christmas fruit and flower design give this chrome glass ball the appearance of fine lacquer boxes. Caption: "Love, which is the spirit and the heart of Christmas, blossoms all year through. 1984."

Chrome Glass, 2⅞" diam.
450QX247-4, $4.50 ☐

Love

Classic mimes share thoughts of love against a bright red background. Caption: "Love can say the special things that words alone cannot. Christmas 1984."

Chrome Glass, 2⅞" diam.
450QX255-4, $4.50 ☐

Ten Years Together

A white bone china bell features a lovely, frosty blue winter scene inside an oval. Tied in blue fabric ribbon, the bell is captioned, "Ten Years Together. Christmas 1984."

Bone China, 3" tall
650QX258-4, $6.50 ☐

Twenty-Five Years Together

A bone china bell with silver hanging cord pictures an ornate gold and silver sleigh filled with holiday gifts. Caption: "Twenty-Five Years Together. Christmas 1984."

Bone China, 3" tall
650QX259-1, $6.50 ☐

Gratitude

Acrylic teardrop shape is etched with a cheery design of ribbon and sleigh bells. Caption is applied with silver foil stamping. Caption: "The spirit of Christmas lives in every heart that gives."

Acrylic, 4½" tall
600QX344-4, $6.00 ☐

The Fun of Friendship

Scallops decorate the rim of an acrylic bell etched with a charming portrait of two Arctic pals. Silver foil-stamped caption reads, "A friend is a partner in life's merry moments. 1984."

Acrylic, 3¾" tall
600QX343-1, $6.00 ☐

Heartful of Love, Love...the Spirit of Christmas, Love

Ten Years Together, Twenty-Five Years Together   Gratitude, The Fun of Friendship

Friendship

Carolers sing amidst the gentle fall of snowflakes. Set in a red border, the caption reads, "Let us sing a Christmas song of friendship, joy and cheer. 1984."

Blue-Green Glass, 2⅞" diam
450QX248-1, $4.50 ☐

A Gift of Friendship

Muffin and her white kitten rest on a light peach glass ball. Caption: "Friendship is the happiest gift of all!"

Peach Glass, 3" diam.
450QX260-4, $4.50 ☐

New Home

Pearl blue glass forms the background for a village holiday snow scene. Caption: "Home is where the heart is and a new home always seems the happiest of places, for it is filled with all your dreams. Christmas 1984."

Pearl Blue Glass, 2⅞" diam.
450QX245-4, $4.50 ☐

From Our Home to Yours

Sampler design, reproduced from original stitchery, shows an inviting home with family enjoying the snow. Caption: "The spirit of Christmas adorns a home with love. Christmas 1984."

Green Glass, 2⅞" diam.
450QX248-4, $4.50 ☐

Teacher

Whimsical elves deliver a big red apple to teacher. Caption: "1984 Merry Christmas, Teacher."

White Glass, 3" diam.
450QX249-1, $4.50 ☐

Baby-sitter

A charming group of mice depict the fun of Christmas and the closeness shared by children and baby-sitter. Caption: "Thank heaven for Baby-sitters like you."

Green Glass, 3" diam.
450QX253-1, $4.50 ☐

Friendship, A Gift of Friendship, New Home

From Our House to Yours, Teacher, Baby-sitter

Property Ornaments

Betsey Clark Angel
Betsey Clark's hand-painted, fine porcelain angel is dressed in a soft pink dress and white pinafore. The angel plays a holiday song on her mandolin.

Hand-Painted Porcelain, 3½″ tall
900QX462-4, $9.00 ☐

Katybeth
Katybeth is a new Hallmark property in the Keepsake line in 1984. Holding a friendly star, this freckled-faced angel wears a golden halo...a little off-center.

Hand-Painted Porcelain, 2¼″ tall
900QX463-1, $9.00 ☐

PEANUTS ®
SNOOPY ® watches as WOODSTOCK and friends build a gallery of snowmen. SNOOPY'S ® red banner says, "Merry Christmas." Ornament is dated "1984."

Light Blue Soft Sheen Satin, 2⅞″ diam.
450QX252-1, $4.50 ☐

DISNEY
The Disney gang — Mickey, Minnie, Donald, Daisy and Pluto — sends holiday greetings. Caption: "Friends put the merry in Christmas. 1984."

White Glass, 2⅞″ diam.
450QX250-4, $4.50 ☐

The MUPPETS™
KERMIT™, framed by a Christmas wreath, dons a Santa cap to wish us, "Hoppy, Hoppy Holidays!" MISS PIGGY™, framed by a heart-shaped wreath, says, "Merry Kissmas!"

Chrome Glass, 2⅞″ diam.
450QX251-4, $4.50 ☐

Norman Rockwell
This gold ball shows three famous paintings from the Hallmark Collection of Norman Rockwell artwork. Each panel depicts the artist's intepretation of Dickens Christmas characters. Caption: "Good friends, good times, good health, good cheer and happy days throughout the year. From the Norman Rockwell Collection 1984."

Gold Glass, 2⅞″ diam.
450QX251-1, $4.50 ☐

Currier & Ives
Always a favorite, Currier & Ives artwork is carefully reproduced on white blown glass. Caption: "American Winter Scenes, Evening, Christmas 1984."

White Glass, 2⅞″ diam.
450QX250-1, $4.50 ☐

Betsey Clark, Katybeth, PEANUTS®, DISNEY

MUPPETS™, Norman Rockwell, Currier & Ives, Shirt Tales™

Shirt Tales™

The Shirt Tales™ join in a merry snowball fight. Ball is capped with a golden crown. Caption: "Joy in the air, good time to share — Christmas, Christmas everywhere."

Aqua-Blue Satin, 2⅞" diam.
450QX252-4, $4.50 ☐

SNOOPY® and WOODSTOCK

Everyone's favorite beagle takes to the slopes with his faithful pal WOODSTOCK leading the way. But it's cold outside, so SNOOPY® wears a warm fabric scarf.

Handcrafted, 4¼" wide
750QX439-1, $7.50 ☐

Muffin

You'll always know Muffin by the red knitted cap she wears everywhere she goes. She's bringing a holiday gift to her friend Kit.

Handcrafted, 2¾" tall
550QX442-1, $5.50 ☐

Kit

Muffin's special friend Kit is known for his green cap. He brings a candy cane to sweeten your Christmas. Kit and Muffin make a perfect pair on the tree.

Handcrafted, 2¾" tall
550QX453-4, $5.50 ☐

Traditional Ornaments

White Christmas

The hustle and bustle of Christmas time is shown in a wintry town square of yesteryear. Caption: "At Christmas time, love shines in every smile, glows in every heart." Melody: "White Christmas."

Musical, Classic Shape, 4½" tall
1600QX905-1, $16.00 ☐

Twelve Days of Christmas

This musical ornament was originally part of Hallmark's Musical Decoration line. In 1984 it was re-introduced as a Keepsake Ornament. Melody: "The Twelve Days of Christmas."

Musical, Handcrafted, 3¾" tall
1500QX415-9, $15.00 ☐

Gift of Music

A colorfully dressed, bearded elf ties his holiday gift with red ribbon. The label on the blue wrapped gift says, "Jolly Holidays!" Melody: "Jingle Bells."

Musical, Handcrafted, 3" tall
1500QX451-1, $15.00 ☐

SNOOPY®, and WOODSTOCK, Muffin, Kit

White Christmas, Twelve Days of Christmas, Gift of Music

Amanda

Dressed in ruffled frock and bonnet of bright green fabric, Amanda is ready for a Christmas party. Her face and hands are fashioned of fine porcelain and painted by hand.

Fabric, Hand-Painted Porcelain, 4¾" tall
900QX432-1, $9.00 ☐

Holiday Jester

Looking as if he may have played to royal audiences, this jester wears the traditional black and white costume with gold shoes. His arms and legs are movable.

Handcrafted, 5¼" tall
1100QX437-4, $11.00 ☐

Uncle Sam

A pressed tin Uncle Sam, holding a teddy bear and flags, wears an "84" badge to remind us of that Presidential election year.

Pressed Tin, 5" tall
600QX449-1, $6.00 ☐

Chickadee

Hand-painted porcelain chickadee brings a cluster of mistletoe to your tree. A metal clip keeps the bird perched on the branch.

Hand-Painted Porcelain, 3¼" wide
600QX451-4, $6.00 ☐

Cuckoo Clock

"Merry Christmas" is the "time" etched on the brass face of this intricately detailed clock that comes complete with pinecone pendulums. Santa's face decorates the top and a reindeer adorns the bottom.

Handcrafted, 3¼" tall
1000QX455-1, $10.00 ☐

Alpine Elf

Holiday messages echo through the Alps when this elf plays his long carved horn.

Handcrafted, 3½" wide
600QX452-1, $6.00 ☐

Nostalgic Sled

This classic-style sled evokes memories of childhood fun. Sled has real string rope and metal runners. Caption: "Season's Greetings."

Handcrafted, 3½" wide
600QX442-4, $6.00 ☐

Amanda

Holiday Jester, Uncle Sam

Chickadee, Cuckoo Clock, Alpine Elf, Nostalgic Sled

Santa Sulky Driver

Santa races along in his etched brass rig that displays a "Season's Greetings" banner.

Etched Brass, 1¾" tall
900QX436-1, $9.00 ☐

Old Fashioned Rocking Horse

A new look for the Keepsake line, this ornament features a finely etched rocking horse embedded in acrylic.

Brass, Acrylic, 3¼" diam.
750QX346-4, $7.50 ☐

Madonna and Child

The Madonna cradles the Holy Child as a dove of peace watches in this loving scene etched in acrylic. The gold foil-stamped caption reads, "All is calm, all is bright..."

Acrylic, 4" tall
600QX344-1, $6.00 ☐

Holiday Friendship

This panorama peek-through ball depicts the friendship shared by a little boy and girl. Both hide gifts as they wave to each other through a frosty window.

Peek-Through Ball, 3¼" diam.
1300QX445-1, $13.00 ☐

Peace on Earth

Oval red cameo shows a beautiful old-world angel in ivory relief playing a harp. Caption: "Peace on Earth."

Cameo, 3" tall
750QX341-4, $7.50 ☐

A Savior is Born

A Nativity scene with holiday flowers brings the most important message of the season: "For unto you is born this day in the City of David a Savior which is Christ the Lord. Luke 2:11."

Purple Glass, 2⅞" diam.
450QX254-1, $4.50 ☐

Holiday Starburst

Holiday ribbons wrap around the silver starburst seen inside this clear glass ball. The caption, "Christmas 1984" is printed in gold.

Clear Glass, 2⅞" diam.
500QX253-4, $5.00 ☐

Santa Sulky Driver, Rocking Horse, Madonna and Child

Holiday Friendship, Peace on Earth, A Savior is Born, Holiday Starburst

Santa

Santa rides a reindeer over lush green hillsides filled with blooming flowers.

Hand-Embroidered Fabric, 4″ tall
750QX458-4, $7.50 ☐

Needlepoint Wreath

The delicate intricacy of needlepoint is beautifully displayed in this handmade wreath of bright holiday poinsettias.

Needlepoint-Fabric, 3½″ diam.
650QX459-4, $6.50 ☐

Christmas Memories Photoholder

A striking array of holiday fabrics forms a wreath fashioned to display a special Christmas photo. Caption: "Christmas is a remembering time 1984."

Fabric, 3″ diam.
650QX300-4, $6.50 ☐

Embroidered Heart

Reissue from 1983. (See 1983 Annual Collection.)

Hand-Embroidered Fabric, 4¾″ tall
650QX421-7, $6.50 ☐

Embroidered Stocking

Reissue from 1983. (See 1983 Annual Collection.)

Hand-Embroidered Fabric, 3¼″ tall
650QX479-6, $6.50 ☐

Holiday Humor

Bell Ringer Squirrel

A handcrafted squirrel swinging from an acorn forms the unique clapper in this clear glass bell.

Glass, Handcrafted, 4″ tall
1000QX443-1, $10.00 ☐

Raccoon's Christmas

Handcrafted raccoon is at home in his snow-covered tree house. Both he and his little neighbor have hung their Christmas stockings.

Handcrafted, 2¾″ tall
900QX447-4, $9.00 ☐

Three Kittens in a Mitten

Three kittens — black, tan, and gold — have found themselves in a dilemma. A real knitted red and green mitten.

Handcrafted, 3½″ tall
800QX431-1. $8.00 ☐

Marathon Santa

Santa carries a torch dated "1984." He's a gold medalist on December 25!

Handcrafted, 2¼″ tall
800QX456-4, $8.00 ☐

Santa, Needlepoint Wreath, Christmas Memories Photoholder

Bell Ringer Squirrel, Raccoon's Christmas, Three Kittens in a Mitten, Marathon Santa

Santa Star
A shining example of Santa! He's designed in the shape of a five-pointed star.

Handcrafted, 3½" tall
550QX450-4, $5.50 ☐

Snowmobile Santa
Santa goes out in his shiny new snowmobile. He loves the ride, but he has reasurred his reindeer that he won't be snowmobiling on Christmas Eve!

Handcrafted, 2¾" wide
650QX431-4, $6.50 ☐

Snowshoe Penguin
This neighbor of Santa's has set out in his showshoes to deliver his own Christmas gift. His cap has a real pom-pom.

Handcrafted, 3" tall
650QX453-1, $6.50 ☐

Christmas Owl
A wise little owl, wearing Santa's hat, watches from a clear acrylic moon. His Christmas stocking, made to fit his foot, hangs from the moon's tip.

Handcrafted, Acrylic, 3¾" tall
600QX444-1, $6.00 ☐

Musical Angel
This little angel has a unique view of Christmas, but even her position won't stop her from playing a heavenly tune. The banner hanging from her brass horn is stamped with the caption: "Noel."

Handcrafted, 1¼" tall
550QX434-4, $5.50 ☐

Napping Mouse
This little mouse is not "stirring," he's napping in a walnut shell while holding tightly to his "teddy mouse." The blanket is a red and white dotted fabric ribbon.

Handcrafted, 1¾" tall
550QX435-1, $5.50 ☐

Roller Skating Rabbit
The red wheels actually turn on the green and white roller skate shoe in which the white bunny is nestled for a holiday "spin."

Handcrafted, 2½" wide
500QX457-1, $5.00 ☐

Frisbee® Puppy
This playful puppy makes a spectacular leap and catches the "Merry Chrismas" Frisbee®. He wears a green fabric bow for the holidays.

Handcrafted, 2¾" tall
500QX444-4, $5.00 ☐

Santa Star, Snowmobile Santa, Snowshoe Penguin, Christmas Owl

Musical Angel, Napping Mouse, Roller Skating Rabbit, Frisbee® Puppy

Reindeer Racetrack
The race has started and the reindeer runners are off! Santa, in the viewing crowd, encourages his friends with a famous line from Clement C. Moore's "Night Before Christmas": "On, Comet! On, Cupid! On, Donder! On, Blitzen!"

Red Glass, 3″ diam.
450QX254-4, $4.50 ☐

A Christmas Prayer
Mary Hamilton's charming angels frolic in the clouds, chasing stars. Ball is capped with a golden crown. Caption: "Little prayer be on your way...bless our friends on Christmas Day."

Blue Sheen Satin, 2⅞″ diam.
450QX246-1, $4.50 ☐

Flights of Fantasy
Elves take flight on the backs of beautiful birds flying in the moonlight on this fanciful holiday ball. A ribbon banner says, "Christmas 1984."

Blue Glass, 2⅞″ diam.
450QX256-4, $4.50 ☐

Polar Bear Drummer
This white polar bear drums up some holiday spirit while keeping warm with a plaid fabric scarf.

Handcrafted, 2¼″ tall
450QX430-1, $4.50 ☐

Santa Mouse
Mister Mouse dresses as Santa with a jacket and cap and furry plush beard.

Handcrafted, 2″ tall
450QX433-4, $4.50 ☐

Snowy Seal
This soft, flocked white seal with dark eyes is dressed for the holidays in a red fabric ribbon.

Handcrafted, 1½″ wide
400QX450-1, $4.00 ☐

Fortune Cookie Elf
An elf paints your fortune for a holiday fortune cookie. Caption: "May your Christmas be merry."

Handcrafted, 2½″ tall
450Q452-4, $4.50 ☐

Peppermint 1984
The year 1984 in peppermint candy. Two birds enjoy the view from atop the number nine.

Handcrafted, 2¾″ wide
450Q456-1, $4.50 ☐

Reindeer Racetrack, A Christmas Prayer, Flights of Fantasy, Polar Bear Drummer

Santa Mouse, Snowy Seal, Fortune Cookie Elf, Peppermint 1984

Mountain Climbing Santa
Reissue from 1983. (See 1983 Annual Collection.)

Handcrafted, 2½″ tall
650QX407-7, $6.50

Limited Edition

Classical Angel
Limited to an edition size of 24,700 pieces, this elegant, hand-painted porcelain angel is Hallmark's first announced limited edition ornament. She stands five inches tall and comes with her own wood display stand. Dressed in a flowing dress of pink, golden-yellow and white, she carries a chain of brass bells. Dated "1984."

Hand-Painted Porcelain, 5″ tall
2750QX459-1., $27.50 □

Collectible Series

Nostalgic Houses and Shops—First Edition
This elegant "Victorian Dollhouse," scaled one inch to one foot, is perfect for both ornament and dollhouse collectors. The fully decorated interior comes complete with wallpaper, furniture, a Christmas tree and even a miniature dollhouse.

Handcrafted, 3¼″ tall
1300QX448-1, $13.00 □

Wood Childhood Ornaments—First Edition
Hand-painted "Wooden Lamb" evokes memories of Christmas past. Wheels that turn and a red fabric bow at the neck add wonderful touches of authenticity.

Wood, Handcrafted, 2¼″ tall
650QX439-4, $6.50 □

Classical Angel

Nostalgic Houses and Shops, Wood Childhood Ornaments

The Twelve Days of Christmas— First Edition

The popular old Christmas song is immortalized on scalloped acrylic. An etched partridge and pear tree depict the first of the days and the gold-foil stamped caption reads, "The Twelve Days of Christmas 1984...and a partridge in a pear tree."

Acrylic, 3″ tall
600QX348-4, $6.00　　□

Art Masterpiece—First Edition

This series brings timeless works of art into your home. The first ornament offers a classic oil painting reproduced on padded satin. Caption: "Giuliano Bugiardini, 'Madonna and Child and St. John,' (ca. 1505) The Nelson-Atkins Museum of Art, Kansas City, Missouri, (Nelson Fund)."

Bezeled Satin, 2¾″ diam.
650QX349-4, $6.50　　□

Porcelain Bear—Second Edition

An adorable "Cinnamon Bear," fashioned in hand-painted porcelain, holds a gold jingle bell with red bow.

Hand-Painted Porcelain, 2½″ tall
700QX454-1, $7.00　　□

Tin Locomotive—Third Edition

Number three in the pressed Tin Locomotive Series is an antique design with movable wheels; the muted colors are red, soft blue, lavender and steel. Dated "1984."

Pressed Tin, 2½″ tall
1400QX440-4, $14.00　　□

Clothespin Soldier — Third Edition

Red and black uniformed Canadian Mountie proudly bears a holiday flag.

Handcrafted, 2½″ tall
500QX447-1, $5.00　　□

Holiday Wildlife—Third Edition

A pair of graceful Ring-Necked Pheasants are pictured against a snow-covered setting on a porcelain-look inset framed in wood. Caption: "Ring-Necked Pheasant, Phasianus Torquatus, Third in a series, Wildlife Collection, Christmas 1984."

Handcrafted, 3″ diam.
725QX347-4, $7.25　　□

Twelve Days of Christmas, Art Masterpiece, Porcelain Bear

Tin Locomotive, Clothespin Soldier, Holiday Wildlife

Rocking Horse—Fourth Edition

Racing into the holiday season is the fourth of the "Rocking Horse" series. The blue and red saddle and rockers provide a colorful contrast to this white and black speckled appaloosa with gray mane and flying yarn tail. Dated "1984."

Handcrafted, 4" wide
1000QX435-4, $10.00 ☐

Frosty Friends—Fifth Edition

The little Eskimo has gone ice fishing with his penguin pal. The catch of the day is a Christmas gift, all wrapped and dated "1984."

Handcrafted, 2½" tall
800QX437-1, $8.00 ☐

Norman Rockwell—Fifth Edition

Rockwell's famous *Caught Napping* is the subject of this delicate cameo. Santa peeks from behind a high-backed chair at two pajama-clad children who tried their best to stay awake for his visit. The background is deep blue with white relief. Caption: "Caught Napping, Fifth in a Series, The Norman Rockwell Collection, Christmas 1984."

Cameo, 3" diam.
750QX341-1, $7.50 ☐

Here Comes Santa—Sixth Edition

Santa's "free delivery" service carries a load of Christmas trees as its cargo. Called "Santa's Deliveries," this ornament has wheels that actually turn. License plate, "1984."

Handcrafted, 3¼" tall
1300QX432-4, $13.00 ☐

The Bellringer—Sixth and Final Edition

The "Elfin Artist," swinging on the outside of a white, fine porcelain bell, has painted his message in red: "Christmas 1984."

Porcelain, 3½" tall
1500QX438-4, $15.00 ☐

Thimble—Seventh Edition

Heavenly blue-gowned angel holds a shiny thimble full of sparkling acrylic stars.

Handcrafted, 1¾" tall
500QX430-4, $5.00 ☐

Betsey Clark—Twelfth Edition

Artist Betsey Clark's little waifs decorate their home for the holidays. Caption: "Days are merry, hearts are light, and all the world's a lovely sight. Chrismas 1984."

White Frosted Glass, 3¼" diam.
500QX249-4, $5.00 ☐

Rocking Horse, Frosty Friends, Norman Rockwell

Here Comes Santa, Bellringer, Thimble, Betsey Clark

THE 1985 COLLECTION

The 1985 Keepsake Ornament line continued Hallmark's attempts to design ornaments that meet collectors' needs. Collectors expressed a definite interest in ornaments that look homemade and are fashioned of natural materials such as wood and fabric. To respond to this demand, Hallmark offered two special coordinated groups of five ornaments each.

The "Country Christmas Collection" included ornaments created of wood or porcelain, or fashioned in the look of hand-carved wood. The carefully researched designs captured a nostalgic country flavor. The "Heirloom Christmas Collection" used satin, lace, ribbon and intricate crochet work to bring back the romance of another era. These elegant designs were inspired by popular, turn-of-the-century styles, with some even including rose-scented sachets.

Limited Edition and Collectible Series ornaments are also favorites with collectors. The '85 line featured two new series and the second limited edition Keepsake, a fine porcelain angel called "Heavenly Trumpeter" produced in an edition size of 24,700 pieces. The two new series were "Windows of the World," showing children from all around the globe celebrating Christmas, and "Miniature Creche," offering a new Nativity scene fashioned of different materials each year.

Three properties, FRAGGLE ROCK™, Rainbow Brite™, and Hugga Bunch made their debut this year, as did an ornament designed especially for Niece. Among the new formats were a satin-covered container with a card tucked inside for personalization, and an ornament made of stained glass.

Commemoratives

Baby's First Christmas
A beautiful embroidered satin baby block, bordered in lace, plays a lullaby for Baby. The ABC, four-sided caption reads, "A Baby's 1st Christmas 1985." Melody: "Schubert's Lullaby."

Musical, Fabric, 3¼" tall
1600QX499-5, $16.00 ☐

Baby's First Christmas
Baby's out for a ride to deliver a special Christmas gift. This lace-trimmed, rattan-look stroller with real fabric bow and pillow was inspired by a turn-of-the-century mail-order catalog and is built to scale. Caption: "Baby's First Christmas 1985."

Handcrafted, 3¾" tall
1500QX499-2, $15.00 ☐

Baby Locket
Textured brass locket has a space for Baby's photo and for personalizing. The caption, "Baby," is decorated with embossed toys.

Textured Brass, 2¼" diam.
1600QX401-2, $16.00 ☐

Baby's First Christmas
An acrylic baby cup, brimming with toys, is captioned, "Baby's First Christmas 1985" in stamped silver foil.

Acrylic, 3¾" tall
575QX370-2, $5.75 ☐

Baby's First Christmas: Musical, Handcrafted

Baby Locket, Baby's First Christmas: Acrylic

Baby's First Christmas

This hand-embroidered tree is just Baby's size! It's decorated with ribbon and lace and is captioned, "1985 Baby's 1st Christmas."

Embroidered Fabric, 4½″ tall
700QX478-2, $7.00 □

Baby's First Christmas

Dressed in yellow, Baby is delighted by the Christmas toys shown around the center of this green satin ball. Ornament is topped with a handcrafted mouse. Caption: "A Baby keeps the season bright and warms the heart with sweet delight. Baby's First Christmas 1985."

Green Soft-Sheen Satin, 2⅞″ diam.
500QX260-2, $5.00 □

Baby's Second Christmas

An adorable teddy bear rides a stick pony that has a plush mane and fabric reins. Teddy's shirt is captioned, "Baby's Second Christmas 1985."

Handcrafted, 3½″ tall
600QX478-5, $6.00 □

Child's Third Christmas

A brown flocked teddy bear has found a home in a red and white sneaker laced with a real shoestring. Sneaker is bordered with the caption: "A Child's Third Christmas '85."

Handcrafted, 2¼″ tall
600QX475-5, $6.00 □

Grandchild's First Christmas

The elves are busily making Christmas toys on this ecru ball topped with a handcrafted mouse. Sitting on Santa's knee, the adorable little baby can't wait to hug his new teddy bear. The caption reads, "Grandchild's First Christmas 1985."

Ecru Satin, 2⅞″ diam.
500QX260-5, $5.00 □

Grandchild's First Christmas

White hand-knitted bootie with ribbon trim is filled with toys Baby will love. Caption: "Grandchild's First Christmas 1985."

Handcrafted, 3¼″ tall
1100QX495-5, $11.00 □

Baby's First Christmas: Fabric, Satin Ball; Baby's Second Christmas

Child's Third Christmas, Grandchild's First Christmas: Satin Ball, Handcrafted

Grandparents, Niece, Mother

Mother and Dad, Father, Sister, Daughter

Godchild, Son

Grandmother, Grandson, Granddaughter

Grandparents

A white poinsettia appears against a rich garnet background to create a unique lacquer-look that is new to the Keepsake Ornament line. Framed in brass, the design is accented with gold for an extra-festive touch. Caption: "Grandparents have beautiful ways of adding love to the holidays. Christmas 1985."

Bezeled Lacquer-Look, 2¾″ wide
700QX380-5, $7.00 ☐

Niece

A new and sure-to-be-popular caption. Stamped in silver foil on an acrylic teardrop is the sentiment: "A Niece fills hearts with a special kind of love. Christmas 1985."

Acrylic, 3¾″ tall
575QX520-5, $5.75 ☐

Mother

Clear acrylic raindrop, framed in a golden ring, brings a tribute to Mother. The gold foil-stamped caption reads, "Mother is the heart of our happiest holiday memories. Christmas 1985."

Acrylic, 3⅜″ tall
675QX372-2, $6.75 ☐

Mother and Dad

Snowy white, fine porcelain bell has bas-relief paisley design. The trim, caption, tie cord and tassle are all coordinated in soft blue. Caption: "Mother and Dad. Christmas 1985."

Porcelain, 3″ tall
775QX509-2, $7.75 ☐

Father

Filled with gifts and a Christmas tree, this old-fashioned sleigh is printed on hardwood with the look of hand painting. Caption: "A Father sees through the eyes of love and listens with his heart. Christmas 1985."

Wood, 3″ diam.
650QX376-2, $6.50 ☐

Sister

This white porcelain bell, hanging from a red ribbon, has a cheerful heart and holly design that looks as if it were hand-painted especially for Sister. Caption: "For Sister with love. Christmas 1985."

Porcelain, 2¾″ tall
725QX506-5, $7.25 ☐

Daughter

Framed in a wooden embroidery hoop tied with a delicately embroidered fabric ribbon, the design has the look of fine silk-screening. Caption: "A Daughter decorates the holidays with love. Christmas 1985."

Wood, 3¼″ diam.
550QX503-2, $5.50 ☐

First Christmas Together Brass, Love at Christmas, First Christmas Together Acrylic

Godchild

This unique design has been taken from Hallmark's Antique Greeting Card Collection and reproduced on padded satin. The caption on the reverse side is stamped in gold foil. Caption: "A Godchild is a loving gift to treasure through the years. Christmas 1985."

Bezeled Satin, 2¾″ Diam.
675QX380-2, $6.75 ☐

Son

An adorable terrier, with a fabric bow at his neck, fetches the message: "Merry Christmas, Son 1985."

Handcrafted, 2″ tall
550QX502-5, $5.50 ☐

Grandmother

A nostalgic floral design decorates this transparent red, teardrop-shaped ball. The scroll banner bears the caption: "A Grandmother gives the gift of love. Christmas 1985."

Red Glass, 3″ diam.
475QX262-5, $4.75 ☐

Grandson

A bright red, green and yellow antique train chugs around a green glass ball bringing Grandson a Christmas message. Caption: "A Grandson makes holiday joys shine even brighter! Christmas 1985."

Green Glass, 2⅞″ diam.
475QX262-2, $4.75 ☐

Granddaughter

A contemporary American country look is achieved in the design of the vividly colored animals on the center of this ivory ball. Caption: "There's nothing like a Granddaughter to warm the world at Christmas. 1985."

Ivory Glass, 2⅞″ diam.
475QX263-5, $4.75 ☐

First Christmas Together

Romantic embossed hearts surround the caption "First Christmas Together 1985" on the cover of this polished brass locket. With its special hanger, the locket can be displayed closed to show the cover or open to reveal your two photos inside. Locket comes with a special felt storage pouch.

Polished Brass, 2½″ tall
1675QX400-5, $16.75 ☐

Love at Christmas

It's raining romantic red foil hearts on this heart of acrylic etched with the caption: "The spirit of Christmas is love."

Acrylic, 3¼″ wide
575QX371-5, $5.75 ☐

First Christmas Together

On a clear acrylic oval, framed in brass, a graceful pair of etched doves carry a banner bearing the gold foil-stamped caption: "First Christmas Together 1985."

Acrylic, 3½″ wide
675QX370-5, $6.75 ☐

First Christmas Together

A pale green bisque porcelain bell with scalloped, bas-relief design becomes a romantic symbol of love. The red porcelain, double-heart clapper bears the caption: "First Christmas Together 1985."

Porcelain, 2" tall
1300QX493-5, $13.00

Holiday Heart

Colorful flowers and holiday greenery decorate a white, fine porcelain puffed heart. The ornament is captioned with the word "Love" in bas-relief and topped with a white fabric tassel.

Porcelain, 2" tall
800QX498-2, $8.00

First Christmas Together

This design is a unique blend of old-fashioned charm and romance. The red heart is hand-woven inside a wooden frame decorated with a bright red fabric tassel. Caption: "1985 First Christmas Together."

Fabric, Wood, 2½" tall
800QX507-2, $8.00

Heart Full of Love

A lovely winter scene of snow-capped trees, accented by brightly colored cardinals and red berries, is printed on padded satin and framed with a chrome ring. Caption: "The world is full of beauty when hearts are full of love. Christmas 1985."

Bezeled Satin, 3" tall
675QX378-2, $6.75

First Christmas Together

Heart-shaped frames reveal romantic silhouette vignettes painted in shades of blue, green and red. Caption: "Love is a gift from heart to heart. First Christmas Together 1985."

Light Blue Glass, 2⅞" diam.
475QX261-2, $4.75

Twenty-Five Years Together

This miniature porcelain plate, a new format in 1985, is decorated with a gold, silver and blue holly wreath. The border caption on the front reads, "Twenty-Five Years Together." Back: "Christmas 1985." Plate stand included.

Porcelain, 3¼" diam.
800QX500-5, $8.00

First Christmas Porcelain Bell, Holiday Heart, First Christmas Fabric and Wood

Heart Full of Love, First Christmas Together Glass Ball, Twenty-Five Years Together

Friendship

A new format for 1985, this tasseled container, covered in rich Oriental red satin, is hand embroidered with a pine and snowflake design. A gift card for personalizing is tucked inside and the caption reads, "Christmas...a special time for friendship. 1985."

Embroidered Satin, 2" tall
775QX506-2, $7.75 ☐

Friendship

An early American village reflects the warmth of Christmas and of friendship. If you look carefully you'll see Santa standing in the middle of town. Artwork is printed on padded satin and framed with a chrome bezel. Caption: "Christmas ... season bright with friendship. 1985."

Bezeled Satin, 3" tall
675QX378-5, $6.75 ☐

From Our House to Yours

Holiday decorations in the windows of this beautifully detailed, handmade needlepoint house tell visiting neighbors that friendship and Christmas cheer are inside. The caption on red satin reads, "A happy home reflects the joy of Christmas all year round. 1985."

Needlepoint-Fabric, 4" tall
775QX520-2, $7.75 ☐

Teacher

A wise owl is ready for class as he perches on a slate board displaying the lesson, "Merry Christmas to a Grade A Teacher!" The owl's book has the title "School Days 1985." There is room for personalization on the back of the slate.

Handcrafted, 3" tall
600QX505-2, $6.00 ☐

With Appreciation

A lovely combination of silver and gold appears in this acrylic oval framed in brass. Stamped in silver foil, snowflakes surround the gold foil-stamped caption: "Christmas...a time when we think of those who have given us so much. 1985."

Acrylic, 3½" tall
675QX375-2, $6.75 ☐

Special Friends

Unique quadrafoil acrylic shape is the setting for this charming etching of a doll and her "beary" best friend. Caption, stamped in silver foil, says, "Special friends bring special joys to Christmas. 1985."

Acrylic, 3" wide
575QX372-5, $5.75 ☐

Friendship: Embroidered, Bezeled Satin; From Our House to Yours, Teacher

With Appreciation, Special Friends

New Home

Lovely Victorian homes, decorated with wreaths and Christmas greenery, encircle a blue teardrop ball. Caption: "New Home, new joys, new memories to cherish. Christmas 1985."

Blue Glass, 3" diam.
475QX269-5, $4.75 ☐

Baby-sitter

Each of these pandas is preparing for Christmas in his own special way. The red, white and black bears present a striking contrast against the brilliant green teardrop ball. Caption: "A Baby-sitter is a special kind of friend. Christmas 1985."

Green Glass, 3" diam.
475QX264-2, $4.75 ☐

Good Friends

Penguins frolic in the snow, making patterns and words to commemorate the holiday season. Caption on this frosted teardrop ball reads, "Good times with good friends make life's merriest moments. Christmas 1985."

White Frosted Glass, 3" diam.
475QX265-2, $4.75 ☐

Property Ornaments

SNOOPY® and WOODSTOCK

SNOOPY® is practicing for the holiday hockey tournament with the help of his star player, WOODSTOCK. They'll skate their way into your Christmas for many years to come.

Handcrafted, 1¾" tall
750QX491-5, $7.50 ☐

Muffin the Angel

All dressed up as an angel, Muffin is ready for the Christmas pageant wearing a snowy white fabric outfit.

Handcrafted, 2½" tall
575QX483-5, $5.75 ☐

Kit the Shepherd

Kit is a shepherd in the Christmas pageant, dressed in a fabric headdress.

Handcrafted, 2½" tall
575QX484-5, $5.75 ☐

Betsey Clark

This little boy is one of Betsey Clark's most charming angels. On bended knee, he gathers a little lamb into his arms.

Hand-Painted Porcelain, 2½" tall
850QX508-5, $8.50 ☐

New Home, Baby-sitter, Good Friends

SNOOPY® and WOODSTOCK, Muffin the Angel, Kit the Shepherd, Betsey Clark

Hugga Bunch™

These little cuties share warm hugs and Christmas fun as they make their debut in the Keepsake line. Caption: "Huggy Holidays!"

Light Blue Glass, 2⅞" diam.
500QX271-5, $5.00 ☐

FRAGGLE ROCK™ Holiday

The dog, SPROCKET™, peeks in on the holiday activities of the FRAGGLE ROCK™ gang. A new property in the Keepsake Ornament line. Caption: "Happy Holidays '85."

Light Blue Glass, 3" diam.
475QX265-5, $4.75 ☐

PEANUTS®

SNOOPY® directs a Christmas chorus starring WOODSTOCK and his friends on a teardrop-shaped ball. Caption: "Sing a song of Christmas joy! 1985."

Blue Glass, 3" diam.
475QX266-5, $4.75 ☐

Norman Rockwell

Three favorite Rockwell Santa paintings appear on this frosted white ball. The caption describes the portrayals perfectly: "...He was chubby and plump, a right jolly old elf, and I laughed when I saw him, in spite of myself...C.C. Moore. From the Norman Rockwell Collection 1985."

Frosted White Glass, 2⅞" diam.
475QX266-2, $4.75 ☐

Rainbow Brite™ and Friends

Rainbow Brite and the Sprites make their first appearance in the Keepsake line amid a rainbow of colorful stars and snowflakes. Visible inside the clear glass ball is a bright gold starburst. Caption: "1985."

Clear Glass, 2⅞" diam.
475QX268-2, $4.75 ☐

A DISNEY Christmas

It's stocking-hanging time at Mickey Mouse's house as Mickey dons a Santa suit complete with a pillow for stuffing. This ornament displays a new process that allows printing directly on the glass. Dated "1985."

Pearl Blue Glass, 3" diam.
475QX271-2, $4.75 ☐

Merry Shirt Tales™

The Shirt Tales, all bundled up for winter, go skating, skiing and sledding on a teardrop-shaped ball. Caption: "Every day's a holiday when good friends get together. Christmas 1985."

Light Blue Glass, 3" diam.
475QX267-2, $4.75 ☐

Hugga Bunch, FRAGGLE ROCK™ Holiday, PEANUTS®, Norman Rockwell

Rainbow Brite™ and Friends, A DISNEY Christmas, Merry Shirt Tales™

Traditional Ornaments

Porcelain Bird
This Tufted Titmouse looks so real you might think he flew into your home to celebrate the holidays. He's fashioned of hand-painted porcelain and perches on your tree with the help of a specially designed clip.

Hand-Painted Porcelain, 2″ tall
650QX479-5, $6.50 ☐

Sewn Photoholder
A cheery array of holiday hearts and Christmas flowers are embroidered on this red fabric photoholder. Caption: "Cherished times that mean the most are kept in memory ever close. Christmas 1985."

Embroidered Fabric, 3¼″ diam.
700QX379-5, $7.00 ☐

Candle Cameo
The warmth and cheer of Christmas are captured in this portrayal of traditional holiday symbols. Subtle shadings in the ivory design accentuate the bas-relief detailing. Gold foil-stamped caption reads, "Christmas...the season that brightens the world. 1985."

Bezeled Cameo, 3″ tall
675QX374-2, $6.75 ☐

Santa Pipe
A pipe with the look of carved antique meerschaum displays a bas-relief Santa and reindeer on their Christmas Eve ride.

Handcrafted, 4½″ tall
950QX494-2, $9.50 ☐

Old-Fashioned Wreath
An intricate etched brass wreath of Christmas toys is embedded in clear acrylic. The gold foil-stamped caption says, "Christmas 1985."

Etched Brass, Acrylic, 3¼″ diam.
750QX373-5, $7.50 ☐

Peaceful Kingdom
Etched onto an acrylic oval, the lion and lamb symbolize the words that are so much a part of the meaning of Christmas: "...and peace will reign in the kingdom...Christmas 1985." Caption is stamped in gold foil.

Acrylic, 3″ wide
575QX373-2, $5.75 ☐

Christmas Treats
In the tradition of beautiful stained glass, this ornament depicts holiday candies in bright shades of red and green. A lead frame encircles the glass design. This is a new format in the Keepsake line.

Bezeled Glass, 3¼″ tall
550QX507-5, $5.50 ☐

Porcelain Bird, Sewn Photoholder, Candle Cameo, Santa Pipe

Old-Fashioned Wreath, Peaceful Kingdom, Christmas Treats

The Spirit of Santa Claus-Special Edition
Driving a green and gold sleigh laden with a bag of toys and a Christmas tree, Santa holds the reins to a beautiful prancing reindeer. The complexity and detailing of this ornament make it a true work of art. A special wishbone-shaped hanger comes with the ornament.

Handcrafted, 4¾" tall
2250QX498-5, $22.50 ☐

Nostalgic Sled
Reissue from 1984. (See 1984 Annual Collection.)

Handcrafted, 3½" wide
600QX442-4, $6.00

Holiday Humor

Night Before Christmas
This favorite Christmas story is at your fingertips. When you push the button, 30 pages depicting the story flip over before your eyes. Ornament comes with special stand for off-tree display.

Panorama Ball, 3¼" diam.
1300QX449-4, $13.00 ☐

Nativity Scene
The birds and bunnies gather 'round as a group of adorable little angels welcome the Baby. This delicately detailed design illustrates the caption: "O come, all ye faithful...Christmas 1985."

Light Blue Glass, 3" diam.
475QX264-5, $4.75 ☐

Santa's Ski Trip
Santa waves his hat as he rides to the slopes in gondola "Snowflake Mountain No. 1985." The gondola hangs by a pully with a real string "rope."

Handcrafted, 3¾" tall
1200QX496-2, $12.00 ☐

Mouse Wagon
Bringing a gift of his favorite cheese, a white mouse rides into the Christmas season in his little red wagon. Dated "1985," the wagon has wheels that turn and a movable handle.

Handcrafted, 2" tall
575QX476-2, $5.75 ☐

Children in the Shoe
Inspired by the nursery rhyme, this ornament depicts an old shoe house with sparkling snow on the roof, a wreath on the door and, of course, children everywhere.

Handcrafted, 3¼" tall
950QX490-5, $9.50 ☐

The Spirit of Santa Claus

Night Before Christmas, Nativity Scene, Santa's Ski Trip, Mouse Wagon, Children in the Shoe

Do Not Disturb Bear
His green stocking is hung with care and so is his "Do not disturb 'til Christmas" sign, as the flocked bear snoozes snugly in his log. Pillow and blanket are fabric.

Handcrafted, 3" wide
775QX481-2, $7.75

Sun and Fun Santa
Santa loves the beach but he wouldn't think of going into the water without his reindeer inner tube. His bathing cap is dated " '85."

Handcrafted, 2¾" tall
775QX492-2, $7.75

Bottlecap Fun Bunnies
Mommy bunny, wearing a real pom-pom on her hat, gives baby bunny a ride. Her sled is a metal bottle cap from the "Santa Soda, North Pole Bottling Co."

Handcrafted, 2¼" tall
775QX481-5, $7.75

Lamb in Legwarmers
Little flocked lamb is ready to exercise in green, red and white crocheted fabric legwarmers.

Handcrafted, 3" tall
700QX480-2, $7.00

Candy Apple Mouse
With his tummy filled, a little white mouse naps on a partially eaten candied red apple at the end of a "1985" stick.

Handcrafted, 3¾" tall
650QX470-5, $6.50

Skateboard Raccoon
Flocked raccoon is going for a ride on a red skateboard with green, movable wheels. The design on his skateboard proclaims his star status!

Handcrafted, 2½" tall
650QX473-2, $6.50

Stardust Angel
A darling angel brushes the excess stardust from her star and keeps it in her handy "Stardust" bag.

Handcrafted, 2" tall
575QX475-2, $5.75

Soccer Beaver
This energetic beaver, dressed in red, is ready for a holiday game of soccer.

Handcrafted, 2½" tall
650QX477-5, $6.50

Beary Smooth Ride
Like children everywhere, Teddy enjoys riding all around the neighborhood. His colorful tricycle has wheels that turn.

Handcrafted, 1¾" tall
650QX480-5, $6.50

Do Not Disturb Bear, Sun and Fun Santa, Bottlecap Fun Bunnies, Lamb in Legwarmers

Candy Apple Mouse, Skateboard Raccoon, Stardust Angel, Soccer Beaver, Beary Smooth Ride

Swinging Angel Bell
Riding on a bright red swing, a little angel is the clapper of this sparkling clear bell.

Handcrafted, Glass, 3¾″ tall
1100QX492-5, $11.00 ☐

Doggy in a Stocking
Santa delivers a puppy for Christmas and he's a stocking full of charm. This tan terrier is snuggled in a stocking of crocheted red and green yarn.

Handcrafted, 3″ tall
550QX474-2, $5.50 ☐

Engineering Mouse
A white mouse is the engineer of this bright red and green train styled to look like a windup toy.

Handcrafted, 2″ tall
550QX473-5, $5.50 ☐

Kitty Mischief
Yellow and white kitten is all tangled up with a ball of real red yarn.

Handcrafted, 2″ tall
500QX474-5, $5.00 ☐

Baker Elf
An elf puts the finishing touch of green icing on his bell-shaped cookie. Centered on the cookie, "1985" appears in red icing.

Handcrafted, 3″ tall
575QX491-2, $5.75 ☐

Ice-Skating Owl
Cute white owl, wearing a red and white hat of real yarn, seems to be a bit unsteady on his new ice skates.

Handcrafted, 2″ tall
500QX476-5, $5.00 ☐

Dapper Penguin
Sporting a red top hat, gold cane and green bow tie, this dashing penguin is ready for a holiday gala.

Handcrafted, 2¼″ tall
500QX477-2, $5.00 ☐

Trumpet Panda
This flocked panda practices his holiday music for the Christmas Day parade.

Handcrafted, 2″ tall
450QX471-2, $4.50 ☐

Merry Mouse
Wearing a hat just like Santa's, this mouse can't wait until Christmas arrives. His tail is fashioned of real leather.

Handcrafted, 2½″ tall
450QX403-2, $4.50 ☐

Snow-Pitching Snowman
Flocked white snowman wearing a red and green baseball cap is all wound up and ready to pitch his snowball.

Handcrafted, 2″ tall
450QX470-2, $4.50 ☐

Swinging Angel Bell, Doggy in a Stocking, Engineering Mouse, Kitty Mischief, Baker Elf

Ice Skating Owl, Dapper Penguin, Trumpet Panda, Merry Mouse, Snow-Pitching Snowman

Three Kittens in a Mitten
Reissue from 1984. (See 1984 Annual Collection.)

Handcrafted, 3½" tall
800QX431-1, $8.00

Roller Skating Rabbit
Reissue from 1984. (See 1984 Annual Collection.)

Handcrafted, 2½" wide
500QX457-1, $5.00

Snowy Seal
Reissue from 1984. (See 1984 Annual Collection.)

Handcrafted, 1½" wide
400QX450-1, $4.00

Country Christmas Collection

Old-Fashioned Doll
She's a real Colonial lady, dressed in a holiday costume trimmed with lace. The doll has hand-painted porcelain arms, legs and head.

Hand-Painted Porcelain, Fabric, 5½" tall
1450QX519-5, $14.50 ☐

Country Goose
This delicate print on natural wood brings back memories of a simpler time. Caption: "This original design, styled in the American Country Tradition, has been printed on hardwood."

Wood, 3" diam.
775QX518-5, $7.75 ☐

Rocking Horse Memories
Silk-screen applique rocking horse is a lovely contrast against a holly-patterned background framed in an authentic wooden embroidery hoop. Caption: "Christmas 1985."

Wood, Fabric, 3¼" diam.
1000QX518-2, $10.00 ☐

Whirligig Santa
A real wood Whirligig Santa with arms that move is modeled after a popular Colonial toy.

Wood, 4" tall
1250QX519-2, $12.50 ☐

Sheep at Christmas
Reminiscent of olden-day carvings, this sheep wears a bell that rings in the holidays. Caption: "Season's Greetings 1985."

Handcrafted, 3¼" tall
825QX517-5, $8.25 ☐

Old Fashioned Doll, Country Goose, Rocking Horse Memories, Whirligig Santa, Sheep at Christmas

Keepsake Basket, Victorian Lady, Charming Angel, Lacy Heart, Snowflake

Heirloom Christmas Collection

Keepsake Basket
Hand-crocheted basket is trimmed with satin and lace. A pearl-like button closure opens to a rose-scented sachet.
Fabric, 2½″ tall
1500QX514-5, $15.00 □

Victorian Lady
Hand-painted porcelain doll rests on a burgundy satin, lace-trimmed cone.
Hand-Painted Porcelain, Fabric, 3¾″ tall
950QX513-2, $9.50 □

Charming Angel
A precious angel with yarn hair and wings of sheer netting wears a hand-sewn lace dress and holds a satin rose.
Fabric, 3¾″ tall
975QX512-5, $9.75 □

Lacy Heart
A romantic padded satin heart is lavishly trimmed with lace and scented with a rose sachet.
Fabric, 3″ tall
875QX511-2, $8.75 □

Snowflake
This hand-crocheted snowflake is padded with burgundy satin and laced with intricate detail.
Fabric, 4¼″ diam.
650QX510-5, $6.50 □

Limited Edition

Heavenly Trumpeter
The second limited edition ornament is a hand-painted porcelain angel, playing a golden trumpet to announce the joyous tidings of the season. The ornament, limited to an edition size of 24,700, comes with a wooden display stand.
Hand-Painted Porcelain, 5″ tall
2750QX405-2, $27.50 □

Collectible Series

Windows of the World—First Edition
An adorable Mexican child sits in a brick and stucco window in this first of a series of worldwide celebrations of Christmas. A "1985" pinata and Christmas greeting, "Feliz Navidad," decorate the archway.
Handcrafted, 3″ tall
975QX490-2, $9.75 □

Miniature Creche—First Edition
A series of unique Nativities fashioned in different media such as wood and porcelain.
1985 875QX482-5 Wood and Straw □

Heavenly Trumpeter

Windows of the World, Miniature Creche

Limited Edition

Magical Unicorn

This fine porcelain unicorn may, indeed, be magical because it has become one of the most sought after ornaments in the history of the Keepsake line. Hand-painted pastel flowers circle the unicorn's neck and are woven through his mane. Matching green and pink fabric ribbons are draped around his body, and his hooves and horn are painted silver. Limited to an edition size of 24,700 pieces, the ornament comes with a wooden display stand.

Hand-Painted Fine Porcelain, 4½" tall
2750QX429-3, $27.50 □

Christmas Medley Collection

Joyful Carolers

This design, sculpted to look like hand-carved wood, is reminiscent of the "Nostalgia" ornaments from years past. Dressed in the style of Dickens' characters, the carolers are fully dimensional. Caption on front and back: "Joy to the World 1986."

Handcrafted, 3¼" diam.
975QX513-6, $9.75 □

Festive Treble Clef

Let the music begin! A tiny brass bell dangles from a shiny treble clef, accented with translucent red and tied with a striped fabric ribbon.

Handcrafted, 3⅞" tall
875QX513-3, $8.75 □

Favorite Tin Drum

The tin drum, a favorite of children for generations, is reproduced in miniature including two tiny drumsticks. A delicate holly design decorates both drumheads, and the bindings are made of gold cord.

Tin, 2" diam.
850QX514-3, $8.50 □

Christmas Guitar

Decorated front and back with a green and red holly design, this miniature guitar is dated "1986" and hangs from its own guitar strap made of striped fabric ribbon. The tiny frets are accented with gold.

Handcrafted, 3" tall
700QX512-6, $7.00 □

Holiday Horn

Made of velvety bisque porcelain, this graceful horn is accented with touches of gold and tied with a striped fabric ribbon. The holly design seen on the "Favorite Tin Drum" adorns the ivory surface outside the horn's mouth.

Fine Porcelain, 3" tall
800QX514-6, $8.00 □

Magical Unicorn

Country Treasures Collection

All of the ornaments in this collection are packaged in a wooden Shaker box.

Country Sleigh

Modeled after an antique sleigh, this ornament evokes memories of an old-fashioned Christmas. Dated "1986," the sleigh holds a plaid fabric blanket—just the right thing for a crisp country morning!

Handcrafted, 2" tall
1000QX511-3, $10.00 □

Remembering Christmas

The vivid country quilt pattern re-created on this fine porcelain ornament will appeal to both plate and ornament collectors. Dated "1986," the back of the miniature plate displays the sentiment, "Christmas memories are keepsakes of the heart." Plate stand included.

Fine Porcelain, 3¼" diam.
875QX510-6, $8.75 □

Little Drummers

Motion is the special feature of this unique ornament. The three little drummer boys, fashioned to look like wood, actually play their drums when you tap or shake the ornament's platform. A novel variation on a favorite symbol of the season.

Handcrafted, 4" tall
1250QX511-6, $12.50 □

Nutcracker Santa

This Santa's not a real nutcracker, of course, but he's crafted to look like one. When you lift the tassel on his cap, his mouth pops open. Carefully painted and antiqued, the design resembles hand-carved wood.

Handcrafted, 3⅜" tall
1000QX512-3, $10.00 □

Welcome, Christmas

Dangling inside a heart-shaped frame, a little angel brings a warm country welcome. The frame, decorated with a delicate stencil-look design of hearts and greenery, carries the caption, "Welcome, Christmas! 1986."

Handcrafted, 2⅝" tall
825QX510-3, $8.25 □

Joyful Carolers, Festive Treble Clef

Favorite Tin Drum, Christmas Guitar, Holiday Horn

Country Sleigh, Remembering Christmas

Little Drummers, Nutcracker Santa, Welcome, Christmas

Traditional Ornaments

Holiday Jingle Bell
Crafted in the shape of a jingle bell, this French blue and white musical ornament plays a very appropriate melody: "Jingle Bells." Eight tiny bas-relief reindeer race gracefully around a band in the center. Caption: "Merry Christmas 1986."

Handcrafted, 2¾" diam.
1600QX404-6, $16.00 ☐

Memories to Cherish
A braided ceramic wreath, with brightly painted bow and holly, is a photoholder for the holiday tree. Caption: "A memory to cherish. Christmas 1986."

Ceramic, 3⅛" tall
750QX427-6, $7.50 ☐

Bluebird
This red-breasted bluebird, a symbol of happiness, appears to have just landed on a Christmas tree branch. He's made of hand-painted fine porcelain and attaches with a special clip.

Hand-Painted Fine Porcelain, 3⁵⁄₁₆" tall
725QX428-3, $7.25 ☐

Glowing Christmas Tree
A lacy brass Christmas tree, trimmed with colorful stars, is embedded in a teardrop acrylic ornament. The date, "1986," appears on the tree's base.

Embedded Acrylic, 3¼" diam.
700QX428-6, $7.00 ☐

Heirloom Snowflake
Delicate hand-crocheted trim decorates padded lavender-blue satin to create this lacy snowflake.

Fabric, 4¾" tall
675QX515-3, $6.75 ☐

Christmas Beauty
Inspired by the sensitive and subtle designs of the Orient, this lacquer-look ornament reflects the spirit of the season. Caption: "Christmas comes gently, touching the world with beauty, filling it with joy."

Lacquer-Look, 2¾" diam.
600QX322-3, $6.00 ☐

Star Brighteners
Two charming etched angels polish a star for Christmas. The gold foil-stamped caption, "Joy at Christmas 1986," makes the star glow.

Acrylic, 2¾" diam.
600QX322-6, $6.00 ☐

The Magi
On a gold glass teardrop ball, the Magi come to Christmas once more. Caption: "O come let us adore Him. Christmas 1986."

Gold Glass, 3" diam.
475QX272-6, $4.75 ☐

Holiday Jingle Bell, Memories to Cherish, Bluebird, Glowing Chritmas Tree

Heirloom Snowflake, Christmas Beauty, Star Brighteners, The Magi

Mary Emmerling: American Country Collection

Mary Emmerling is a well-known designer and authority on country decor. Her collection of four coordinated glass balls has the speckled look of spatterware and was inspired by popular design motifs found in 19th-century American homes.

White and Blue Glass, 2⅞″ diam.
795QX275-2, $7.95 ☐

Collectible Series

Mr. and Mrs. Claus—First Edition

Mrs. Claus starts this series out with a holiday kiss for her hubby. Standing under the mistletoe she thoughtfully provides, he holds a list dated "1986." Aptly named "Merry Mistletoe Time," the ornament is first in this new series.

Handcrafted, 3⁷⁄₁₆″ tall
1300QX402-6, $13.00 ☐

Reindeer Champs—First Edition

"Dasher" lives up to his name as he jogs around Santa's workshop in preparation for his Christmas Eve journey. Wearing a shirt that says "Dasher 86," he's the first in this series of reindeer sports stars.

Handcrafted, 2⅞″ tall
750QX422-3, $7.50 ☐

Betsey Clark: Home for Christmas—First Edition

The first Betsey Clark ball series ended in 1985, but this new one brings the artist's children back to the Keepsake line. Smaller in diameter, the balls in this second series show Betsey and her friends celebrating Christmas around the home. On the first ornament, they are busy decorating. Caption on Wall Poster: "May Christmas love fill every little corner of your world." On Calendar: "1986."

Pink Glass, 2⅞″ diam.
500QX277-6, $5.00 ☐

Windows of the World—Second Edition

A happy Dutch girl peeks over the half-door in her Holland home to greet the holiday. Someone has filled her little wooden shoes with Christmas goodies. "Vrolyk Kerstfeest 1986" is the Christmas greeting written above the door.

Handcrafted, 3″ tall
1000QX408-3, $10.00 ☐

Miniature Creche—Second Edition

Simple and elegant, this fine porcelain portrait of the Holy Family is second in the series of creches fashioned in different media. The velvety bisque of the figures contrasts beautifully with the satiny glow of the glazed arch. A brass star shines above.

Fine Porcelain, 3¾″ tall
900QX407-6, $9.00 ☐

American Country Collection   *Mr. and Mrs. Claus*

Reindeer Champs, Betsey Clark: Home for Christmas, Windows of the World, Miniature Creche

Nostalgic Houses and Shops—Third Edition

What town would be complete without a "Christmas Candy Shoppe?" This ornament has two rooms: one downstairs where the sweets and confections are sold, and another upstairs, where the mixing and baking are done. A sign above the door says, "Candies 1986."

Handcrafted, 4⁵⁄₁₆″ tall
1375QX403-3, $13.75 ☐

Wood Childhood Ornaments—Third Edition

This "Wooden Reindeer" takes a holiday ride on a wagon with wheels that turn. As he rolls along, he makes a galloping motion. The wagon is dated "1986."

Hand-Painted Wood, 2½″ tall
750QX407-3, $7.50 ☐

Twelve Days of Christmas—Third Edition

On the third day of Christmas, three French hens nesting on holly leaves were etched onto a glowing acrylic teardrop. Gold foil-stamped caption reads, "The Twelve Days of Christmas 1986...Three French Hens."

Acrylic, 3⅜″ tall
650QX378-6, $6.50 ☐

Art Masterpiece—Third and Final Edition

This ornament is the last featuring classic paintings of the Madonna and Child reproduced on padded satin. Bezeled in brass, it carries the caption, "Lorenzo Di Cridi, Madonna and Child with the Infant St. John, The Nelson-Atkins Museum of Art, Kansas City, Missouri (Nelson Fund)."

Bezeled Satin, 3¼″ tall
675QX350-6, $6.75 ☐

Porcelain Bear—Fourth Edition

"Cinnamon Bear" is carrying a surprise—a brightly wrapped Christmas package for a special friend. This fine porcelain ornament is painted by hand to accentuate the subtle detail.

Hand-Painted Fine Porcelain, 2¹¹⁄₁₆″ tall
775QX405-6, $7.75 ☐

Tin Locomotive—Fifth Edition

The stencil-look holly design on the cabin of this pressed "Tin Locomotive" tell us the ornament is the Christmas Express. A mixture of interesting shapes and patterns, the train has wheels that turn as it rolls past your tree. It carries the date "1986."

Pressed Tin, 3¹⁷⁄₃₂″ tall
1475QX403-6, $14.75 ☐

Nostalgic Houses and Shops, Wood Childhood Ornaments, Twelve Days of Christmas

Art Masterpiece, Porcelain Bear, Tin Locomotive

Holiday Wildlife—Fifth Edition

While one Cedar Waxwing samples a berry, another looks on nearby. Framed in wood, this ornament presents a lifelike vision of nature. Caption: "Cedar Waxwing, (Cedarbird), BOMBYCILLA CEDORUM, Fifth in a series, Wildlife Collection, Christmas 1986."

Wood, 2½" diam.
750QX321-6, $7.50 ☐

Clothespin Soldier—Fifth Edition

Napoleon would have been proud to have this "French Officer" in his troop. Dressed in holiday colors and a hat decorated with holly, the soldier has movable arms.

Handcrafted, 1 ²⁷⁄₃₂" tall
550QX406-3, $5.50 ☐

Rocking Horse—Sixth Edition

A golden palomino, with brown and blue saddle and trappings, is proud to ride on your tree this Christmas. He stands on sea-green rockers dated "1986" and has a flowing white yarn tail.

Handcrafted, 4" wide
1075QX401-6, $10.75 ☐

Norman Rockwell—Seventh Edition

Santa peers through his telescope to check up on all the good boys and girls before Christmas. Against the red background, the white bas-relief cameo has subtle variations in shading. Framed in brass, the ornament carries a gold foil-stamped caption on the back: "Checking Up, Seventh in a Series, Christmas 1986, The Norman Rockwell Collection."

Cameo, 3¼" diam.
775QX321-3, $7.75 ☐

Frosty Friends—Seventh Edition

This little Eskimo places a wreath around the neck of his new pal—a flocked baby reindeer whose antlers are just beginning to bud. They sit on a clear acrylic ice floe dated "1986."

Handcrafted, 2¼" tall
850QX405-3, $8.50 ☐

Here Comes Santa—Eighth Edition

A chrome bell announces that Santa has arrived with "Kringle's Kool Treats." The freezer advertises "Ice Cream" and "Snow Cones" made by "Kringle's," of course. Fitted with movable wheels, Santa's cart has a license plate dated "1986."

Handcrafted, 3¹⁵⁄₁₆" tall
1400QX404-3, $14.00 ☐

Thimble—Ninth Edition

This "Thimble Partridge" is sitting pretty. She has found the perfect nesting place atop a silvery thimble filled with holiday greenery and fruit.

Handcrafted, 1 ²¹⁄₃₂" tall
575QX406-6, $5.75 ☐

Holiday Wildlife, Clothespin Soldier, Rocking Horse

Norman Rockwell, Frosty Friends, Here Comes Santa, Thimble

THE 1987 COLLECTION

Three limited edition ornaments highlighted the 1987 Keepsake line. The annual fine porcelain limited edition, "Christmas Time Mime," is a combination of fantasy and tradition, limited to an edition size of 24,700.

The two other limited editions introduced new formats and new kinds of markings on the designs. "Christmas is Gentle," a basket holding two lambs, brought bone china into the line and was the first ornament to be individually numbered by hand. The number appears on the bottom of the basket along with the ornament's edition size of 24,700. The "Holiday Heirloom" ornament, a bell framed by a sculpted wreath, was the first limited edition Collectible Series, and the first design to feature silver plating and lead crystal. The edition size of 34,600 is embossed on a sculpted bow.

Designed for both plate and ornament collectors, the new "Collector's Plate" series began with a miniature porcelain plate decorated with artwork of children trimming the tree. The "Clothespin Soldier" series came to an end with the sixth edition — a "Sailor."

Three new collections of ornaments appeared in 1987. The designs in the new "Artists' Favorites" collection feature subject matter, such as bears and mice, that has been historically popular with collectors. These ornaments, however, are also favorites of the Hallmark artists who sculpted them. That's how the collection got its name! Each ornament carries the artist's signature or initials. The "Christmas Pizzazz" collection offers a lighthearted, contemporary look at the season. And the third group, the "Old-Fashioned Christmas" collection consists of traditional designs that look hand carved or homemade.

The Property ornaments in 1987 were integrated into other portions of the line such as "Holiday Humor." New properties were "Jammie Pies™," "Crayola®" and "Dr. Seuss." Back by popular demand were two satin balls — "Baby Boy" and "Baby Girl" for "Baby's First Christmas." The "Dad" ornament was humorous for the first time, and there was a special ornament for business use, "Holiday Greetings."

Commemoratives

Baby's First Christmas
Holding onto a tiny rattle, this baby has a lot of fun in the real spring seat swing. The ornament carries the caption, "Baby's First Christmas 1987," on the back of the seat.
Handcrafted, 4¼" tall
975QX411-3, $9.75 ☐

Baby's First Christmas Photoholder
An ecru fabric wreath, trimmed in lace and ribbon and embroidered with toys and holly, frames a favorite photo of Baby. "Baby's First Christmas 1987" is embroidered on the front, and a sentiment is silk-screened on the flocked back: "Welcome to Christmas, Baby dear. Everyone is glad you're here."
Fabric, 3¼" diam.
750QX461-9, $7.50 ☐

Baby's First Christmas
Baby's acrylic booties are decorated with etched jingle bells and holly. The caption, "Baby's First Christmas 1987," is stamped on the bow in gold foil.
Acrylic, 3½" tall
600QX372-9, $6.00 ☐

Baby's First Christmas: Handcrafted, Photoholder, Acrylic

Baby's First Christmas—Baby Girl

Dressed in rosy pink, the rag doll on this white satin ball is so proud she can spell "BABY GIRL" with her blocks. Caption: "A Baby Girl, so dear and sweet, makes your Christmas joy complete. Baby's First Christmas 1987."

White Satin, 2⅞" diam.
475QX274-7, $4.75   ☐

Baby's First Christmas—Baby Boy

A cuddly blue bear and a train carrying holly keep Baby's blocks from tumbling down. The blocks spell "BABY BOY," and the caption on this white satin ball reads, "A Baby Boy, so darling and dear, makes Christmas extra special this year. Baby's First Christmas 1987."

White Satin, 2⅞" diam.
475QX274-9, $4.75   ☐

Grandchild's First Christmas

A teddy bear plays with his blocks inside a jenny lind style playpen lined with a green and red quilt sprinkled with stars. The blanket carrying the caption, "Grandchild's First Christmas 1987," is made of fabric. The bottom of the ornament has room for personalization.

Handcrafted, 1¾" tall
900QX460-9, $9.00   ☐

Baby's Second Christmas

A cheery clown-in-the-box bounces on a real spring as he wishes Baby a happy holiday. Caption: "Baby's 2nd Christmas 1987." The ornament attaches to your tree with a special clip.

Handcrafted, 2¾" tall
575QX460-7, $5.75   ☐

Child's Third Christmas

Dressed in bright red with a real pompom on his cap, the child enjoys a holiday ride. The reindeer makes a galloping motion when it is tapped gently. Caption: "My 3rd Christmas 1987."

Handcrafted, 3" tall
575QX459-9, $5.75   ☐

Baby Locket

Baby's photo will look festive inside this special locket that has the shimmery look of silver. Embossed on the front is the word "Baby" and on the back, "1987." The locket has a special insert for personalization and comes with a wishbone hanger.

Textured Metal, 2¼" diam.
1500QX461-7, $15.00   ☐

Baby's First Christmas: Baby Girl, Baby Boy; Grandchild's First Christmas

Baby's Second Christmas, Child's Third Christmas, Baby Locket

Mother and Dad

Tied with a red satin ribbon, this deep blue porcelain bell carries a loving tribute: "For a Mother and Dad who give the gift of love. Christmas 1987." The tree on the front has a sponged stencil look.

Fine Porcelain, 4¾" tall
700QX462-7, $7.00   ☐

Mother

This acrylic oval's intricately cut beveled edge, a design seen for the first time in the Keepsake line, gives the ornament the look of cut glass. An etched sprig of holly accents the gold foil-stamped caption, "Mother is another word for love. Christmas 1987." The ornament is framed in brass.

Acrylic, 3½" tall
650QX373-7, $6.50   ☐

Dad

What does Dad want for Christmas? Another tie, of course! This polar bear has some special favorites—even one with a bright Hawaiian motif. Caption: "For Dad Christmas 1987."

Handcrafted, 3" tall
600QX462-9, $6.00   ☐

Husband

The sentiment and design on this ornament remind us that Christmas is the season of love and sharing. Against a sky blue background, the ivory cameo sleigh has delicate bas-relief detailing. Front Caption: "For My Husband." Back Caption: "The nicest part of Christmas is sharing it with you. 1987."

Cameo, 3¼" diam.
700QX373-9, $7.00   ☐

Sister

A lovely basket of poinsettias has been tied with a bright green bow especially for Sister. The design, a bright stencil look printed on wood, reflects the message on the back: "A Sister brings happiness wrapped in love. Christmas 1987."

Wood, 2¾" tall
600QX474-7, $6.00   ☐

Daughter

A pair of prancing reindeer pull a graceful swan sleigh, just like the ones seen in carousels. Fashioned to look like wood, the ornament carries the caption: "Daughter Christmas 1987."

Handcrafted, 1¼" tall
575QX463-7, $5.75   ☐

Son

This colorful train races across the tree to wish Son a happy holiday. It looks like an old-fashioned toy. Caption: "For Son Christmas 1987."

Handcrafted, 1" tall
575QX463-9, $5.75   ☐

Mother and Dad, Mother, Dad

Niece

Accented with touches of red, a flock of snowy white lambs frolic around a turquoise blue teardrop ball. The caption, printed in the lower border, reflects the cheery look of the design: "Christmas is happier...merrier...cheerier...because of a Niece's love. 1987."

Turquoise Blue Glass, 3" diam.
475QX275-9, $4.75   ☐

Grandmother

The loving caption on this frosted pink teardrop ball is illustrated with delicately painted roses and carnations. Caption: "Grandmothers, like flowers, fill the world with beauty, the heart with joy. Christmas 1987."

Pink Glass, 3" diam.
475QX277-9, $4.75   ☐

Grandparents

Building a snowman, skating on a frozen stream, and riding in a horse-drawn sleigh are just some of the activities depicted in this country portrait. The scene, reminiscent of American folk art, captures the warmth of the holiday and echoes the special message: "Grandparents...so warm, so loving, so like the Christmas season. 1987."

Porcelain White Glass, 2⅞" diam.
475QX277-7, $4.75   ☐

Grandson

Dressed in holiday uniforms, a musical marching band parades around this sky blue teardrop ball carrying a banner with a special message: "Grandsons have a talent for making wonderful memories." The drum reads, "Christmas 1987."

Sky Blue Glass, 3" diam.
475QX276-9, $4.75   ☐

Granddaughter

Filled with toys, the antique sleigh on this padded satin ornament offers a nostalgic look at the joys of the holiday. The ornament is bezeled in brass and carries the caption, "A Granddaughter makes each day a holiday in the heart. Christmas 1987."

Bezeled Satin, 2¾" diam.
600QX374-7, $6.00   ☐

Godchild

This vivid blue ball looks as if it were sprinkled with snow. The brightly lit holiday tree on the front, designed to resemble torn paper, symbolizes the warmth of the season and reflects the caption: "A Godchild makes Christmas glow a little brighter. 1987."

Blue Glass, 2⅞" diam.
475QX276-7, $4.75   ☐

Husband, Sister

Daughter, Son, Niece

Grandmother, Grandparents

Grandson, Granddaughter, Godchild

First Christmas Together

Displayed open or closed, this heart-shaped brass locket is a loving memento of the season. Embossed lovebirds decorate the back, and the embossed caption, "First Christmas Together 1987," adorns the front. The ornament comes with a wishbone hanger.

Textured Brass, 2¼" tall
1500QX446-9, $15.00 ☐

First Christmas Together

Home is where the heart is, especially in this Alpine cottage captioned, "First Christmas Together 1987." The room inside holds a bottle-brush tree and a sampler with, "Love Sweet Love."

Handcrafted, 3" tall
950QX446-7, $9.50 ☐

First Christmas Together

Two raccoons snuggle inside a fabric sweatshirt with "First Christmas Together" silk-screened on the front. The date "1987" appears inside a heart on the back.

Handcrafted, 2½" tall
800QX445-9, $8.00 ☐

First Christmas Together

Two exquisitely etched swans float across an acrylic oval framed in brass. The caption, stamped in gold foil, says "First Christmas Together 1987."

Acrylic, 2½" tall
650QX371-9, $6.50 ☐

First Christmas Together

A garden of pastel poinsettias touched with silver decorates this frosted white glass ball. Two lovebirds appear on the front with the caption, "First Christmas Together 1987." On Back: "To all who love, love is all the world."

White Glass, 2⅞" diam.
475QX272-9, $4.75 ☐

Ten Years Together

A heart-shaped floral wreath frames the caption "Ten Years Together" on this snow white porcelain bell. The ornament is tied with a bright red satin ribbon and carries "Christmas 1987" on the back.

Fine Porcelain, 4¾" tall
700QX444-7, $7.00 ☐

Twenty-Five Years Together

A crisply painted pair of cardinals enjoys the holiday season on a miniature porcelain collector's plate that celebrates a life of sharing. The lettering on front and back is printed in traditional silver. Front Caption: "25 Years Together Christmas 1987." Back: "Love is for always." Plate stand included.

Fine Porcelain, 3¼" diam.
750QX443-9, $7.50 ☐

First Christmas Together: Textured Brass, Handcrafted, Handcrafted, Acrylic

Fifty Years Together

The velvety bisque finish of this unique porcelain bell contrasts beautifully with the glazed finish of the bas-relief poinsettia design and sculpted handle. "Fifty Years Together" and "Christmas 1987" are printed in gold.

Fine Porcelain, 5" tall
800QX443-7, $8.00 ☐

Word of Love

There's no other word that means so much. This fine bisque porcelain ornament is accented with touches of gold and a tiny red dangling heart. Caption: "Christmas 1987."

Fine Porcelain, 2⅛" tall
800QX447-7, $8.00 ☐

Heart in Blossom

A single rose is a timeless symbol of love. It has been carefully etched into this heart-shaped acrylic ornament to reflect the message stamped in gold foil: "Love is the heart in blossom. Christmas 1987."

Acrylic, 2¾" tall
600QX372-7, $6.00 ☐

Sweetheart

A package labeled "For My Sweetheart" is about to be delivered in this surrey with the fabric fringe on top. Beautifully detailed, the vehicle has wheels that turn and room for personalization underneath.
"Christmas 1987" is printed in gold on the front of the surrey, and the word "Sweet" printed above two entwined hearts appears on the back.

Handcrafted, 3⅛" tall
1100QX447-9, $11.00 ☐

Love Is Everywhere

Against a shiny chrome background, a winter landscape echoes the peace and serenity of the holiday season. A pair of cardinals brings a bright splash of color to the silvery sky. Caption: "Beautifully, peacefully, Christmas touches our lives...love is everywhere. 1987."

Chrome and Frosted Blue Glass, 2⅞" diam.
475QX278-7, $4.75 ☐

First Christmas Together White Glass

Ten Years Together, Twenty-Five Years Together, Fifty Years Together

Word of Love, Heart in Blossom

Sweetheart, Love is Everywhere

Holiday Greetings

This elegant ornament features a graphic silver Christmas tree and lettering against a shimmery blue and violet foil background. Bezeled in chrome, the ornament has been designed to be especially appropriate for use by businesses. The ornament box provides room for personalization. Caption on Front: "Season's Greetings." On Back: "Wishing you happiness at this beautiful time of year. 1987."

Bezeled Foil, 2¾ " diam.
600QX375-7, $6.00 ☐

Warmth of Friendship

The gold foil caption stamped on this acrylic ornament displays the classic beauty of calligraphy. Caption: "As Christmas warms the world friendship warms our hearts. 1987."

Acrylic 3¾ " tall
600QX375-9, $6.00 ☐

Time for Friends

Two white mice hang garland around a red glass teardrop ball. They're hurrying to meet each other in the center because the caption says, "When good friends meet, good times are complete! Christmas 1987."

Red Glass, 3 " diam.
475QX280-7, $4.75 ☐

From Our Home to Yours

A friendly welcome awaits you at every door in this neighborhood. Decorated for the holidays, the doors circle a frosted white glass teardrop ball that carries the caption, "From Our Home...To Yours...At Christmas 1987."

White Glass, 3 " diam.
475QX279-9, $4.75 ☐

New Home

The scene on this ornament brings back memories of holidays long ago, but the format is new to the Keepsake line. Printed in white on a mirrored acrylic background is a snug and cozy cottage. Caption: "A New Home is a wonderful beginning to wonderful memories. Christmas 1987."

Mirrored Acrylic, 2¾ " diam.
600QX376-7, $6.00 ☐

Babysitter

The scenes on this porcelain white teardrop ball symbolize the love given to children by those special people who take care of them. One bunny is reading a book titled "Bunny Tales," and a calendar on the wall says it's "1987." Caption: "For bringing children such special gifts...gentleness, caring, and love. Merry Christmas."

Porcelain White Glass, 3 " diam.
475QX279-7, $4.75 ☐

Holiday Greetings, Warmth of Friendship, Time for Friends

From Our Home to Yours, New Home, Babysitter

Teacher

This beary good student has a message for teacher and room for personalization on his slate: "Merry Christmas, Teacher From (name)." But the bear can be mischievous since he carved "1987" into the desk.

Handcrafted, 2" tall
575QX466-7, $5.75 ☐

Holiday Humor

SNOOPY® and WOODSTOCK

SNOOPY® and WOODSTOCK have decorated a bottle-brush tree for the holiday. WOODSTOCK perches on top—the perfect angel. On Dish: "SNOOPY."

Handcrafted, 2½" tall
725QX472-9, $7.25 ☐

Bright Christmas Dreams

Wearing colorful nightcaps, four mice dream of a bright Christmas in an authentic Crayola® box made of varnished paper. Front of Box: "Crayola® Crayons, Bright Christmas Dreams, Binney & Smith®." Back, Sides and Bottom of Box: "Crayola® Crayons." The back of the box also carries the caption, "Christmas 1987" designed to look like part of a store code.

Handcrafted, 4" tall
725QX473-7, $7.25 ☐

Joy Ride

Santa and a reindeer take a holiday spin on Santa's new motorcyle. The "wheels" really do spin and the reindeer wears a fabric muffler. Caption on Front Fender: "Joy Ride." On License Plate: "1987."

Handcrafted, 3½" tall
1150QX440-7, $11.50 ☐

Pretty Kitty

This little kitten is all tangled up in some red beads. He has to hold on tight because he's the clapper inside the clear glass bell.

Handcrafted, Glass, 3½" tall
1100QX448-9, $11.00 ☐

Santa at the Bat

Santa is the star of the team because his signature "Santa Claus" bat connects with a pearlized snowball. His uniform reads: "North Pole Nicks 87."

Handcrafted, 3¼" tall
775QX457-9, $7.75 ☐

Jogging Through the Snow

Carrying his radio and wearing headphones, this rabbit listens to Christmas music, of course. His shirt carries his number "87" and "Holiday Run."

Handcrafted, 3" tall
725QX457-7, $7.25 ☐

Teacher   *SNOOPY®, Bright Christmas Dreams*

Joy Ride, Pretty Kitty, Santa at the Bat, Jogging Through the Snow

Jack Frosting

Jack dips his brush into an acorn filled with sparkling frost and brushes the glitter onto each leaf, creating a winter wonderland for all to enjoy. This ornament attaches to your tree with a special clip.

Handcrafted, 2½" tall
700QX449-9, $7.00 ☐

Raccoon Biker

This fellow rides the trails on his dirt bike to deliver a Christmas gift cross country. The front of the bike is marked "87."

Handcrafted, 3" tall
700QX458-7, $7.00 ☐

Treetop Dreams

The squirrel was nestled all snug in his bed while visions of acorns danced in his head! His blanket is polka dot fabric, and a matching fabric ribbon decorates the wreath. To achieve an especially authentic look, real sticks were used to mold this design.

Handcrafted, 3" tall
675QX459-7, $6.75 ☐

Night Before Christmas

It's the night before Christmas, and this mouse isn't stirring. He'd much rather be sleeping in Santa's hat. The flocked hat has furry trim and a pompom at the top. A tiny chunk of cheese is tucked into the trim at the back.

Handcrafted, 2¾" tall
650QX451-7, $6.50 ☐

"Owliday" Wish

Wearing brass spectacles, this owl helps us all get a clear vision of his "owliday" wish on the eyechart: "SEASONS GREETINGS TO YOU." Real sticks were used to mold his perch and pointer.

Handcrafted, 2" tall
650QX455-9, $6.50 ☐

Let It Snow

This little tyke is dressed for cold weather—but he won't feel it wearing his knitted cap and muffler and real pompom earmuffs.

Handcrafted, 3" tall
650QX458-9, $6.50 ☐

Hot Dogger

Santa is king of the hill, a champion skier and, as his ski jacket says, a "Hot Dogger" on the slopes! His ski outfit is decorated with snowflake patches.

Handcrafted, 2½" tall
650QX471-9, $6.50 ☐

Spots 'n Stripes

Santa has left a special gift in this Dalmatian pup's Christmas stocking—a candy cane made to order in his favorite shape.

Handcrafted, 2¼" tall
550QX452-9, $5.50 ☐

Jack Frosting, Raccoon Biker, Treetop Dreams, Night Before Christmas

"Owliday" Wish, Let It Snow, Hot Dogger, Spots 'n Stripes

Seasoned Greetings

This elf has a very important job to do—placing salt on all the holiday pretzels. He uses a silvery shaker that he fills from his salt bag labeled, "Seasoned Greetings SALT."

Handcrafted, 2" tall
625QX454-9, $6.25 ☐

Chocolate Chipmunk

Has this chipmunk confiscated a chip from his cookie, or is he looking for a place to add one chip more? He'll never tell! He's dressed for the winter in a knitted red muffler. A real cookie was used to mold the design, and the ornament attaches with a special clip.

Handcrafted, 2" tall
600QX456-7, $6.00 ☐

Fudge Forever

Sitting in a dark blue spatterware ladle, this little mouse is so full of fudge he can hardly budge! But that doesn't stop him from scooping up just a little bit more with his own mouse-sized spoon.

Handcrafted, 3" tall
500QX449-7, $5.00 ☐

Seasoned Greetings, Chocolate Chipmunk, Fudge Forever

Sleepy Santa

If there's one person who deserves a nap after Christmas—it's Santa. He lounges in his favorite chair, soaking his feet and dreaming of next year's toys. The chair is flocked and the calendar page reads, "DEC. 26."

Handcrafted, 2¾" tall
625QX450-7, $6.25 ☐

Reindoggy

This little puppy may be wearing antlers, but his expression shows he isn't ready to pull Santa's sleigh. The antlers were molded from real sticks and are tied to the puppy's head with a red satin bow.

Handcrafted, 2¾" tall
575QX452-7, $5.75 ☐

Christmas Cuddle

Wearing matching Santa hats in honor of the holiday, these two buddies enjoy a warm Christmas hug. The kitten's hat is topped with a real pompom.

Handcrafted, 2¾" tall
575QX453-7, $5.75 ☐

Paddington™ Bear

Paddington™ likes to eat what he bakes! Perhaps he has flavored the cookies with his favorite food—honey. He wears a red apron marked "Paddington™ Bear" and a chef's hat tagged, "Please look after this Bear Thank You."

Handcrafted, 3" tall
550QX472-7, $5.50 ☐

Sleepy Santa, Reindoggy, Christmas Cuddle, Paddington™ Bear

Nature's Decorations

The painted animals and birds on this light blue glass ball are Mother Nature's way of decorating her wintry world. Caption: "The nicest Christmas decorations start with Nature's own creations. 1987."

Blue Glass, 2⅞" diam.
475QX273-9, $4.75 ☐

Dr. Seuss: The Grinch's Christmas

Framed by a colorful Christmas wreath, the Grinch is smiling at last. He and a chorus of Whos from Who-ville celebrate the holiday on a blue glass ball. Caption: "A very merry wish for a merry, merry Christmas."

Blue Glass, 2⅞" diam.
475QX278-3, $4.75 ☐

Jammie Pies™

A new Hallmark property, Jammie Pies™, makes its Keepsake debut on this porcelain white glass ball. The swan arrives from the "Land of Sweet Dreams" bringing the child a visitor—a Jammie Pies friend who knows a world of stories. Caption: "When Jammie Pies are close to you, all your Christmas dreams come true. 1987."

Porcelain White Glass, 2⅞" diam.
475QX283-9, $4.75 ☐

PEANUTS®

Wearing their cool dark glasses, SNOOPY®, WOODSTOCK and his friends, and even a snowman show that the caption on this chrome teardrop ball tells the truth: "Everyone's cool at Christmastime!" The supper dish carries the date "1987."

Chrome Glass, 3" diam.
475QX281-9, $4.75 ☐

Happy Santa

Carrying a shiny brass bell, Santa uses his candy cane to swing from a branch on your tree.

Handcrafted, 2½" tall
475QX456-9, $4.75 ☐

Icy Treat

This penguin knows what's good to eat—especially in the cool North Pole. His shimmery cherry treat is just the thing for a frosty afternoon snack.

Handcrafted, 2¼" tall
450QX450-9, $4.50 ☐

Mouse in the Moon

Reissue from 1986. (See 1986 Annual Collection.)

Handcrafted, 2¾" tall
550QX416-6, $5.50

L'il Jingler

Reissue from 1986. (See 1986 Annual Collection.)

Handcrafted, 2" tall
675QX419-3, $6.75

Nature's Decorations, Dr. Seuss: The Grinch's Christmas, Jammie Pies™

PEANUTS®, Happy Santa, Icy Treat

Walnut Shell Rider

Reissue from 1986. (See 1986 Annual Collection.)

Handcrafted, 1¾" tall
600QX419-6, $6.00

Treetop Trio

Reissue from 1986. (See 1986 Annual Collection.)

Handcrafted, 2" tall
1100QX425-6, $11.00

Jolly Hiker

Reissue from 1986. (See 1986 Annual Collection.)

Handcrafted, 2" tall
500QX483-2, $5.00

Merry Koala

Reissue from 1986. (See 1986 Annual Collection.)

Handcrafted, 2" tall
500QX415-3, $5.00

The Constitution

An acrylic oval, framed in brass, commemorates the 200th anniversary of the signing of the Constitution. Stamped in silver foil, the quill design complements the gold foil caption: "We the People, The Constitution of the United States, 200 Years, 1787-1987."

Acrylic, 2½" tall
650QX377-7, $6.50 ☐

Old-Fashioned Christmas Collection

Nostalgic Rocker

Looking as if it were crafted by hand, this subtlly painted pony is fashioned of wood and has fabric ears. The clean lines and simple design reflect an American country styling.

Wood, 2½" tall
650QX468-9, $6.50 ☐

Little Whittler

The little carver prides himself on the craftsmanship he puts into the reindeer toy he is carving. This ornament, sculpted and painted to resemble carved wood, display the same craftmanship and a touch of whimsy.

Handcrafted, 3" tall
600QX469-9, $6.00 ☐

Country Wreath

The warm old-fashioned design of this straw wreath reminds us of Christmas in the country. Tied with burgundy yarn, the ornament is decorated with tiny wooden hearts and trees and a wooden house.

Wood and Straw, 4¾" tall
575QX470-9, $5.75 ☐

In a Nutshell

There's a world of Christmas inside this nutshell. Two intricately detailed scenes show a teddy bear beneath a Christmas tree and fireplace with two tiny stockings. Molded from a real walnut, the ornament is hinged so it can be displayed open and stored closed.

Handcrafted, 1 ½" tall
550QX469-7, $5.50 ☐

Folk Art Santa

Carefully painted and antiqued, this Old-World Santa reflects the rich tradition of folk art. His deeply sculpted face and beard and the details of his clothing give him the appearance of hand-carved wood. Carrying a bottle-brush tree, he wears a long coat accented with touches of gold.

Handcrafted, 4" tall
525QX474-9, $5.25 ☐

The Constitution

Nostalgic Rocker, Little Whittler

Country Wreath, In a Nutshell, Folk Art Santa

Christmas Pizzazz Collection

Doc Holiday
Santa becomes a hero of the Old West when he rides the spring-powered mechanical reindeer. When you set the ornament on a mantel or table and gently tap it, Santa gets a bouncy ride. His cowboy shirt carries his name, "Doc Holiday."

Handcrafted, 4″ tall
800QX467-7, $8.00 ☐

Christmas Fun Puzzle
A favorite childhood puzzle is updated in a whimsical ball ornament. Divided horizontally into three movable sections, this blue ball is decorated with three bas-relief figures—Santa, mouse and reindeer. As you turn the sections, you mix the top, middle and bottom parts of the figures creating new characters such as a Rein-mouse or a Santa-deer.

Handcrafted, 2½″ diam.
800QX467-9, $8.00 ☐

Jolly Follies
Dressed in tuxes and tails, three dapper penguins actually kick up their heels and dance each time you pull the string. The sparkling acrylic stage carries the name of their act, "Jolly Follies."

Handcrafted, 2″ tall
850QX466-9, $8.50 ☐

St. Louie Nick
He's cool, he's hot, he's a jazzy dresser from his beret to his spats. Santa blows the sweetest horn this side of the North Pole and wears a vest with his stage name, "St. Louie Nick."

Handcrafted, 3½″ tall
775QX453-9, $7.75 ☐

Holiday Hourglass
Designed to be displayed in two different ways, this realistic hourglass celebrates both Christmas and the New Year. Through Christmas Day, the ornament can be displayed so that the "Merry Christmas" wish and snowman in Santa cap appear. After Christmas, the hourglass can be flipped over to display the snowman in top hat and "Happy New Year" wish.

Handcrafted, 3″ tall
800QX470-7, $8.00 ☐

Doc Holiday, Christmas Fun Puzzle

Jolly Follies, St. Louie Nick, Holiday Hourglass

Mistletoad

You don't have to kiss this whimsical fellow to get a special Christmas surprise. When you pull the cord, he gives you a wide holiday grin and a loud greeting in a very froggy voice. His hat is decorated with a pompom and his name, "Mistletoad."

Handcrafted, 3¾" tall
700QX468-7, $7.00 ☐

Happy Holidata

Two little programmers watch the message "Happy Holidata" flash onto the computer screen in alternating colors of green and red. On the back of the terminal, the name "Cranberry Computer" tells you this ornament is a high-tech edition.

Handcrafted, 1½" tall
650QX471-7, $6.50 ☐

Traditional Ornaments

Goldfinch

This realistic Goldfinch looks as if he has paused in flight to admire the scenery below. Fashioned of fine porcelain, he has been painted by hand to accentuate detail. Unlike the previous porcelain birds in the Keepsake line, this ornament attaches to your tree with a traditional hook instead of a clip.

Hand-Painted Fine Porcelain, 2½" tall
700QX464-9, $7.00 ☐

Heavenly Harmony

This little angel brings Christmas music for all the world to hear. Reminiscent of an Old-World Spanish belltower, the ornament plays "Joy to the World." The music is started by a key at the back.

Musical, Handcrafted, 4¼" tall
1500QX465-9, $15.00 ☐

Special Memories Photoholder

Both needlepoint and embroidery decorate the front of this bright holiday wreath. Trimmed in lace, it will display one of your cherished photographs. The wreath hangs from a green satin ribbon accented with a red satin rosette. Caption on Back: "Every Christmas brings special moments to remember. 1987."

Fabric, 3¼" diam.
675QX464-7, $6.75 ☐

Joyous Angels

Three intricately sculpted angels join hands and dance their joy beneath a brass star. Their halos and the trim on their snowy white dresses are touched with gold.

Handcrafted, 4" tall
775QX465-7, $7.75 ☐

Mistletoad, Happy Holidata

Goldfinch, Heavenly Harmony, Special Memories Photoholder, Joyous Angels

Promise of Peace

Carrying a gold foil olive branch, the Christmas dove spreads a timeless message of the season. To enhance the dimension of the design, the dove was etched into the back of the acrylic piece and the caption into the front, along the bevel. The ornament is framed in brass. Caption: "a season of hope, a reminder of miracles, a promise of peace."

Acrylic, 2¾" diam.
650QX374-9, $6.50   ☐

Christmas Keys

A miniature upright piano, decorated with festive green and red holly, brings to mind those happy times spent caroling with family and friends. The music is captioned, "Carols."

Handcrafted, 2" tall
575QX473-9, $5.75   ☐

I Remember Santa

Taken from the Hallmark Historical Collection, three antique post card paintings are reproduced on this porcelain white glass ball. They offer a vision of Santa Claus that brings back memories of Christmas long ago. Caption: "At Christmastime, especially, those magic memories start...those memories of yesterday that so delight the heart. 1987."

Porcelain White Glass, 2⅞" diam.
475QX278-9, $4.75   ☐

Norman Rockwell: Christmas Scenes

A hearty toast, a joyful dance, a stolen kiss under the mistletoe—all of these are depicted with warmth and gentle humor in the Norman Rockwell paintings on this gold glass ball. The three "Christmas Scenes" come from the Hallmark Collection of Norman Rockwell originals. Caption: "O gather friends, at Christmastime, to sing a song of cheer, to reminisce the days gone by, to toast the bright new year. From the Norman Rockwell Collection 1987."

Gold Glass, 2⅞" diam.
475QX282-7, $4.75   ☐

Currier & Ives: American Farm Scene

Porcelain white glass is the perfect setting for this nostalgic portrait of a wintry morning on the farm. The caption is decorated with painted holly and ribbon. Caption: "Christmas 1987, American Farm Scene, Currier & Ives."

Porcelain White Glass, 2⅞" diam.
475QX282-9, $4.75   ☐

Promise of Peace, Christmas Keys

I Remember Santa, Norman Rockwell, Currier & Ives

Limited Editions

Christmas Time Mime
Wearing a Santa hat and beard, the mime shares a moment of Christmas with a friend. His bag, tied with a golden chain, is filled with stars and magic. This ornament, made of fine porcelain and painted by hand, is limited to an edition size of 24,700 pieces. A wooden display stand is included in the box as well as the following poem that tells a charming story about the design:

The Mime looks deep in the
teddy bear's eyes.
The teddy bear looks at the Mime,
And they feel they have known each other
From some other place and time.
There's a magical bond between them
From the silent world they share,
And now they know, wherever one goes,
The other will always be there.

Hand-Painted Fine Porcelain, 2½" tall
2750QX442-9, $27.50 ☐

Christmas is Gentle
Two little lambs...one fast asleep...the other ready to play...embody the gentle spirit of the season. This ornament, issued in an edition limited to 24,700 pieces, is the first in the Keepsake line to be individually numbered by hand. It is made of white bone china accented with gold and subtle touches of color. Caption on the Bottom: "Christmas is gentle, Bone China, Limited Edition of 24,700 Max., Number: (hand-written number)."

Hand-Painted Bone China, 3" tall
1750QX444-9, $17.50 ☐

Christmas Time Mime, Christmas is Gentle

Special Edition

Favorite Santa
Like previous Special Edition ornaments, this one is designed for display on table or mantel as well as the tree. Fashioned of fine porcelain and painted by hand, Santa carries a long, long stocking which is the subject of the following legend printed on a card tucked into the ornament box:

One day Old St. Nick found a stocking—
It was threadbare, and tattered, and torn,
But his elves fixed it up with their magic,
And a new Christmas legend was born.
They say that it's loaded with presents
That are tied up with ribbons and bows;
For each gift he gives, a new one appears,
How it works—only Santa Claus knows!

Hand-Painted Fine Porcelain, 5½" tall
2250QX445-7, $22.50 ☐

Favorite Santa

Artists' Favorites

Three Men in a Tub
Inside the tub the famous trio—butcher, baker and candlestick maker—hold sausages, a cake with holly icing, and a Christmas candle. Donna Lee, the sculptor of this ornament, likes to bring classic nursery ryhmes to life with a contemporary look that is often whimsical. The tub looks like wood and carries the caption, "Rub-A-Dub-Dub."

Handcrafted, 3" tall
Artist: Donna Lee
800QX454-7, $8.00 ☐

Wee Chimney Sweep
Artist Ed Seale's mouse sweeps the chimney so Santa will stay neat and clean on Christmas Eve. A hard worker, the mouse carries a real brush. Seale commented that his design reflects the increased use of fireplaces and woodburning stoves to keep homes warm in the winter.

Handcrafted, 3" tall
Artist: Ed Seale
625QX451-9, $6.25 ☐

December Showers
Sitting on an acrylic cloud, this angel stays dry under her holly-trimmed umbrella. She checks to see if the shower has stopped because she wants to play. Artist Donna Lee designed the angel to resemble a real child—full of fun and mischief.

Handcrafted, 2½" tall
Artist: Donna Lee
550QX448-7, $5.50 ☐

Beary Special
This cuddly flocked bear reaches up to put his ornament on your tree. It's a tiny green ball decorated with his own likeness. Artist Bob Siedler explained that he likes sculpting bears because they are his daughter's favorite and part of everyone's childhood memories.

Handcrafted, 2½" tall
Artist: Bob Siedler
475QX455-7, $4.75 ☐

Collectible Series

Holiday Heirloom—First Edition/Limited Edition
This elegant new series introduces lead crystal and a precious metal into the Keepsake line. The intricately sculpted wreath has been plated in silver and frames a bell made of 24 percent lead crystal with a silver-plated holly clapper inside. The series also is the first to be offered in a limited edition. The date "1987" is embossed on the front of the wreath, and the edition size is embossed on the back: "Limited Edition 34,600."

Lead Crystal, Silver Plating, 3¼" tall
2500QX485-7, $25.00 ☐

Three Men in a Tub, Wee Chimney Sweep

December Showers, Beary Special

Holiday Heirloom

Collector's Plate—First Edition

The first collector's plate, issued in the late 1800s, offered a beautiful Christmas scene. This new ornament continues that meaningful tradition in miniature plates fashioned of fine porcelain. Each edition will bring a vision of children celebrating the season and a message on the back. The first plate shows children decorating the family tree. Caption: "Light Shines at Christmas. 1987." Plate stand included.

Fine Porcelain, 3¼" diam.
800QX481-7, $8.00 ☐

Mr. and Mrs. Claus—Second Edition

Mrs. Claus baked her spouse a plateful of cookies to give him energy for his Christmas Eve ride. His calendar reads, "1987 Dec. 24," so it's almost time to go. But Santa won't leave without his snack because he knows there's nothing better than "Home Cooking."

Handcrafted, 3" tall
1325QX483-7, $13.25 ☐

Reindeer Champs—Second Edition

Warmly dressed in a skating sweater monogrammed with her name "Dancer" and the date "'87," this reindeer is a star on ice. She whirls and twirls on skates trimmed with real pompoms.

Handcrafted, 3½" tall
750QX480-9, $7.50 ☐

Betsey Clark: Home for Christmas—Second Edition

While Santa peers around the porch of the house addressed "1987," Betsey and her friends trim the outdoor trees and paint holiday messages on the windows. One window says, "There's no place like Christmas," and the other reads, "Noel."

Gold Glass, 2⅞" diam.
500QX272-7, $5.00 ☐

Windows of the World—Third Edition

Sitting by the sea, a little Polynesian child strums a holiday tune on her ukulele. She has written "1987" in the sand and hung her stocking out for Santa. Her thatched window seat carries the Christmas greeting, "Mele Kalikimaka."

Handcrafted, 3" tall
1000QX482-7, $10.00 ☐

Miniature Creche—Third Edition

Multiple layers of delicately etched brass, washed in gold, nickel and copper, create a stunning three-dimensional Nativity. Gold wire starbeams shine on the Holy Family from a Christmas star above the stable.

Multi-Plated Brass, 3½" tall
900QX481-9, $9.00 ☐

Collector's Plate, Mr. and Mrs. Claus, Reindeer Champs

Betsey Clark: Home for Christmas, Windows of the World, Miniature Creche

Nostalgic Houses and Shops— Fourth Edition

The Victorian "House on Main St." has an exclusive "1987" address. Its spacious upstairs bedroom is decorated in shades of lavender and mauve; the downstairs parlor has a blue chair, matching drapes and a tiny bottle-brush Christmas tree.

Handcrafted, 4¼" tall
1400QX483-9, $14.00 ☐

Twelve Days of Christmas—Fourth Edition

Four etched colly birds gather in the center of a beveled acrylic diamond because it is the fourth day of Christmas. Stamped in gold foil, the caption reads, "The Twelve Days of Christmas 1987...four colly birds..." The four classic acrylic shapes used in this series—quadrafoil, heart, teardrop and diamond—will be repeated three times.

Acrylic, 4" tall
650QX370-9, $6.50 ☐

Wood Childhood Ornaments— Fourth Edition

Saddled in festive green and red and carefully groomed from his plush mane to his yarn tail, this "Wooden Horse" is ready to lead the Christmas parade. His cart has wheels that turn as he is pulled along. He is dated "1987."

Wood, 2¼" tall
750QX441-7, $7.50 ☐

Nostalgic Houses and Shops, Twelve Days of Christmas, Wood Childhood Ornaments

Porcelain Bear—Fifth Edition

What is "Cinnamon Bear" searching for inside his Christmas stocking? Maybe he'll find some honey candy stuck in the toe! Made of fine porcelain, the ornament has been painted by hand.

Hand-Painted Fine Porcelain, 2⅛" tall
775QX442-7, $7.75 ☐

Tin Locomotive—Sixth Edition

Ringing its brass bell and chugging along on wheels that actually roll, this Tin Locomotive ornament arrives at the North Pole station. The spoke pattern of the large rear wheels resembles a circle of cut-out hearts. The train is dated "1987."

Pressed Tin, 3½" tall
1475QX484-9, $14.75 ☐

Holiday Wildlife—Sixth Edition

Framed in wood, two snow geese fly across the starry Christmas sky, creating a picture of beauty and grace. The caption on the back reads, "Snow Goose, CHEN HYPERBOREA, Sixth in a Series, Wildlife Collection, Christmas 1987."

Wood, 2½" diam.
750QX371-7, $7.50 ☐

Porcelain Bear, Tin Locomotive, Holiday Wildlife

Clothespin Soldier—Sixth and Final Edition
Fashioned with movable arms, this "Sailor" in a crisp white uniform signals all hands on deck to bid farewell to the Clothespin series. His signals are easy to see because his flags display bright green trees against a red background.

Handcrafted, 2¼" tall
550QX480-7, $5.50　☐

Frosty Friends—Eighth Edition
This little flocked seal has jumped up through a hole in the ice to deliver a gift to his Eskimo friend. He's carrying the package the best way he can—balancing it ever so carefully on his nose. The ice is made of clear acrylic and the package is dated "1987."

Handcrafted, 2" tall
850QX440-9, $8.50　☐

Rocking Horse—Seventh Edition
A fitting steed for any prince or princess, this white charger is saddled in red, blue and gold and rides on royal purple rockers dated "1987." His mane and graceful yarn tail are the color of cream.

Handcrafted, 3¾" wide
1075QX482-9, $10.75　☐

Norman Rockwell—Eighth Edition
Norman Rockwell is one of America's most beloved artists. His delightful painting of a little girl dancing with her dog has been transformed into a delicate bas-relief cameo against a light blue background. Framed in chrome, the ornament carries the caption, "The Christmas Dance, Eighth in a Series, Christmas 1987, The Norman Rockwell Collection."

Cameo, 3¼" diam.
775QX370-7, $7.75　☐

Here Comes Santa—Ninth Edition
All the toys are packed, and Santa is driving through town in his sporty new car. "Santa's Woody" has whitewalls that turn, custom paneling, and two personalized license plates. The rear plate carries the date "1987," and the front one conveys Santa's special wish: "JOY-2-U."

Handcrafted, 2" tall
1400QX484-7, $14.00　☐

Thimble—Tenth Edition
A bunny plays his silvery thimble drum to celebrate the tenth year of this series. The "Thimble Drummer" has a fluffy pompom tail, and the strap around his drum is made of striped fabric ribbon.

Handcrafted, 2" tall
575QX441-9, $5.75　☐

Clothespin Soldier, Frosty Friends, Rocking Horse

Norman Rockwell, Here Comes Santa, Thimble

THE 1988 COLLECTION

The 1988 Keepsake Ornament line provided collectors with a unique image of Santa Claus. A group of eight "lifestyle" Santas depicts the jolly old elf enjoying contemporary pastimes, hobbies, and sports — and he's wearing an appropriate outfit for each activity!

A logo design from Hallmark's early years was featured on a Keepsake Ornament for the first time, as "Hall Bro's Card Shop" became the fifth edition of the Collectible Series "Nostalgic Houses and Shops." A new Collectible Series, "Mary's Angels," premiered with "Buttercup." This new series is based on drawings by popular Hallmark stylist Mary Hamilton. Two series were retired this year. The "Norman Rockwell Cameo" bid farewell with its ninth edition, "And to All a Good Night." The "Holiday Wildlife" series concluded with its seventh edition, "Purple Finch."

The commemorative caption "Five Years Together" made its first appearance in the Keepsake line. Two designs with patriotic themes, "Americana Drum" and "Uncle Sam Nutcracker," were issued in observance of the 1988 election year. Limited edition ornaments were offered exclusively to members of the Hallmark Keepsake Ornament Collector's Club for the first time.

Collectors interested in new techniques and materials discovered colors embedded in acrylic, in the "Our First Christmas Together" ornament, and a new rubbery material that added to the fun of the "Child's Third Christmas" design.

Keepsakes artists found new subjects for the line with "Jolly Walrus" and "Santa Flamingo." Three designs gave collectors food for thought, featuring national brands filled with memories. These designs were "Party Line" with Campbell's Soup, "OREO® Chocolate Sandwich Cookies," and "A KISS™ From Santa" with HERSHEY'S® KISSES.

The country look continued to be a popular decorating theme, echoed in "Twirl-About" ornaments, and the wood "Old-Fashioned Schoolhouse" and "Old-Fashioned Church." Tribute was paid to early American craftsmen with designs in both tin and multi-dimensional brass. Ornaments also featured the look of old-world wood carvings.

Commemoratives

Baby's First Christmas
All bundled up in a softly flocked, snow-white bunting, Baby enjoys a gentle ride in a beautifully detailed rocking horse suspended from a wishbone hanger. The green fabric blanket is edged with real lace. Caption: "Baby's First Christmas 1988."

Handcrafted, 3⅝" tall
975QX470-1, $9.75 ☐

Baby's First Christmas Photoholder
A padded fabric heart, embroidered with golden-haired angels and sprigs of holly, frames a treasured photograph. The eggshell-colored fabric is trimmed with matching lace. Front Caption: "Baby's First Christmas 1988." Back Caption: "A Baby is a gift of joy, a gift of love at Christmas."

Fabric, 5" tall
750QX470-4, $7.50 ☐

Baby's First Christmas: Handcrafted, Photoholder

Baby's First Christmas: Acrylic, Baby Boy, Baby Girl

Baby's First Christmas
A proud bunny holds a heart fashioned from two candy canes. Stamped in gold foil, the caption reads, "Baby's 1st Christmas 1988." The acrylic is carefully etched to suggest the bunny's soft fur.

Acrylic, 4" tall
600QX372-1, $6.00 ☐

Baby's First Christmas—Baby Boy
Peering out from his sky-blue blanket and cap, this little boy is being delivered by a flying white stork. Caption: "From the moment a new Baby Boy arrives, he's the love of your heart, the light in your eyes. Baby's First Christmas 1988."

White Satin, 2⅞" diam.
475QX272-1, $4.75 ☐

Baby's First Christmas—Baby Girl
Safe and snug in her pink blanket, this little girl is arriving by stork express. The caption reads, "A sweet Baby Girl, so tiny and new, is a bundle of joy and a dream come true. Baby's First Christmas 1988."

White Satin, 2⅞" diam.
475QX272-4, $4.75 ☐

Baby's Second Christmas
A softly flocked bear with a hammer discovers the fun of a classic childhood toy, the pounding bench. The captions "1988" and "Baby's 2nd Christmas" are printed on the ends of the bench.

Handcrafted, 1¾" tall
600QX471-1, $6.00 ☐

Child's Third Christmas
This little one is ready for adventure! He rides a reindeer bouncy-ball made of a flexible new material that makes it feel like rubber. The commemorative caption printed on the side of the bright red ball reads, "My Third Christmas 1988."

Handcrafted, 2½" tall
600QX471-4, $6.00 ☐

Daughter
The gingerbread girl presents a tray with four tiny gingerbread girls. The caption, "Daughter," is in pink icing. There's a pink bow on her sparkly white cap, and pink flowers border her skirt. The year date "1988" decorates her frosty white apron.

Handcrafted, 3⅝" tall
575QX415-1, $5.75 ☐

Son
All set to satisfy a Christmas sweet tooth, the gingerbread boy holds a cookie sheet with four small gingerbread boys and the icing caption, "Son." He's donned a sparkly white baker's cap, a white neckerchief, and an apron with the year date "1988."

Handcrafted, 3⅝" tall
575QX415-4, $5.75 ☐

Baby's Second Christmas, Child's Third Christmas, Daughter, Son

Mother, Dad, Mother and Dad

Sister

Grandmother, Grandparents

Granddaughter, Grandson, Godchild

Mother

The delicate filigree design echoes the outline of a heart tied with a ribbon and bow. The gold foil design and calligraphy sentiment are embedded in clear acrylic. Captions: "Mother puts love inside each moment of Christmas" and "1988."

Acrylic, 3¾" tall
650QX375-1, $6.50 ☐

Dad

This polar bear is so proud of his new socks, he can't wait to try them on. He's starting with bright red-and-green argyles, a pattern that's sure to keep his paws warm. The gift box reads, "For Dad 1988."

Handcrafted, 2¾" tall
700QX414-1, $7.00 ☐

Mother and Dad

Accents of gold give this traditional design of holly and a glowing red candle the look of cloisonné. The white, fine porcelain bell is tied with a red satin ribbon. Captions: "Mother and Dad 1988" and "You give Christmas a special warmth and glow."

Fine Porcelain, 3" tall
800QX414-4, $8.00 ☐

Sister

Wearing a candy-apple red pinafore dress and a ruffled white bonnet, this little girl puts a gold star atop a Christmas tree that's just her size. The white, fine porcelain bell is tied with a lacy red ribbon. Caption: "Sisters know so many ways to brighten up the holidays! 1988."

Fine Porcelain, 3" tall
800QX499-4, $8.00 ☐

Grandmother

The partridge-in-a-pear-tree theme is beautifully expressed in a richly colored design that looks like crewel embroidery. The caption on the teardrop-shaped ball reads, "Grandmother makes love a Christmas tradition. 1988."

Gold Glass, 2⅞" diam.
475QX276-4, $4.75 ☐

Grandparents

An old-fashioned tree is decorated with lots of toys for the little ones, and kitty naps nearby. The appreciative caption on this teardrop ball reads, "Grandparents are the heart of so many treasured memories. Christmas 1988."

Red Glass, 2⅞" diam.
475QX277-1, $4.75 ☐

Granddaughter

For the first time, a Keepsake glass ball ornament has been painted in two contrasting background colors that softly blend, adding depth to the design. Here, an angel reaches for a star in a sunset-colored sky. Caption: "A Granddaughter is a delight to love! Christmas 1988."

Red and White Glass, 2⅞" diam.
475QX277-4, $4.75 ☐

Sweetheart, First Christmas Together: Handcrafted, Acrylic, Ball

Grandson

Santa's catching snowflakes to share with someone special, and the caption tells us who it is: "A Grandson makes Christmas merry! 1988." The background colors of green and white gradually blend, the result of the new design technique.

Green and White Glass, 2⅞" diam.
475QX278-1, $4.75 ☐

Godchild

Carrying an old-fashioned lamp, a bell, and a songbook, these three children go a-caroling. And their little dog joins right in. This charming scene celebrates a special relationship: " A Godchild brings joy to the world...especially at Christmas. 1988."

Gold Glass, 2⅞" diam.
475QX278-4, $4.75 ☐

Sweetheart

A romantic swan sleigh features pearly colors that shimmer in the light. Inside the sleigh, a single rose signifies true love. Front Caption: "Sweetheart." Back Caption: "Christmas 1988." Beneath the sleigh is a place for personalization: "For (name), Love (name)."

Handcrafted, 3⅜" tall
975QX490-1, $9.75 ☐

First Christmas Together

This happy couple is ready to exchange presents, and both have heart-shaped packages! They stand on a braided rug, inside a heart-shaped frame that is styled to look like wood. Front Caption: "First Christmas Together." Back Caption: "1988."

Handcrafted, 3¼" tall
900QX489-4, $9.00 ☐

First Christmas Together

Using a technique new to the Keepsake line, subtle colors are embedded in acrylic to add depth to holiday greenery in a graceful Art Nouveau design. The gold foil caption reads, "Our First Christmas Together 1988." The oval ornament has a beveled edge and is framed in brass.

Acrylic, 4" tall
675QX373-1, $6.75 ☐

First Christmas Together

A pair of cardinals symbolizes lasting love in this wintry scene that features snow-covered evergreens and a sparkling sky. The caption reads, "Beauty is found in many things, but most of all in love. Our First Christmas Together 1988."

Sparkling Glass, 2⅞" diam.
475QX274-1, $4.75 ☐

Five Years Together
This glass ball introduces a new commemorative to the Keepsake line. It features five trees composed of green hearts. Each tree also contains a number of red hearts, from one to five, to celebrate the passing years. Caption: "5 Years Together Christmas 1988."

White Glass, 2⅞" diam.
475QX274-4, $4.75 ☐

Ten Years Together
Two deer stand on a hill overlooking a quiet village. The snow is falling gently. Caption: "Love warms every moment, brightens every day. Ten Years Together Christmas 1988."

White Glass, 2⅞" diam.
475QX275-1, $4.75 ☐

Twenty-Five Years Together
Stamped in silver foil to commemorate a Silver Anniversary, this lovely acrylic ornament is beveled to catch the light. It is framed in chrome. Caption: "25 Years Together Christmas 1988."

Acrylic, 3⅛" tall
675QX373-4, $6.75 ☐

Fifty Years Together
For a Golden Anniversary celebration, the decorative numerals and caption appear in gold foil: "50 Years Together Christmas 1988." The beveled edge and brass frame enrich the design.

Acrylic, 3⅛" tall
675QX374-1, $6.75 ☐

Love Fills the Heart
A delicate pattern of holly leaves and berries repeats the silhouette of this finely etched acrylic heart. Two birds and a gold foil sentiment complete the design. Caption: "Love fills the heart forever."

Acrylic, 3" tall
600QX374-4, $6.00 ☐

Love Grows
Flowers in full bloom are accented with pale green leaves and displayed against black to achieve a rich, lacquered look. The caption on this chrome teardrop ball reads, "Patiently, joyfully, beautifully, Love grows. Christmas 1988."

Chrome Glass, 2⅞" diam.
475QX275-4, $4.75 ☐

Spirit of Christmas
Dressed in the costumes of their native lands, children hold hands as they encircle a teardrop ball. They represent the universal wish for peace. Caption: "Love begins changing the world by awakening one heart at a time. Christmas 1988."

Chrome Glass, 2⅞" diam.
475QX276-1, $4.75 ☐

Five Years Together, Ten Years Together

Twenty-Five Years Together, Fifty Years Together, Love Fills the Heart

Love Grows, Spirit of Christmas

Year to Remember, Gratitude, New Home

Year to Remember
Designed for business use, this distinctive filigree ornament clearly commemorates the year, "1988." Fashioned of ivory ceramic, the motif incorporates holly leaves and berries, as well as an oval frame. A slender red satin ribbon and bow complete the design.
Ceramic, 3¾" tall
700QX416-4, $7.00 ☐

Gratitude
Snowflakes and a graceful evergreen tree highlight this etched acrylic teardrop. The sparkling silver foil caption reads, "Christmas fills our hearts with thoughts of those who care. 1988."
Acrylic, 3⅜" tall
600QX375-4, $6.00 ☐

New Home
Santa and his reindeer fly over a house nestled among the trees. The frosted bas-relief design is on the front of the acrylic oval, while the gold foil stars and caption are stamped on the back for added depth. Caption: "A new home makes Christmas merry and bright." The year date "1988" is etched into the design.
Acrylic, 2½" tall
600QX376-1, $6.00 ☐

From Our Home to Yours
Scenes of playful snow-people alternate with homes decorated for the holidays on a sparkling glass teardrop ball. Caption: "Merry Christmas From Our Home to Yours. 1988."
Sparkling Glass, 2⅞" diam.
475QX279-4, $4.75 ☐

Babysitter
Building a snowman, throwing snowballs, and sledding are depicted in appealing childlike drawings. The green glass ball is speckled with white to suggest a gentle snowfall. The snowman holds a sign that reads, "May the love you show children return to you this holiday. 1988."
Green Glass, 2⅞" diam.
475QX279-1, $4.75 ☐

PEANUTS®
Flying across the sky, WOODSTOCK and pals pull SNOOPY® on a gift-laden sled. The caption on the blue teardrop ball explains, "Where friendship goes, happiness follows! Christmas 1988."
Blue Glass, 2⅞" diam.
475QX280-1, $4.75 ☐

From Our Home to Yours, Babysitter, PEANUTS®

Teacher

This thoughtful, flocked bunny has created a special card "For Teacher." He's drawn a carrot inside, and now he's using his favorite "CRAYOLA® Crayon" to add "Merry Christmas 1988." There's a place for your name on the back of the card where it says, "From."

Handcrafted, 2¼" tall
625QX417-1, $6.25 ☐

Holiday Traditions

Jingle Bell Clown

This musical ornament plays "Jingle Bells" for a very merry clown. Dashing through the snow in his wood-look reindeer sleigh, he thinks it's fun to ring a bright brass bell all the way. The year date "1988" appears on the license plate.

Handcrafted, Musical, 3" tall
1500QX477-4, $15.00 ☐

Travels With Santa

Mrs. Claus joins Santa as he decides to see the world at a more leisurely pace. You can catch a glimpse of them inside this shiny trailer — enjoying their picture window view, portable TV, and tiny green bottle-brush tree. The trailer wheels turn, and the license plate reads, "B MERRY."

Handcrafted, 2" tall
1000QX477-1, $10.00 ☐

Party Line

Two chatty little raccoons have recycled cans of "Campbell's Chicken Noodle Soup" to start their own phone company. It's a local call or long distance, depending on whether you place the pals close together or on separate branches of your tree.

Handcrafted, 1¾" tall
875QX476-1, $8.75 ☐

Goin' Cross-Country

Now that he's mastered those bright red skis, this confident bear would rather glide than walk. His warm white coat is accented with a jaunty muffler of ribbon, and there's a real pompom on his cap.

Handcrafted, 3¼" tall
850QX476-4, $8.50 ☐

Winter Fun

It's a wide-eyed ride for a happy, three-kid crew on a brand-new toboggan. Two face forward, one's riding backwards. The design includes a real rope for controlling the sled.

Handcrafted, 2" tall
850QX478-1, $8.50 ☐

Teacher *Jingle Bell Clown*

Travels with Santa, Party Line, Goin' Cross Country, Winter Fun

Go for the Gold, Soft Landing, Feliz Navidad, Squeaky Clean

Christmas Memories Photoholder, Purrfect Snuggle, SNOOPY® and WOODSTOCK

Go for the Gold
An exuberant Santa dashes by, celebrating an exciting year in sports. Outfitted in a red-white-and-blue jogging suit, he carries a golden torch with a light-catching, translucent flame. The caption on Santa's jacket reads "88."

Handcrafted, 3½" tall
800QX417-4, $8.00 ☐

Soft Landing
Santa beams with confidence as he glides across the ice. From the back, you can see his secret — a real fabric pillow in holiday green and white, tied around his waist with a green fabric ribbon.

Handcrafted, 3" tall
700QX475-1, $7.00 ☐

Feliz Navidad
This little gray burro wears a *sombrero* and carries two saddlebags with the look of hand-tooled leather. One saddlebag holds a green bottle-brush tree. The other contains a holiday package with the caption "Feliz Navidad," the traditional Spanish wish for a happy holiday.

Handcrafted, 2⅞" tall
675QX416-1, $6.75 ☐

Squeaky Clean
'Twas the night before Christmas...time for this little mouse to relax in a bubble-filled tub, molded from a walnut shell. The tub stands on four golden feet, and there's a tiny golden shower overhead.

Handcrafted, 2⅜" tall
675QX475-4, $6.75 ☐

Christmas Memories Photoholder
Silver foil snowflakes encircle an acrylic wreath, while holly leaves appear on the bow at the top. The year date "1988" is shown on the front. The silvery caption on the back reads, "Christmas is more than a day in December...it's the magic and love we'll always remember."

Acrylic, 3¾" tall
650QX372-4, $6.50 ☐

Purrfect Snuggle
This gray-and-white striped kitten is purring his way into the heart of a new friend — a teddy bear, all decked out for Christmas with a handcrafted, red-and-green plaid bow.

Handcrafted, 2" tall
625QX474-4, $6.25 ☐

SNOOPY® and WOODSTOCK
These two special friends are so eager to be part of the holiday scene, they've tucked themselves inside a real knit stocking to decorate your tree. They even brought along a bow-tied gift bone.

Handcrafted, 2⅜" tall
600QX474-1, $6.00 ☐

The Town Crier

Dressed in Colonial clothing from his hat to his buckle shoes, the rabbit rings a bell and reads the holiday proclamation. The caption facing him says, "Hear Ye! Hear Ye! Christmas time has come to cheer ye!" Front caption: "Hear Ye! Hear Ye! Christmas joy is always near ye!"

Handcrafted, 2¼″ tall
550QX473-4, $5.50
☐

Norman Rockwell: Christmas Scenes

These gentle portrayals of children are carefully reproduced to reflect the charm of the original paintings. The scene of a child saying bedtime prayers is captioned, "Christmas...the season that blesses the world. 1988." Two children dressed for a holiday pageant are shown with the caption: "Christmas...the season that touches the heart. From the Norman Rockwell Collection."

White Glass, 2⅞″ diam.
475QX273-1, $4.75
☐

The Town Crier, Norman Rockwell: Christmas Scenes

Jolly Walrus

Proud to be the first walrus featured in a Keepsake Ornament, this fellow flashes a toothsome smile. He's donned a wreath of shiny green foil and bright red satin ribbon to celebrate the occasion.

Handcrafted, 1⅞″ tall
450QX473-1, $4.50
☐

Slipper Spaniel

Sound asleep in a flocked red slipper, this little puppy dreams that Santa will fill his Christmas stocking with puppy treats instead of sugarplums.

Handcrafted, 3″ tall
425QX472-4, $4.25
☐

Arctic Tenor

This penguin is wearing his everyday-best tuxedo, a green bow tie and colorful spats to perform his holiday program. Musical notes are printed on the pages of his open songbook titled "Arctic Arias."

Handcrafted, 1¾″ tall
400QX472-1, $4.00
☐

Jolly Walrus, Slipper Spaniel, Arctic Tenor

St. Louie Nick

Reissue from 1987. (See 1987 Annual Collection.)

Handcrafted, 3½″ tall
775QX453-9, $7.75
☐

Mistletoad

Reissue from 1987. (See 1987 Annual Collection.)

Handcrafted, 3¾″ tall
700QX468-7, $7.00
☐

Treetop Dreams

Reissue from 1987. (See 1987 Annual Collection.)

Handcrafted, 3″ tall
675QX459-7, $6.75
☐

Night Before Christmas

Reissue from 1987. (See 1987 Annual Collection.)

Handcrafted, 2¾″ tall
650QX451-7, $6.50
☐

Owliday Wish

Reissue from 1987. (See 1987 Annual Collection.)

Handcrafted, 2″ tall
650QX455-9, $6.50
☐

Happy Holidata

Reissue from 1987. (See 1987 Annual Collection.)

Handcrafted, 1½″ tall
650QX471-7, $6.50
☐

Reindoggy

Reissue from 1987. (See 1987 Annual Collection.)

Handcrafted, 2¾″ tall
575QX452-7, $5.75
☐

In a Nutshell

Reissue from 1987. (See 1987 Annual Collection.)

Handcrafted, 1½″ tall
550QX469-7, $5.50
☐

The Wonderful Santacyle

Special Edition

The Wonderful Santacycle

Santa really rolls along on this fanciful three-wheeler. It's reminiscent of that childhood favorite — a rocking horse — but this one sits atop golden-spoked wheels that turn. Special details include a brass bell on Santa's cap.

Handcrafted, 4¼″ tall
2250QX411-4, $22.50

New Attractions

Christmas Cuckoo

This is one of three ornaments in the 1988 Keepsake line to feature a special, non-electronic movement. When you hold the clock by its sides, and gently tap the pendulum, two things happen. The cuckoo's door opens, revealing a tiny blue bird inside, and the clock's face turns from 12:00 to 3:00. The pendulum is molded from a real pinecone.

Handcrafted, 4⅞″ tall
800QX480-1, $8.00   ☐

Peek-a-Boo Kitties

These kitties are really having fun! Hold the basket by its sides, and gently tap the kitten swinging on the ball of yarn. As it moves to and fro, the lid of the basket opens on first one side and then the other — disclosing two more playful kittens hiding inside. One is white; the other, charcoal gray.

Handcrafted, 5″ tall
750QX487-1, $7.50   ☐

Cool Juggler

This clever snowman is waiting to entertain you. Just hold this ornament by the base, and gently tap the snowball below. The snowman's arms move up and down, while three sparkling snowballs glide from hand to hand.

Handcrafted, 4¾″ tall
650QX487-4, $6.50   ☐

Santa Flamingo

This whimsical fellow knows how to stand out in a crowd. He's wearing a red fabric Santa hat with fluffy white trim and real pompom. And his long, stilt-like legs really move, enabling him to take the holidays in stride.

Handcrafted, 5½″ tall
475QX483-4, $4.75   ☐

Christmas Cuckoo; Peek-a-Boo Kitties, Cool Juggler, Santa Flamingo

Par for Santa

This group of lifestyle ornaments shows what Santa does for fun! In this design, he's playing golf. Holding a scorecard for the "St. Nick Open," he waits to tee off with his favorite wood.

Handcrafted, 2⅝" tall
500QX479-1, $5.00

Hoe-Hoe-Hoe!

Santa likes to tend his garden. He orders his gardening clothes in Christmas colors — a red visor cap and green overalls.

Handcrafted, 2⅜" tall
500QX422-1, $5.00

Nick the Kick

Santa's keeping pace with the popular game of soccer. The team emblem, a snowflake, is emblazoned on the front of his sweater. The team name, "Blizzard," as well as Santa's number, "OO," appear on the back.

Handcrafted, 2¼" tall
500QX422-4, $5.00

Holiday Hero

Quarterback Claus steps back to pass the football for a touchdown. He's very sure-footed, thanks to the tiny cleats on the soles of his shoes. The back of his shirt carries his name, "S. Claus," and also makes it official — he's number "1."

Handcrafted, 2⅝" tall
500QX423-1, $5.00

Polar Bowler

Santa practices bowling with a polished green bowling ball, and there's a green towel in his hip pocket. The back of his shirt reads, "North Pole Bowl."

Handcrafted, 2¼" tall
500QX478-4, $5.00

Gone Fishing

Santa's equipped for fishing success, and he has the catch to prove it. A rare blue fish swings from the nylon line connected to a flexible rod. He carries a creel to hold fish.

Handcrafted, 2½" tall
500QX479-4, $5.00

Love Santa

Santa skillfully returns a serve. The soft pompom ball is attached to his silvery racket. His attire for the courts includes a green headband and matching wristbands.

Handcrafted, 2½" tall
500QX486-4, $5.00

Kiss the Claus

Santa will be happy to serve his specialty — a cheeseburger on a bun. Be sure to dress casually, Santa's wearing thongs. His apron reads, "Kiss the Claus."

Handcrafted, 2¾" tall
500QX486-1, $5.00

Par for Santa, Hoe-Hoe-Hoe!, Nick the Kick, Holiday Hero

Polar Bowler, Gone Fishing, Love Santa, Kiss the Claus

Sweet Star, Filled With Fudge, Teeny Taster

Sweet Star

Chocolate lovers find several 1988 Keepsake Ornaments especially tempting. Claiming this chocolate-rimmed sugar cookie for his very own, a mischievous squirrel begins nibbling on the maraschino cherry he found on top. The cookie clips onto a branch of your tree.

Handcrafted, 1 ¾" tall
500QX418-4, $5.00 □

Filled With Fudge

This little mouse found his favorite dessert and jumped right in. Now he's holding out a spoon to signal that he's ready for a second helping. The mouse's red fabric ribbon is tied in a bow in back.

Handcrafted, 3 ⅜" tall
475QX419-1, $4.75 □

Teeny Taster

Who wants to wait for Christmas when the batter tastes so good! Not this happy chipmunk, who insists on a big spoonful. He'll be careful not to spill a drop on his green fabric neck-ribbon and bow.

Handcrafted, 4 ⅜" tall
475QX418-1, $4.75 □

A KISS™ From Santa

Looking just like chocolate, this Keepsake Ornament is a treat that can be enjoyed season after season. The sculpted Santa wears a bright red hat with silvery trim, and he's holding a silvery likeness of the popular candy. The attached plume reads, "HERSHEY'S® KISSES."

Handcrafted, 3 ¼" tall
450QX482-1, $4.50 □

OREO®Chocolate Sandwich Cookies

This life-size cookie is hinged and can be displayed closed or open. Inside, Santa's smiling face appears in the creamy filling. Caption: "ho ho ho!"

Handcrafted, 1 ⅞" diam.
400QX481-4, $4.00 □

A KISS™ From Santa, OREO® Chocolate Sandwich Cookies (shown both open and closed)

Uncle Sam Nutcracker, Old-Fashioned Schoolhouse, Church

Noah's Ark, Sailing! Sailing!, Americana Drum

Kringle Portrait, Kringle Tree, Kringle Moon

Glowing Wreath, Sparkling Tree, Shiny Sleigh

Loving Bear, Starry Angel, Christmas Cardinal

Uncle Sam Nutcracker
This traditional American figure wears his hair pulled back in a ponytail. Lift it, and his mouth moves in true Nutcracker fashion. Uncle Sam has a soft plush beard, and wears a campaign button dated "1988."

Handcrafted, 5¼" tall
700QX488-4, $7.00

Old-Fashioned Schoolhouse
The little red schoolhouse is made of wood. It represents the hand-made villages which were favorite folk-art decorations. The design is complete with an American flag over the door, as well as a tower to house the bell that called children to class.

Wood, 3" tall
400QX497-1, $4.00

Old-Fashioned Church
The nostalgic village church, the hub of the holiday celebration, also reflects the American Country motif. Its classic lines include an arched doorway and windows, and a tall steeple.

Wood, 4½" tall
400QX498-1, $4.00

Noah's Ark
Reminiscent of antique pull toys, this colorful and highly detailed craft is filled with passengers from stem to stern. It is one of two nautical pressed tin designs in the 1988 Keepsake Ornament line. The wheels on the ark really turn, and there's a metallic pull-cord.

Pressed Tin, 2⅛" tall
850QX490-4, $8.50

Sailing! Sailing!
This year's second nautical pressed tin ornament also features a nostalgic pull-toy design. Here, a sailor enjoys a breezy day. Water laps against the sides of his boat, and fish jump over the waves. Pull the metallic cord, and the sailboat's wheels roll along.

Pressed Tin, 2⅞" tall
850QX491-1, $8.50

Americana Drum
The sides of this colorful tin drum are decorated with a holiday version of a traditional American eagle-and-banner design. The eagle holds evergreen branches and holly. The caption, "Merry Christmas U.S.A. 1988," appears on both drumheads. Gold metallic cord forms the bindings, and a set of drumsticks is attached.

Tin, 2" diam.
775QX488-1, $7.75

Kringle Portrait
This highly detailed image of Santa's face and flowing beard is encircled by a wreath. Another sculpted design appears on the back — Santa's sleigh, complete with Christmas tree and teddy bear.

Handcrafted, 3¼" tall
750QX496-1, $7.50

Kringle Tree
Two favorite symbols of Christmas — Santa and a tree — are combined in one ornament, carefully sculpted to give the appearance of an Old World carving. The antiqued finish contributes to the timeless quality of the design.

Handcrafted, 3⅜" tall
650QX495-4, $6.50

Kringle Moon
The man in the moon is Santa himself, and he's catching 40 winks. There's a tiny brass jingle bell at the tip of his cap. The carving appears on both sides of the ornament.

Handcrafted, 3⅜" tall
550QX495-1, $5.50

Glowing Wreath
This year's trio of multi-dimensional brass ornaments is a tribute to early American artisans who created their decorations from simple metal shapes. This gleaming brass wreath begins with a circle and the silhouettes of a house and a heart. Nine additional silhouettes are then added, extending forward from the wreath at various levels, to achieve the layered appearance.

Dimensional Brass, 3½" tall
600QX492-1, $6.00

Sparkling Tree
The brass silhouette of a Christmas tree is layered with additional brass silhouettes that symbolize the season — a home, a reindeer, two doves of peace, a heart, and a star. Tiny cut-outs in the tree itself let the light shine through.

Dimensional Brass, 3⅜" tall
600QX493-1, $6.00

Shiny Sleigh
Fashioned from one continuous piece of metal, this multi-dimensional design is created by careful bending and shaping. The red cord in Santa's hand serves as the reins for his reindeer, as well as a means of suspending the light-catching brass ornament from your tree.

Dimensional Brass, 1⅜" tall
575QX492-4, $5.75

Loving Bear
"Twirl-Abouts," ornaments with rotating center designs, were introduced in 1976. Three new ornaments similar to Twirl-Abouts appeared in 1988. This teddy bear twirls inside a holiday wreath decorated with folk-art shapes of hearts and holly.

Handcrafted, 3¼" tall
475QX493-4, $4.75

Starry Angel
Her white robe trimmed in red and green, this angel twirls about inside the silhouette of a star. The stencil-like design on the star reflects a Scandinavian influence.

Handcrafted, 2⅞" tall
475QX494-4, $4.75

Christmas Cardinal
A cheerful cardinal twirls about inside the silhouette of an evergreen tree. The folk art flavor of the design is emphasized by a pattern that suggests pine branches accented with white ornaments.

Handcrafted, 2⅞" tall
475QX494-1, $4.75

Artists' Favorites

Merry-Mint Unicorn
When she was a child, artist Anita Marra loved to draw pictures of unicorns with big doe eyes and curly manes. Now she's recreated her favorite design in fine porcelain. The unicorn appears to be balancing on a piece of peppermint candy.

Hand-Painted Fine Porcelain, 3¾" tall
Artist: Anita Marra
850QX423-4, $8.50 ☐

Little Jack Horner
Artist Bob Siedler thinks this nursery rhyme is especially appropriate for the holiday season, so he's sculpted his vision of the well-known lad pulling a plum out of his Christmas pie. The boy's hat, adorned with a handcrafted yellow feather, is captioned: "Little Jack Horner."

Handcrafted, 2½" tall
Artist: Bob Siedler
800QX408-1, $8.00 ☐

Midnight Snack
This whimsical white mouse waits for Santa and enjoys a treat, thanks to his artist, Bob Siedler. The handcrafted doughnut is topped with make-believe icing and red sparkles. And the mouse wears a green fabric ribbon bow.

Handcrafted, 2½" tall
Artist: Bob Siedler
600QX410-4, $6.00 ☐

Cymbals of Christmas
Artist Donna Lee explains that this playful angel wants everyone to know she's there. So she's pulled two golden stars out of the sky to make a big ka-boom! Her halo is brass, and her frosted acrylic cloud is decorated with holly and stars.

Handcrafted, Acrylic, 2⅛" tall
Artist: Donna Lee
550QX411-1, $5.50 ☐

Very Strawbeary
Artist Peter Dutkin remembers waiting for the ice-cream truck when he was a boy, so he's given this softly flocked teddy bear a special treat. The decorated cone carries the artist's initials, "PDII." Sparkling red acrylic ice crystals add a holiday flavor.

Handcrafted, 2¼" tall
Artist: Peter Dutkin
475QX409-1, $4.75 ☐

Baby Redbird
This cheerful fellow reminds artist Robert Chad of cardinals who feast on sunflower seeds at feeding stations, then rest like lovely decorations in nearby trees. "Baby Redbird" has a clip-on design that enables it to perch realistically on a branch.

Handcrafted, 2⅝" tall
Artist: Robert Chad
500QX410-1, $5.00 ☐

Merry-Mint Unicorn, Little Jack Horner, Midnight Snack

Cymbals of Christmas, Very Strawbeary, Baby Redbird

Mary's Angels, Collector's Plate, Mr. and Mrs. Claus

Collectible Series

Mary's Angels—First Edition

"Buttercup" is the first angel in a series of new designs by Hallmark stylist Mary Hamilton. This little angel has a pastel yellow dress and pearly wings. She's napping on a frosted acrylic cloud that displays the signature "Mary" on the bottom.

Handcrafted, 2¼" tall
500QX407-4, $5.00 ☐

Collector's Plate —Second Edition

The tree is decorated, the stockings are hung by the chimney with care, and there's a plateful of cookies on the table. Brother and sister nap, while their puppy peers up the fireplace. The caption says, "Waiting for Santa 1988." Plate stand included.

Fine Porcelain, 3¼" diam.
800QX406-1, $8.00 ☐

Mr. and Mrs. Claus —Third Edition

When the North Pole radio request-line plays their special song, this loving couple always has time for a waltz. Santa carries a gift list, dated "1988," in his pocket. The graceful wishbone hanger enhances the design, titled "Shall We Dance."

Handcrafted, 4¼" tall
1300QX401-1, $13.00 ☐

Reindeer Champs —Third Edition

During basketball season, "Prancer" flies down the court and scores with a unique overhoof shot. The back of his shirt shows his name and number, "Prancer 88."

Handcrafted, 3½" tall
750QX405-1, $7.50 ☐

Betsey Clark: Home for Christmas —Third Edition

Baking cookies, stitching a quilt, and pressing a red stocking captioned "Noel," Betsey and her friends show the love that goes with every gift. The caption appears on a wall poster: "A homemade touch can do so much to make each Christmas special!" A wall clock reads, "1988."

Light Blue Glass, 2⅞" diam.
500QX271-4, $5.00 ☐

Windows of the World —Fourth Edition

On a cozy hearth, a poodle keeps his young master company while they wait for Santa. Overhead, two red bows hold a banner with the Christmas greeting in French, "Joyeux Noël." The yule logs in the fireplace show the year date "1988."

Handcrafted, 3½" tall
1000QX402-1, $10.00 ☐

Reindeer Champs, Betsey Clark: Home for Christmas, Windows of the World

Miniature Crèche
—Fourth Edition
This serene Nativity is depicted in frosted acrylic and silhouetted within a clear acrylic star. The sides of the star have been faceted to reflect the light, then painted in gold. A golden, star-shaped finding covers the top point of the design.

Acrylic, 2¾" tall
850QX403-4, $8.50 □

Nostalgic Houses and Shops
—Fifth Edition
Take a trip back in time, when "Cards" and "Gifts" were selected at "Hall Bro's," the original name of Hallmark Cards, Inc. Inside, there's an old-fashioned cash register on the counter, and a greeting card display nearby. The second floor holds an artist's studio. "Hall Bro's Card Shop" enjoys a prime corner location with a "1988" address.

Handcrafted, 4¼" tall
1450QX401-4, $14.50 □

Wood Childhood Ornaments
—Fifth Edition
The propeller spins, and the wheels really roll on this nostalgic "Wooden Airplane." Hand-painted details and a green yarn pull-cord help bring back warm memories. The design is dated "1988."

Wood, 1⅝" tall
750QX404-1, $7.50 □

The Twelve Days of Christmas
—Fifth Edition
The quadrafoil shape of this ornament complements the jewelry named in the song. Each of the five rings has its own special design, and the rings are linked with a ribbon and bow. The design is etched into clear acrylic, and the caption is stamped in gold foil: "The Twelve Days of Christmas 1988...five golden rings..."

Acrylic, 3" tall
650QX371-4, $6.50 □

Porcelain Bear—Sixth Edition
This year, "Cinnamon Bear" is playing Santa! He's wrapped up a heart full of memories for someone special. Careful painting by hand gives this fine porcelain teddy his winsome expression.

Hand-Painted Fine Porcelain, 2¼" tall
800QX404-4, $8.00 □

Tin Locomotive—Seventh Edition
This colorful "Tin Locomotive" has a distinctive, pierced-tin cowcatcher. The wheels are decorated with bright embossed patterns, which add to the sense of motion as the wheels turn. The year date "1988" appears on the boiler.

Pressed Tin, 3" tall
1475QX400-4, $14.75 □

Miniature Crèche, Nostalgic Houses and Shops, Wood Childhood Ornaments

The Twelve Days of Christmas, Porcelain Bear, Tin Locomotive

Holiday Wildlife, Rocking Horse, Frosty Friends

Holiday Wildlife—Seventh and Final Edition

Perched on a pine branch, a pair of purple finches is realistically depicted on this porcelain-look inset framed in wood. Caption: "Purple Finch, CARPODACUS PURPUREUS, Seventh in a Series, Wildlife Collection, Christmas 1988."

Wood, 2½" diam.
775QX371-1, $7.75 ☐

Rocking Horse—Eighth Edition

Hurrying to the festivities, this dapple gray pony brings happy memories of childhood. His red and green trappings are accented with gold, and the red and green rockers read "1988." The pony's mane and forelock are dark gray, and he boasts the first two-tone yarn tail in the series.

Handcrafted, 3¼" wide
1075QX402-4, $10.75 ☐

Frosty Friends—Ninth Edition

A polar bear cub holds one end of a real fabric ribbon while his Eskimo pal wraps the "North Pole" in holiday style. They stand on an icy base of acrylic, dated "1988."

Handcrafted, 3⅜" tall
875QX403-1, $8.75 ☐

Norman Rockwell—Ninth and Final Edition

Back home after a whirlwind tour of the world, Santa relaxes in his chair. The wall calendar reads "Dec 25," and Santa holds the "Dec 24" page in his hand. The white bas relief cameo appears against a red background. The ornament is framed in brass and carries a gold-foil stamped caption on the back. An appropriate way to end the series, it reads: "And to All a Good Night, Ninth in a Series, Christmas 1988, The Norman Rockwell Collection."

Cameo, 3¼" diam.
775QX370-4, $7.75 ☐

Here Comes Santa— Tenth Edition

Wearing a ten-gallon hat, Santa's in the driver's seat waiting for his team. Gift packages ride in the luggage rack, and there's a bottle-brush tree in the boot. A teddy bear waves from the inside. The door next to the bear opens and carries the caption, "Kringle Koach 1988." The opposite door also reads, "Kringle Koach."

Handcrafted, 3¼" tall
1400QX400-1, $14.00 ☐

Thimble—Eleventh Edition

"Thimble Snowman" has discovered that a silvery thimble makes a marvelous hat. The pearly snowman's attire includes a red muffler and green mittens.

Handcrafted, 2⅜" tall
575QX405-4, $5.75 ☐

Norman Rockwell, Here Comes Santa, Thimble

THE 1989 COLLECTION

Attention focused on Collectible Series in 1989, as five new series made their debut. They were "The Gift Bringers," "Hark! It's Herald," "Christmas Kitty," "Winter Surprise," and "CRAYOLA® Crayon." Especially notable was "The Gift Bringers." Not only was it the first new ball series since 1986, but Hallmark announced at the outset that a total of five editions would be offered. Four series were retired this year: "Thimble," "Wood Childhood Ornaments," "Tin Locomotive," and "Miniature Crèche."

For many people who enjoy collecting ornaments for children, the 1989 Keepsake offering introduced an appealing group of bear ornaments that commemorates a child's first five Christmases. The group included two new captions: "Child's Fourth Christmas" and "Child's Fifth Christmas." Grandchildren were remembered with acrylic ornaments commemorating "Grandson's First Christmas" and "Granddaughter's First Christmas." Other new captions for relatives were "Brother" and "Mom and Dad." The latter design presented a whimsical view of these two special people, which was a departure from the more traditional "Mother and Dad" ornaments of previous years.

Ornaments that celebrate "Twenty-Five" and "Fifty Years Together" appeared as lovely photoholders. And, for the first time, a Keepsake Ornament celebrated "Forty Years Together." All three of these commemoratives were attractive variations of the same photoholder design.

Continuing the Keepsake tradition of commemorating events of historical or popular interest, the '89 line included an ornament honoring the 200th anniversary of the first presidential inauguration. It is called "George Washington Bicentennial." And, on a lighter note, a "PEANUTS®" ball ornament marked the 25th anniversary of the television special, "A Charlie Brown Christmas."

Collectors who loved the 1987 ornament "In a Nutshell" were pleased to find three new ornaments in this format in '89. There were also new ornament designs that featured movement, and new lifestyle Santa designs. The 1989 Special Edition was "The Ornament Express," a three-ornament train set which consists of a "Locomotive," "Coal Car," and "Caboose."

Commemoratives

Baby's First Christmas Photoholder
The sentiment on the back of this star-shaped photoholder announces that Baby is "A new star on the family tree!" Decorated with toys, the ornament holds a favorite photo and carries the caption, "Baby's First Christmas 1989."

Handcrafted, 3¾" tall
625QX468-2, $6.25   ☐

Baby's First Christmas—Baby Girl
Sleeping sweetly through her first Christmas Eve, the Baby Girl on this pink satin ball doesn't see Santa standing by her cradle. Caption: "A New Baby Girl To Love. Baby's First Christmas 1989."

Pink Satin, 2⅞" diam.
475QX272-2, $4.75   ☐

Baby's First Christmas—Baby Boy
Like the Baby Girl, the Baby Boy on this blue satin ball is fast asleep on his first Christmas Eve. Santa motions for quiet while he watches the little one slumber. Caption: "A New Baby Boy To Love. Baby's First Christmas 1989."

Blue Satin, 2⅞" diam.
475QX272-5, $4.75   ☐

Baby's First Christmas: Photoholder, Baby Girl, Baby Boy

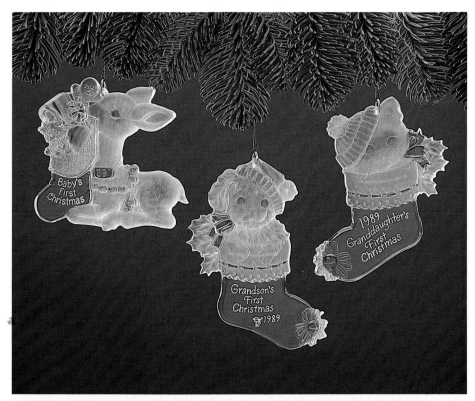

Baby's First Christmas, Granddaughter's First Christmas, Grandson's First Christmas

Baby's First Christmas

An acrylic reindeer brings gifts for Baby. The stocking holds etched toys and the gold foil caption, "Baby's First Christmas." The collar is dated "89."

Acrylic, 3 7/16" tall
675QX381-5, $6.75 ☐

Granddaughter's First Christmas

An acrylic stocking is the perfect place for a kitty to play, especially when it carries the gold foil caption, "Granddaughter's First Christmas 1989." This ornament is a new commemorative caption.

Acrylic, 4¼" tall
675QX382-2, $6.75 ☐

Grandson's First Christmas

A puppy finds a hideaway inside an acrylic stocking. The ornament is a new commemorative caption. Stamped in gold foil, the caption reads, "Grandson's First Christmas 1989."

Acrylic, 4¼" tall
675QX382-5, $6.75 ☐

Children's Age Collection

Parents and relatives will want to collect this group of ornaments for a child. The bears commemorate a child's first five Christmases. Each bear wears a flocked hat and has a pearly candy cane number.

Baby's First Christmas

Wearing a green bow, this bear holds a big candy cane number "1" dated "1989." The entire bear is flocked and wears a flocked hat. Caption: "Baby's 1st Christmas."

Handcrafted, 2⅝" tall
725QX449-2, $7.25 ☐

Baby's Second Christmas

A friendly polar bear holds a candy cane "2" and waves a Christmas "hello." Caption: "Baby's 2nd Christmas '89."

Handcrafted, 2 13/16" tall
675QX449-5, $6.75 ☐

Child's Third Christmas

This honey bear hugs a candy cane number "3" and is having fun celebrating a third Christmas. Caption: "My 3rd Christmas '89."

Handcrafted, 2½" tall
675QX469-5, $6.75 ☐

Child's Fourth Christmas

A panda marches proudly in the Christmas parade and carries a candy cane "4." Caption: "My 4th Christmas '89."

Handcrafted, 3" tall
675QX543-2, $6.75 ☐

Child's Fifth Christmas

Hanging on to a candy cane "5," a smiling koala commemorates a fifth Christmas. Caption: "My 5th Christmas '89."

Handcrafted, 2⅜" tall
675QX543-5, $6.75 ☐

Children's Age Collection: First, Second, Third, Fourth and Fifth Christmas

Mother, Mom and Dad, Dad

Daughter, Son

Brother, Sister

Grandparents, Grandmother

Granddaughter, Grandson, Godchild

Mother
Delicately designed Christmas flowers frame a loving sentiment on the front of a fine porcelain heart. Caption: "Mother is the heart of the family. 1989." The ornament is tied with a red fabric ribbon.

Fine Porcelain, 2½" tall
975QX440-5, $9.75 ☐

Mom and Dad
This cozy penguin duo loves to go skating and also enjoys commemorating two very special people! "MOM" and "DAD" appear on the penguins' shirts, and "1989" is printed on Dad's scarf.

Handcrafted, 2⅜" tall
975QX442-5, $9.75 ☐

Dad
The designer shorts are just a tiny bit too big for this polar bear dad. Painted a pearly white, the shorts look like silk. Caption: "For Dad 1989."

Handcrafted, 2⅞" tall
725QX441-2, $7.25 ☐

Daughter
This rosy-cheeked girl has just purchased a new bonnet. She's bringing it home in a hatbox captioned, "Daughter Christmas 1989." Her colorful attire is designed after American folk art.

Handcrafted, 3" tall
625QX443-2, $6.25 ☐

Son
Dressed for frosty weather, this boy is carrying home a gift that bears the caption: "SON Christmas 1989." His knickers and hose give him an appealing old-fashioned look.

Handcrafted, 3" tall
625QX444-5, $6.25 ☐

Brother
This commemorative caption makes its first appearance in the Keepsake line. The high-top shoe, tied with a real shoelace, is captioned especially for "Brother." The two snowflake insignia are dated "1989," and the bottom of the shoe carries a warm compliment: " No one else can fill your shoes!"

Handcrafted, 3¼" tall
725QX445-2, $7.25 ☐

Sister
Reminiscent of American folk art designs, a trio of large Christmas hearts appears on a porcelain white ball for Sister. The caption is divided into three parts — one under each heart: "Having a Sister means happiness. Loving a Sister means joy. Christmas 1989."

Porcelain White Glass, 2⅞" diam.
475QX279-2, $4.75 ☐

Grandparents
A delicately painted winter scene on a pearly glass ball evokes memories of home and Christmas and grandparents. The caption is a loving compliment: "Grandparents make Christmas welcome in their home and in their hearts. 1989."

Peach Glass, 2⅞" diam.
475QX277-2, $4.75 ☐

Grandmother
This teardrop ball is decorated with a bright garland of poinsettias, pinecones, and Christmas greenery. The stencil-look design frames the caption: "A Grandmother is thought about often... and always with love. Christmas 1989."

Tan Glass, 2⅞" diam.
475QX277-5, $4.75 ☐

Granddaughter
A wonderful time is had by all the forest animals as they skate around this two-toned glass ball. The "star skater" bunny etches "1989" in the ice. Caption: "A Granddaughter makes Christmastime one of the best times of all!"

White and Green Glass, 2⅞" diam.
475QX278-2, $4.75 ☐

Grandson
The stylized design on this glass ball shows Santa climbing into a chimney. He's bringing gifts to the children of the house. Printed on Santa's bag, the caption reflects a similar idea: "A Grandson brings joy to everyone...just like Christmas!" One of the reindeer wears a blanket dated "1989."

Periwinkle Blue Glass, 2⅞" diam.
475QX278-5, $4.75 ☐

Godchild
Etched onto an acrylic oval, a little angel delivers a big star with a very special wish: "Merry Christmas, Godchild 1989." The stars, caption, and angel's halo are stamped in gold foil.

Acrylic, 2¾" tall
625QX311-2, $6.25 ☐

Sweetheart

A bicycle built for two will take a pair of Sweethearts on a charming holiday ride. The wheels turn, and a package in the basket carries the caption: "Merry Christmas, Sweetheart." The license plate reads "1989."

Handcrafted, 4⅝" wide
975QX486-5, $9.75 □

First Christmas Together

Real branches were used to mold the heart-shaped wreath in this romantic ornament. Attached with red cord, the dangling swing proved irresistible to these loving chipmunks! Caption: "Our First Christmas Together 1989."

Handcrafted, 3½" tall
975QX485-2, $9.75 □

First Christmas Together

In a wintry forest, two deer share the beauty of the season. This acrylic commemorative is engraved on both front and back to enhance the dimension of the design. A caption in gold foil reads, "Our First Christmas Together 1989."

Acrylic, 2⁷/₁₆" tall
675QX383-2, $6.75 □

First Christmas Together

Mr. Polar Bear holds a sprig of mistletoe above his sweetie! The back of this ball presents a whimsical back view of the same couple. Front Caption: "Our First Christmas Together." Back Caption: " 'Tis the season to be cuddly." The year date, "1989," appears on a log.

White Glass, 2⅞" diam.
475QX273-2, $4.75 □

Five Years Together

A wintry Christmas scene provides a lovely setting for two serene swans. They symbolize a couple celebrating their fifth Christmas. The sentiment on the back of the teardrop ball reflects the mood of the design: "Love makes the world a beautiful place to be." Front Caption: "Five Years Together Christmas 1989."

Blue-Green Glass, 2⅞" diam.
475QX273-5, $4.75 □

Ten Years Together

What could be more romantic than sharing Christmas number ten in a one-horse open sleigh? This nostalgic scene appears on a white teardrop ball carrying the caption: "Ten Years Together Christmas 1989." Back Caption: "There's joy in each season when there's love in our hearts."

White Glass, 2⅞" diam.
475QX274-2, $4.75 □

Sweetheart, First Christmas Together: Handcrafted, Acrylic

First Christmas Together, Five Years Together, Ten Years Together

Commemorative Photoholders: 25 Years Together, 40 Years Together, 50 Years Together

Language of Love, World of Love

Commemorative Photoholders

Three lovely photoholders offer a unique way to preserve a memory forever. Fashioned in snow-white fine porcelain, each ornament is a bas-relief wreath decorated with a hand-painted green and red holly design. The photoholders carry front and back captions and are tied with fabric ribbons.

Twenty-Five Years Together Photoholder

Printed in silver, the front caption of this ornament reads, "25 Years Together." The back caption, printed in red, says "Christmas 1989." The photoholder is tied with a red ribbon.

Hand-Painted Fine Porcelain, 3¾" tall
875QX485-5, $8.75 □

Forty Years Together Photoholder

Both the front and back captions of this new commemorative in the Keepsake line are printed in red. The ornament is tied with a ribbon of holiday green. Front Caption: "40 Years Together." Back Caption: "Christmas 1989."

Hand-Painted Fine Porcelain, 3¾" tall
875QX545-2, $8.75 □

Fifty Years Together Photoholder

This photoholder, suspended from a white fabric ribbon, is captioned on the front in gold: "50 Years Together." The reverse side carries the caption in red: "Christmas 1989."

Hand-Painted Fine Porcelain, 3¾" tall
875QX486-2, $8.75 □

Language of Love

Just as Christmas goes with love, so does the poinsettia complement the romantic sentiment on this acrylic ornament. Beneath the etched flower, the gold foil caption reads, "Together...the most caring word in the language of love. 1989."

Acrylic, 3" tall
625QX383-5, $6.25 □

World of Love

"Christmas is here, and the sound of love echoes all over the world." This sentiment, as well as the artwork on the glass ball, reflects the loving spirit of brotherhood. The design shows children from countries throughout the world enjoying the season together. A sleigh carries the date "1989."

Silver-Blue Glass, 2⅞" diam.
475QX274-5, $4.75 □

Friendship Time

Like special friends everywhere, the two charmingly gowned mice in this teacup enjoy a holiday chat. The cup carries a warm message: "... Always time for friendship." Back: "Christmas 1989."

Handcrafted, 2½" tall
975QX413-2, $9.75 ☐

Teacher

Homework is lots of fun for this little student. He has a leather tail and is writing a message in his book: "For a Nice Teacher." The other books are titled, "Christmas" and "1989." The word "From" appears on the bottom of the ornament, indicating a place for personalization.

Handcrafted, 2¼" tall
575QX412-5, $5.75 ☐

New Home

Two lovely tones of pearlized lavender and white provide the background for a nostalgic winter scene. The home and tree glow with light, illustrating the words of the caption: "Love is the light in the window of your new home. Christmas 1989."

Lavender and White Glass, 2⅞" diam.
475QX275-5, $4.75 ☐

Festive Year

The combination of silver foil and glowing color gives this acrylic ornament the appearance of stained glass. Specially designed to be appropriate for business use, the ornament carries a silver foil date, "1989," and is bezeled in chrome.

Acrylic, 2¹³/₁₆" tall
775QX384-2, $7.75 ☐

Gratitude

Bezeled in brass, this acrylic ornament evokes feelings of warmth and friendship. A finely etched design of holly tied with flowing ribbons accents the graceful calligraphy of the sentiment. Gold Foil Caption: "Thankful feelings flow from heart to heart at Christmas. 1989."

Acrylic, 2¾" diam.
675QX385-2, $6.75 ☐

From Our Home to Yours

Intricately etched onto an acrylic oval, the design on this ornament reminds us of home and friends we hold dear. Two cardinals perch atop a mailbox filled with gifts. Below, an old-fashioned milk can and festive packages complete the welcoming scene. Stamped in gold foil, the caption reads, "From Our Home to Yours at Christmas." The address on the mailbox reads, "1989."

Acrylic, 3½" tall
625QX384-5, $6.25 ☐

Friendship Time, Teacher, New Home

Festive Year, Gratitude, From Our Home to Yours

Joyful Trio, Old-World Gnome, Hoppy Holidays, The First Christmas

Holiday Traditions

Joyful Trio
A whimsical trio of angels sings in perfect harmony, even though one of the three is having a little bit of halo trouble! Wearing pearly white, the angels symbolize Christmas love and brotherhood. Caption: "Joy To You."

Handcrafted, 2¼" tall
975QX437-2, $9.75 ☐

Old-World Gnome
The special care that is equated with Old-World craftsmanship went into the creation of this appealing gnome. Dressed like Santa, he has been sculpted and painted to resemble a fine European wood carving.

Handcrafted, 3¼" tall
775QX434-5, $7.75 ☐

Hoppy Holidays
Christmas shopping can be fun when you ride through the store like this flocked bunny. He's selected two gifts, captioned, "Hoppy Holidays" and "1989."

Handcrafted, 2¾" tall
775QX469-2, $7.75 ☐

The First Christmas
A beloved Bible quotation is stamped in gold foil on the back of this exquisitely sculpted cameo design. Framed in brass, the Nativity scene is presented in an ivory color, with subtle variations in shading and depth, against a blue background. Caption: "For unto you is born this day in the city of David a Saviour, which is Christ the Lord. LUKE 2:11."

Cameo, 3⅛" tall
775QX547-5, $7.75 ☐

Gentle Fawn
This fawn's softly flocked coat emphasizes his large shiny eyes that melt your heart. He wears a real fabric ribbon and a sprig of fabric holly.

Handcrafted, 2 5/16" tall
775QX548-5, $7.75 ☐

Spencer® Sparrow, Esq.
Spencer enjoys a holiday hors d'oeuvre! Molded from a real cracker, his sesame treat carries the Spencer® Sparrow logo on the bottom.

Handcrafted, 1 ¾" tall
675QX431-2, $6.75 ☐

SNOOPY® and WOODSTOCK
These two dapper pals perform a snappy soft-shoe routine for the holidays. Coordinated from head to toe, they wear matching costumes complete with shiny top hats and bow ties.

Handcrafted, 3" tall
675QX433-2, $6.75 ☐

Gentle Fawn, Spencer® Sparrow, Esq., SNOOPY® and WOODSTOCK

Sweet Memories Photoholder

Designed to look like peppermint candy, this handcrafted wreath will hold a treasured photograph. The wreath is trimmed with a handcrafted bow and holly. Back Caption: "Christmas is the perfect time for making sweet memories. 1989."

Handcrafted, 3 1/16" tall
675QX438-5, $6.75 ☐

Stocking Kitten

The fluffy pompom on the toe of the brightly flocked stocking is irresistible to this playful kitten. He'll soon discover it's a real pompom.

Handcrafted, 2 3/4" tall
675QX456-5, $6.75 ☐

George Washington Bicentennial

A beautifully engraved acrylic commemorates the bicentennial of the first American presidential inauguration. The likeness of Washington, designed to resemble his most famous portrait, is framed by a stamped gold foil caption. Top Caption: "1789 - 1989 American Bicentennial." Bottom Caption: "George Washington First Presidential Inauguration."

Acrylic, 3 9/16" tall
625QX386-2, $6.25 ☐

Feliz Navidad

Elaborately textured to look like a real piñata, this colorful bull carries a cheery message on both sides of his fringed blanket: "Feliz Navidad." This phrase is the traditional Christmas greeting in Spanish. The bull's tail is made out of red yarn.

Handcrafted, 2" tall
675QX439-2, $6.75 ☐

Cranberry Bunny

This flocked bunny likes cranberries almost as much as carrots! He strings a garland of "cranberry" beads with a real metal needle and fabric thread.

Handcrafted, 2 5/8" tall
575QX426-2, $5.75 ☐

Deer Disguise

Two children peek out of their reindeer costume to decide which way they're going. When the front wants to veer right, the back wants to step left! The costume is fashioned with antlers and tail, and a little patch at the back.

Handcrafted, 1 3/4" tall
575QX426-5, $5.75 ☐

Paddington™ Bear

Paddington™ likes to play his drum almost as much as he likes to eat honey! His name, "Paddington™ Bear," appears on his hat, and his familiar tag is attached with a red fabric ribbon. Tag: "Please look after this Bear Thank You."

Handcrafted, 4 1/4" tall
575QX429-2, $5.75 ☐

Sweet Memories Photoholder, Stocking Kitten, George Washington Bicentennial

Feliz Navidad, Cranberry Bunny, Deer Disguise, Paddington™ Bear

Snowplow Santa, Kristy Claus, Here's the Pitch, North Pole Jogger

Snowplow Santa

The North Pole is the ideal place for skiing. Wearing a shirt that carries the caption, "I ♥ Skiing," Santa executes a smooth snowplow stop.

Handcrafted, 2 5/16" tall
575QX420-5, $5.75 ☐

Kristy Claus

A vision on ice, Santa's lovely spouse is about to perform a figure eight. She wears green earmuffs and a skating sweater captioned with her name: "Kristy Claus."

Handcrafted, 2 15/16" tall
575QX424-5, $5.75 ☐

Here's the Pitch

It's the ninth inning, and Santa is only one strike away from a perfect game! His major league outfit includes a red baseball cap, cleated shoes, and a uniform printed with his name and number: "SANTA 1."

Handcrafted, 2 3/8" tall
575QX545-5, $5.75 ☐

North Pole Jogger

The race is on, and Santa leads the pack! He listens to his favorite North Pole radio station as he nears the finish line. His red jogging suit carries the caption: "North Pole 1K."

Handcrafted, 2 1/4" tall
575QX546-2, $5.75 ☐

Camera Claus

Of course Santa is an expert photographer. Everyone who sees him greets him with a smile! Carrying his camera and camera case, he plans to fill an entire album with snapshots.

Handcrafted, 2 3/8" tall
575QX546-5, $5.75 ☐

Sea Santa

Santa has all the latest scuba gear, including flippers, goggles, and a silvery tank of air. Perhaps he's bringing gifts to his pals beneath the ocean. Caption: "Sea Santa."

Handcrafted, 2 1/2" tall
575QX415-2, $5.75 ☐

Gym Dandy

Santa stays in shape by exercising with small weights. He has a lifetime membership at the local health club advertised on his shirt: "Kringle's Gym."

Handcrafted, 2 1/2" tall
575QX418-5, $5.75 ☐

On the Links

Santa shows perfect form as he practices his golf swing. He's fashionably attired in matching slacks and sunshade, a diamond patterned shirt, and white golf shoes.

Handcrafted, 2 1/2" tall
575QX419-2, $5.75 ☐

Camera Claus, Sea Santa, Gym Dandy, On the Links

Special Delivery

An appealing, flocked seal couldn't wait till Christmas to pop out of his box. Decorated with a fancy handcrafted red bow, the box carries the pun: "Signed, Sealed, & Delivered." The ornament displays the words "For:" and "From:" on the bottom, indicating a place for personalization.

Handcrafted, 2" tall
525QX432-5, $5.25 ☐

Hang in There

Why won't the little mouse let go of his hat? Because it looks just like the one Santa wears! Dressed for Christmas, the mouse wears a tiny green fabric bow on his leather tail. The loop at the top of his hat provides a place for your ornament hook.

Handcrafted, 3" tall
525QX430-5, $5.25 ☐

Owliday Greetings

Holding a bright red banner, an owl flies from coast to coast spreading cheer. He's covered with carefully textured feathers. Caption: "Owliday Greetings!"

Handcrafted, 1½" tall
400QX436-5, $4.00 ☐

Norman Rockwell

A holly garland frames two covers from *The Saturday Evening Post*, reproduced on a gold glass ball. The picture of Santa looking at a globe is captioned: "*Post* Cover: December 4, 1926." The picture of Santa at his desk is captioned: "*Post* Cover December 21, 1935." The ornament also carries the captions: "Norman Rockwell, Famous Holiday Covers From *The Saturday Evening Post*," and "Santa's seen in the smiles the whole world is sharing, he's found where there's friendship and loving and caring. 1989."

Gold Glass, 2⅞" diam.
475QX276-2, $4.75 ☐

PEANUTS® - A Charlie Brown Christmas

The entire PEANUTS® gang appears on a sky blue ball to commemorate their TV special. The ball shows scenes from the program, including a picture of Charlie Brown's thin little Christmas tree. Captions: " 'A Charlie Brown Christmas' Television Special, Happy 25th Anniversary 1965-1989" and "Christmas...season of love."

Blue Glass, 2⅞" diam.
475QX276-5, $4.75 ☐

Party Line

Reissue from 1988. (See 1988 Annual Collection.)

Handcrafted, 1¾" tall
875QX476-1, $8.75 ☐

Special Delivery, Hang in There, Owliday Greetings

Norman Rockwell, PEANUTS® - A Charlie Brown Christmas

Peek-a-Boo Kitties

Reissue from 1988. (See 1988 Annual Collection.)

Handcrafted, 5" tall
750QX487-1, $7.50 ☐

Polar Bowler

Reissue from 1988. (See 1988 Annual Collection.)

Handcrafted, 2¼" tall
575QX478-4, $5.75 ☐

Gone Fishing

Reissue from 1988. (See 1988 Annual Collection.)

Handcrafted, 2½" tall
575QX479-4, $5.75 ☐

Teeny Taster

Reissue from 1988. (See 1988 Annual Collection.)

Handcrafted, 4⅜" tall
475QX418-1, $4.75 ☐

A KISS™ From Santa

Reissue from 1988. (See 1988 Annual Collection).

Handcrafted, 3¼" tall
450QX482-1, $4.50 ☐

OREO®
Chocolate Sandwich Cookies

Reissue from 1988. (See 1988 Annual Collection.)

Handcrafted, 1⅞" diam.
400QX481-4, $4.00 ☐

Sparkling Snowflake, Festive Angel, Graceful Swan

New Attractions

Sparkling Snowflake
Separate layers of brass, each etched with a delicate lacy design, form a shimmery snowflake. The year date "1989" is etched in the center.
Brass, 3⅜" tall
775QX547-2, $7.75 □

Festive Angel
To create a dimensional design, this glowing angel is fashioned from intricately etched layers of brass. Her wings are formed by pieces of brass that arch together, giving the ornament added depth and beauty.
Dimensional Brass, 3 5/16" tall
675QX463-5, $6.75 □

Graceful Swan
Elaborately etched and detailed, this dimensional brass swan is a vision of elegance. The gleaming wings are created with layers of brass that come together in a graceful curve.
Dimensional Brass, 2¼" tall
675QX464-2, $6.75 □

Nostalgic Lamb
Sculpted to show detail, the lamb's curly coat keeps him warm as he rides in his bright red cart. He has a smooth journey because the cart is fitted with revolving wheels.
Handcrafted, 1¾" tall
675QX466-5, $6.75 □

Horse Weathervane
The craft of creating weathervanes has existed for many centuries throughout Europe. However, it was in America that the weathervane became appreciated as a unique art form. This steed, galloping into the wind, is fashioned to resemble hand-carved wood.
Handcrafted, 3" tall
575QX463-2, $5.75 □

Rooster Weathervane
Designed to capture the look of American folk art, this colorful rooster makes sure everyone is awake on Christmas morning.
Handcrafted, 3½" tall
575QX467-5, $5.75 □

Country Cat
Wearing a polka dot scarf and resting on a real fabric pillow, this cat is ready to ride to a country Christmas picnic. The old-fashioned cart has revolving wheels and is designed to look like wood.
Handcrafted, 2¼" tall
625QX467-2, $6.25 □

Nostalgic Lamb, Horse Weathervane, Rooster Weathervane, Country Cat

Nutshell Trio

The 1989 Keepsake line offered three nutshell ornaments. Each of the shells was molded from a real walnut and designed with hinges. The ornaments can be displayed open and stored closed.

Nutshell Holiday

Two tiny stockings hang from the mantel of the fireplace inside a cozy nutshell. A sampler on the wall says the shell is "Home Sweet Home." The sleepy kitten catches a quick nap before Santa arrives.

Handcrafted, 1½" tall
575QX465-2, $5.75 □

Nutshell Dreams

Inside his nutshell bedroom, a child dreams of Christmas toys. He doesn't know that Santa is in the other room. The jolly old elf motions for quiet because he doesn't want to disturb the little dreamer.

Handcrafted, 1½" tall
575QX465-5, $5.75 □

Nutshell Workshop

A nutshell is transformed into Santa's Workshop. Two industrious elves work as snow falls gently past the windows. One elf fashions a little wooden horse while the other finishes a wagon.

Handcrafted, 1½" tall
575QX487-2, $5.75 □

Claus Construction

Wearing a belt engraved with his name, "NICK," and a shiny hard hat, Santa oversees the progress of his new workshop. Four cords hold the big beam steady so it can display the company name, "Claus Construction."

Handcrafted, 4¾" tall
775QX488-5, $7.75 □

Cactus Cowboy

Trimmed with strings of tiny "cranberry" beads, a colorful cactus is ready for a western-style Christmas. He has a sprig of holly on his cowboy hat and holds a golden star dated "1989."

Handcrafted, 3½" tall
675QX411-2, $6.75 □

Rodney Reindeer

Rodney's a very flexible fellow! You can bend his arms and legs to point in any direction. This ability will come in handy when he guides Santa on Christmas Eve. Rodney's map is titled "Reindeer Route 89," and his shirt says "Rodney."

Handcrafted, 5" tall
675QX407-2, $6.75 □

Nutshell Holiday, Nutshell Dreams, Nutshell Workshop

Claus Construction, Cactus Cowboy, Rodney Reindeer

Let's Play, Wiggly Snowman, Balancing Elf, TV Break

Cool Swing, Goin' South

Peppermint Clown

Let's Play

The puppy and kitten just can't stand still. When you tap the ornament, the pup will wiggle his head up and down, and the kitten will waggle her tail side to side! Their house is decorated with garland. On the roof, two little paw prints and a "1989" trail are visible in the pearly snow.

Handcrafted, 2¾" tall
725QX488-2, $7.25 ☐

TV Break

What is Santa's favorite TV program when he's on vacation? "All My Reindeer," of course. He watches every afternoon as he relaxes in the sun. His hammock was molded from a piece of cloth woven out of string. Suspended from hooks on each end, the ornament can hang from one branch or between two branches of your tree.

Handcrafted, 3" tall
625QX409-2, $6.25 ☐

Balancing Elf

Standing in the center of a big brass ring, one of Santa's elves is ready to perform a circus act. The two brass bells will jingle when you tap them gently.

Handcrafted, 4⅜" tall
675QX489-5, $6.75 ☐

Wiggly Snowman

Tap this pearly snowman gently, and he'll wiggle and jiggle his head. He's wearing a great big smile because he thinks nodding to friends is lots of fun!

Handcrafted, 4¾" tall
675QX489-2, $6.75 ☐

Cool Swing

Wearing a warm winter hat, a penguin has a "cool" time on his icy swing. When you tap the acrylic ice cube gently, it swings back and forth. Caption: "Have a Cool Christmas!"

Handcrafted, Acrylic, 3½" tall
625QX487-5, $6.25 ☐

Goin' South

The suitcase this little mouse carries says he's "Goin' South." He's ready for sun and fun, wearing shiny green sunglasses as he rides on the Redbird Express.

Handcrafted, 1⅞" tall
425QX410-5, $4.25 ☐

Peppermint Clown

Riding a peppermint unicycle, this clown looks forward to entertaining his fans at Christmas. He's painted by hand and fashioned of the finest porcelain.

Hand-Painted Fine Porcelain, 5 1/32" tall
2475QX450-5, $24.75 ☐

Artists' Favorites

Merry-Go-Round Unicorn

Fine porcelain is the ideal medium for portraying a unicorn, says artist Anita Marra. The smooth material captures the subtle lines and grace of the mythical creature. The candy cane pole adds a bright touch of color to the hand-painted design.

Hand-Painted Fine Porcelain, 2 ¹¹/₁₆" tall
Artist: Anita Marra
1075QX447-2, $10.75 ☐

Carousel Zebra

Artist Linda Sickman relates that she's always been fascinated with animals, especially the unusual ones. It follows that her vision of a carousel would include a colorful zebra. The saddle is decorated with roses and dated "1989" on both sides.

Handcrafted, 2 ¾" tall
Artist: Linda Sickman
925QX451-5, $9.25 ☐

Mail Call

A raccoon mail carrier delivers a letter at his own "Branch Office." The whimsical pun and sculpted ornament are the works of artist Ed Seale. He says he enjoys sculpting designs of animals displaying human traits, and then creating an original pun to match! The word "MAIL" is carved in the branch.

Handcrafted, 3" tall
Artist: Ed Seale
875QX452-2, $8.75 ☐

Baby Partridge

Watching the birds who visit his front yard at home is one of artist John Francis' favorite pastimes. Although he hasn't seen a "Baby Partridge" recently, he enjoyed sculpting one for the Keepsake line. The ornament attaches to your tree with a special clip.

Handcrafted, 2 ¾" tall
Artist: John Francis
675QX452-5, $6.75 ☐

Playful Angel

Like a real child, the sculpted angel in this design has fun playing on her swing. The angels that artist Donna Lee creates often act and look like real children, sometimes even getting into mischief! This angel wears a brass halo, and her swing attaches to the frosted acrylic cloud with a red cord.

Handcrafted, Acrylic, 3 ⅛" tall
Artist: Donna Lee
675QX453-5, $6.75 ☐

Merry-Go-Round Unicorn, Carousel Zebra

Mail Call, Baby Partridge, Playful Angel

Cherry Jubilee, Bear-i-Tone

Cherry Jubilee

This little mouse is having a very sweet Christmas. The cherry is bigger than he is — a whimsical size relationship that artist Linda Sickman enjoyed portraying in her cherry tart design. The ornament attaches to your tree from the cherry's stem.

Handcrafted, 2¼" tall
Artist: Linda Sickman
500QX453-2, $5.00 ☐

Bear-i-Tone

Artist Bob Siedler says he pays careful attention to the poses and expressions of the animals he sculpts so that each will have its own personality. This softly flocked bear's personality can only be described as totally lovable. He plays a real metal triangle.

Handcrafted, 2¼" tall
Artist: Bob Siedler
475QX454-2, $4.75 ☐

Special Edition

The Ornament Express

There's a load of excitement at the North Pole Station because this year's Special Edition is a train set featuring three different ornaments. Each is a distinctive collectible that can be displayed separately or with the other two. All of the designs have revolving wheels and carry a caption. Dated "1989," the colorful "Locomotive" has a silvery cowcatcher and a gold-colored whistle. The "Coal Car" is captioned "Ornament Express" and holds a bag of tiny reproductions of past years' Keepsake Ornaments: the 1983 "Tin Locomotive"; 1986 "Porcelain Bear"; and 1985 "Old-Fashioned Toy Shop." The 1987 "Goldfinch" perches on top of the bag. The "Caboose," designed with a bright red roof, completes the set and carries a wish for the holiday: "Merry Christmas."

Handcrafted, Locomotive 2¼" tall, Coal Car 1¾" tall, Caboose 2⅛" tall
2200QX580-5, $22.00 ☐

The Ornament Express

Collectible Series

Christmas Kitty—First Edition
This new Keepsake Ornament series is the first to feature a cat as its star. Each year, the "Christmas Kitty" series will offer a different fine porcelain kitten, festively dressed for the season. Painted by hand, the 1989 edition wears a soft green frock and a crisp white apron. She carries a basket of holiday poinsettias.

Hand-Painted Fine Porcelain, 3 3/16" tall
1475QX544-5, $14.75 ☐

Winter Surprise—First Edition
A sparkling winter world will appear inside each peek-through ornament in this new series. In the first edition, two penguins decorate their Christmas tree. The bottle-brush evergreen is covered with fluffy snow and tiny ornaments. One of the gift boxes under the tree carries a "1989" tag. The penguins will return every year, bringing a new "Winter Surprise" inside their egg-shaped universe.

Handcrafted, 3¼" tall
1075QX427-2, $10.75 ☐

Hark! It's Herald—First Edition
The whimsical name of this new series, a word play on the famous carol, is especially significant because Herald is a musician. He'll play a different instrument each year. Wearing a hat topped with a real pompom, the elf plays golden chimes dated "1989."

Handcrafted, 2" tall
675QX455-5, $6.75 ☐

CRAYOLA® Crayon
—First Edition
This series is off to a great start with a "Bright Journey" on a CRAYOLA® Crayon raft. Crayons bring back childhood memories of merry hours spent coloring and drawing at Christmas and all through the year. The animals in this series will show how inventive they can be with CRAYOLA® Crayons and often with the box as well. Each crayon in the raft is labeled "CRAYOLA® CRAYON," and the sail, dated "1989," duplicates a portion of the box design.

Handcrafted, 3" tall
875QX435-2, $8.75 ☐

The Gift Bringers—First Edition
The myriad traditions of the Christmas "Gift Bringer" have captured the hearts of young and old throughout the world. This new ball series will bring a beautifully painted interpretation of a different gift bringer each year for five years. The first edition features one of the most famous, identified in the caption: "The Gift Bringers, St. Nicholas, Christmas 1989."

White Glass, 2⅞" diam.
500QX279-5, $5.00 ☐

Christmas Kitty, Winter Surprise

Hark! It's Herald, CRAYOLA® Crayon, The Gift Bringers

Mary's Angels, Collector's Plate, Mr. and Mrs. Claus

Reindeer Champs, Betsey Clark: Home for Christmas

Mary's Angels—Second Edition

Pretty "Bluebell" says a Christmas prayer as she kneels on a frosted acrylic cloud. Designed by Mary Hamilton, the angel has pearly wings and wears a light blue gown that inspired her flower name. The artist's signature, "Mary," appears on the bottom of the cloud.

Handcrafted, Acrylic, 3″ tall
575QX454-5, $5.75   ☐

Collector's Plate—Third Edition

Christmas morning is a thrilling time for the two children pictured on this fine porcelain miniature plate. Even their little dog is excited about all the toys Santa has delivered. Caption: "Morning of Wonder 1989." Plate stand included.

Fine Porcelain, 3¼″ diam.
825QX461-2, $8.25   ☐

Mr. and Mrs. Claus
—Fourth Edition

The North Pole's most famous couple performs a "Holiday Duet." Brightly dressed in Christmas red and green, they join voices to sing a favorite carol identified on the front of the songbook: "We Wish You a Merry Christmas 1989." The caption continues inside: "...And a Happy New Year!"

Handcrafted, 3¼″ tall
1325QX457-5, $13.25   ☐

Reindeer Champs
—Fourth Edition

When it comes to tennis, there's no match for this reindeer! Wearing a sporty tennis shirt printed with her name, "Vixen" wins the North Pole Cup every season. Her racket is dated "89."

Handcrafted, 3¼″ tall
775QX456-2, $7.75   ☐

Betsey Clark: Home for Christmas
—Fourth Edition

Wintertime is a favorite time for Betsey and her friends. One little girl ties a warm scarf around her dog's neck, while the others build a snowman and feed the birds. Caption: "Fun and friendship are the things the Christmas season always brings!" The doghouse has a "1989" address.

Blue-Green Glass, 2⅞″ diam.
500QX230-2, $5.00   ☐

Windows of the World
—Fifth Edition
Inside his cozy Alpine cottage, a little German boy plays carols on his concertina. A brightly decorated tree fills the room with holiday cheer. The year date "1989" appears on the back of the ornament, and a Christmas greeting in German appears on the front: "Fröhliche Weihnachten."

Handcrafted, 3¾" tall
1075QX462-5, $10.75   □

Miniature Crèche
—Fifth and Final Edition
Standing on the rooftop, an angel watches over the final ornament in this series. The double-doored design is called a *retablo*. The original *retablos* were miniatures of full sized altar pieces, and were brought to the Americas by the Spanish in the 16th century. Decorated in the style of Southwestern art, this *retablo* Nativity can be displayed open or closed.

Handcrafted, 3" tall
925QX459-2, $9.25   □

Nostalgic Houses and Shops
—Sixth Edition
Christmas is a busy time at the "U.S. Post Office." The main branch is located downstairs. There, behind an old-fashioned counter, packages and letters are ready to be sorted into the correct compartments and pigeon holes. Upstairs, an office is furnished with files, a desk and a telephone for the mysterious occupant identified on the window: "Investigator Private." The front door carries the address "1989."

Handcrafted, 4¼" tall
1425QX458-2, $14.25   □

Wood Childhood Ornaments
—Sixth and Final Edition
The "Wooden Truck" is hauling a festive cargo—a load of bottle-brush Christmas trees! Fashioned with movable wheels and a yarn pull string, the truck rolls down the last stretch of highway because it's the final ornament in the series. A license plate on the back reads "1989."

Wood, 2" tall
775QX459-5, $7.75   □

Twelve Days of Christmas
—Sixth Edition
A graceful design of six geese is etched onto an acrylic heart to illustrate the sixth day of the beloved Christmas carol. The gold foil-stamped caption reads, "The Twelve Days of Christmas 1989...six geese a-laying..."

Acrylic, 3" tall
675QX381-2, $6.75   □

Windows of the World, Miniature Crèche

Nostalgic Houses and Shops, Wood Childhood Ornaments, Twelve Days of Christmas

Porcelain Bear, Tin Locomotive, Rocking Horse

Porcelain Bear—Seventh Edition

Santa has delivered a big bag of peppermint candy to "Cinnamon Bear." He'll eat one piece now and save the rest for later. Carefully painted by hand, the bear is fashioned of fine porcelain.

Hand-Painted Fine Porcelain, 2″ tall
875QX461-5, $8.75   ☐

Tin Locomotive —Eighth and Final Edition

This last "Tin Locomotive" is one of the most complex designs in the series. As the train's wheels turn, the brass bell jingles merrily, signaling that it's been a great journey for all! Caption: "1989."

Pressed Tin, 3 ³/₁₆″ tall
1475QX460-2, $14.75   ☐

Rocking Horse—Ninth Edition

The pony's black yarn tail flies in the wind as he gallops on his gray and aqua rockers, dated "1989." Fitted with shiny brass stirrups and a red yarn rein, the russet and black bay waits for his rider to join him on Christmas.

Handcrafted, 4″ wide
1075QX462-2, $10.75   ☐

Frosty Friends—Tenth Edition

The little husky puppy and his Eskimo pal are rushing to a Christmas party. They hope their sled glides quickly over the sloping acrylic ice because they're carrying a gift captioned "1989."

Handcrafted, Acrylic, 2½″ tall
925QX457-2, $9.25   ☐

Here Comes Santa —Eleventh Edition

Santa leans out of his customized "Christmas Caboose" to wave at his fans. He's hung a stocking in the window on the opposite side of the car for the teddy bear sitting there. The last passenger is a toy soldier on the roof. He'll have fun playing with the ball that's resting on the back platform. The caboose has movable wheels and is dated "1989."

Handcrafted, 3¼″ tall
1475QX458-5, $14.75   ☐

Thimble —Twelfth and Final Edition

This adorable "Thimble Puppy," with his soulful eyes, melts hearts wherever he goes. Wearing a red handcrafted bow, he sits inside a silvery thimble in this last ornament in the series.

Handcrafted, 1¾″ tall
575QX455-2, $5.75   ☐

Frosty Friends, Here Comes Santa, Thimble

THE 1984 LIGHTED ORNAMENT COLLECTION

Ornament collectors surged with excitement as Lighted Ornaments were introduced by Hallmark in 1984. This marked the first time ever that the brilliance of Christmas tree lights was added to ornaments. The warm glow they created was truly special.

The care and attention to detail put into the design of Lighted Ornaments was unsurpassed. As one designer told me, "The only difficulty I had was deciding when the design was complete. I kept on wanting to add more details." Indeed, the designers have added wonderful touches to the ornaments such as real lace trim on the windows of "Santa's Arrival" and the tiny carolers inside the "Village Church."

The beauty of light graced a variety of ornament designs in 1984. Light showed through the windows of a handcrafted house in "Santa's Workshop," lit up the sky of a panorama ball in "Nativity," and even illuminated a traffic signal in "City Lights."

Village Church
This precious clapboard village church looks as if it could have been taken straight from a New England green. The towering spire, topped with a gold cross, rests on a green shingled roof. Candle-lit windows and opened door reveal the inside appointments and holiday carolers.
Handcrafted, 4⅝" tall
1500QLX702-1, $15.00 ☐

Sugarplum Cottage
Sugar-coated gumdrops, lollipops, and peppermint candy canes make this brightly lit cottage look good enough to eat!
Handcrafted, 3" tall
1100QLX701-1, $11.00 ☐

City Lights
To control the flow of forest traffic, Santa and a friendly "traffic squirrel" perch atop the four-way signal that illuminates an animal in each light's surface.
Handcrafted, 3½" tall
1000QLX701-4, $10.00 ☐

Santa's Workshop
Light shines out the window of Santa's workshop as he offers a toy bunny to his cottontail visitor standing outside.
Peek-Through Ball, 3½" diam.
1300QLX700-4, $13.00 ☐

Village Church

Sugarplum Cottage

City Lights

Santa's Workshop

Santa's Arrival

'Tis the night before Christmas and a little boy is sleeping soundly, dreaming of holiday toys. Inside the softly lit room the child's puppy peers out the window and holds up a list of gifts for Santa to read. The window is framed by genuine white eyelet lace.

Peek-Through Ball, 3½" diam.
1300QLX702-4, $13.00 ☐

Nativity

A beautiful vision of that Holy Night. The dark blue of the ball creates a perfect contrast to the warm glow from inside that illuminates the windows of Bethlehem and the Christmas sky. Caption: "Christmas...light through the darkness...love through the ages."

Panorama Ball, 3½" diam.
1200QLX700-1, $12.00 ☐

Stained Glass

Colorful old-fashioned stained glass design glows like a beautiful window when lit.

Golden Classic Shape, 3⅞" diam.
800QLX703-1, $8.00 ☐

Christmas in the Forest

Silver ball evokes the feeling of a moonlit night in a snowy forest. The design looks almost three-dimensional with its varying hues of white, gray and blue, subtly lit from within. Caption: "Christmas ... magical, memorable time of year."

Silver Classic Shape, 3⅞" diam.
800QLX703-4, $8.00 ☐

Brass Carousel

All lit up and reminiscent of an amusement park merry-go-round. You can almost hear the music play as Santa rides by in a gift-laden sleigh pulled by reindeer.

Etched Brass, 3" tall
900QLX707-1, $9.00 ☐

All Are Precious

A delicately etched shepherd, lamb and donkey stand in awe of the brilliant star that sends rays of light over the world. Gold foil-stamped caption: "All are precious in His sight..."

Acrylic, 4" tall
800QLX704-4, $8.00 ☐

Santa's Arrival

Nativity

Stained Glass

Christmas in the Forest

Brass Carousel

All Are Precious

THE 1985 LIGHTED ORNAMENT COLLECTION

The 1985 Lighted Ornament line was filled with firsts. It contained the first series, the first commemorative, the first property and the first dated ornaments to appear in the new lighted format.

A sleepy mouse reading by candlelight was the first edition in the new "Chris Mouse" Collectible Series. Fashioned to clip onto the tree, this ornament is ideal for people who collect designs of mice as well as series ornaments. The first commemorative in the lighted line was "Baby's First Christmas." This caption, the most popular in the Keepsake line, appeared on a handcrafted carousel complete with acrylic ponies. Both the carousel and the ornament called "Swiss Cheese Lane" were dated "1985." Completing the list of firsts in the Lighted Ornament line was the property "Katybeth." This handcrafted angel was seen painting a beautiful acrylic rainbow, shown to wonderful advantage by the addition of light.

Baby's First Christmas
The carousel is aglow with light as two teddy bears ride 'round and 'round on their frosted acrylic ponies. The ornament is trimmed in gold and displays tiny mirrors on the canopy. Caption: "Baby's First Christmas 1985."

Handcrafted, Acrylic, 4″ tall
1650QLX700-5, $16.50 ☐

Katybeth
Both the rainbow and cloud, made of acrylic, light up for the angel Katybeth. She is busily painting the rainbow red, gold and blue so it will shine for the holidays.

Handcrafted, Acrylic, 3⅝″ tall
1075QLX710-2, $10.75 ☐

Chris Mouse—First Edition
This little mouse is the first collectible series in the Lighted Ornament line. Dressed in his blue nightshirt, he's reading a Christmas story before bedtime. The candle illuminates his book, dated "1985." The ornament attaches to your tree with a specially designed clip.

Handcrafted, 3⅞″ tall
1250QLX703-2, $12.50 ☐

Swiss Cheese Lane
A yellow wedge of Swiss cheese forms the adorable A-frame home for a pair of mice. Through holes in the cheese, you can see the brightly lit interior. One mouse sleeps soundly in a four-poster bed while the other trims the tree in a cozy living room warmed by a potbellied stove and decorated with a braided rug. Caption: "1985 Swiss Cheese Lane."

Handcrafted, 2⅝″ tall
1300QLX706-5, $13.00 ☐

Baby's First Christmas

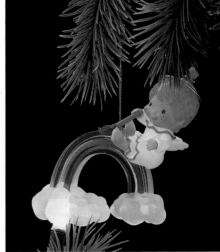
Katybeth

Chris Mouse

Swiss Cheese Lane

Mr. and Mrs. Santa

It's getting late, but Mrs. Santa's home is brightly lit as she trims the tree. Santa waves at passersby from the big picture window and invites us to view the festivities. Inside there's a cozy fireplace with a clock on the mantle and pictures on the wall. The roof is covered with sparkling snow and the chimney wears a holiday wreath. A sign above the door says "The Kringles."

Handcrafted, 3″ tall
1450QLX705-2, $14.50   ☐

Little Red Schoolhouse

The lights are on and the play is about to begin in this intricately detailed schoolhouse. Inside, three parents watch the children perform in a Christmas pageant. Wonderful touches of authenticity include a flagpole in the front, a woodpile at the back, a blackboard inside showing a "chalk" rendition of Bethlehem and a real bell hanging above the front door. A banner announces a "School Play Tonight."

Handcrafted, 2⅝″ tall
1575QLX711-2, $15.75   ☐

Love Wreath

A delicate wreath, decorated with hearts and ribbon, is etched in acrylic and softly illuminated. The special message is stamped in gold foil: "Christmas happens in the heart."

Acrylic, 3½″ tall
850QLX702-5, $8.50   ☐

Sugarplum Cottage

Reissue from 1984. (See 1984 Lighted Ornament Collection.)

Handcrafted, 3″ tall
1100QLX701-1, $11.00

Village Church

Reissue from 1984. (See 1984 Lighted Ornament Collection.)

Handcrafted, 4⅝″ tall
1500QLX702-1, $15.00

Santa's Workshop

Reissue from 1984. (See 1984 Lighted Ornament Collection.)

Peek-Through Ball, 3½″ diam.
1300QLX700-4, $13.00

Nativity

Reissue from 1984. (See 1984 Lighted Ornament Collection.)

Panorama Ball, 3½″ diam.
1200QLX700-1, $12.00

All Are Precious

Reissue from 1984. (See 1984 Lighted Ornament Collection.)

Acrylic, 4″ tall
800QLX704-4, $8.00

Mr. and Mrs. Santa

Little Red Schoolhouse

Love Wreath

Christmas Eve Visit

Christmas Eve Visit

An exquisite, intricately etched brass house glows with light to welcome Santa and his reindeer as they make their rounds on Christmas Eve.

Etched Brass, 2″ tall
1200QLX710-5, $12.00   ☐

Season of Beauty

Blanketed in white, the world reflects the peace and beauty of Christmas. This softly illuminated ornament offers the message, "May joy come into your world as Christmas comes into your heart."

Red and Gold Classic Shape, 3¼″ diam.
800QLX712-2, $8.00   ☐

Season of Beauty

THE 1986 LIGHTED ORNAMENT COLLECTION

Lights! Motion! Action! Hallmark used these three words to describe 1986 Lighted Ornaments and, indeed, the line offered these features and much, much more!

The 1986 ornaments displayed technical advances that quickly enthralled ornament collectors. In addition to light, the designs included electronic motion, scenes that changed before your eyes, and a unique holographic effect.

Two of the ornaments featured motion that was circular. The train in "Village Express" and the sleigh in "Christmas Sleigh Ride" circle scenes under the domes. The motion in "Lighting the Tree" is forward and backward. In this design, Santa moves forward to light the tree and then moves back to his original position.

The "changing scene" feature debuted in the "Baby's First Christmas" ornament. Through the use of alternating lights, it appears as if there are two different scenes inside the panorama ball. Scene one shows a kitten gazing into the empty night sky; scene two shows Santa and his reindeer flying past the window. The new "hologram" feature premiered in the design called "Santa's On His Way." Inside a panorama ball Santa seems to be flying over the city.

Two new Collectible Series were added in '86. The "Sugarplum Fairy" dances in the "Nutcracker Ballet" in the first ornament of the "Christmas Classics" series. And the new "Santa and Sparky" series began with the "light and motion" ornament, "Lighting the Tree."

The commemorative portion of the lighted line increased by three in 1986. The "First Christmas Together" and "Christmas Sleigh Ride" offer romantic designs, and "Sharing Friendship" carries a warm message for a special friend.

Baby's First Christmas

First Christmas Together

Santa and Sparky

Baby's First Christmas
Sitting in front of the nursery window, by the glowing tree, a kitten looks out into the night. Suddenly Santa and his reindeer appear in the sky to deliver something special for Baby. A light illuminates the first scene and then alternates to the second, creating the magical "changing scene" effect. Caption on Front: "Baby's First Christmas 1986." On Back: "There's someone new on Santa's list, someone small and dear, someone Santa's sure to love and visit every year!"

Panorama Ball, 3⅝" tall
Light and Changing Scene
1950QLX710-3, $19.50 ☐

First Christmas Together
A happy teddy bear couple celebrates their first year with a ride in a brightly lit hot-air balloon captioned, "First Christmas Together." Anchoring the basket is a brass heart etched with the date "1986." This caption appears for the first time in the lighted ornament line.

Handcrafted, 5¼" tall
1400QLX707-3, $14.00 ☐

Santa and Sparky — First Edition
Sparky watches eagerly as Santa moves forward and lights the Christmas tree. The excitement of "Lighting the Tree" is just one of the many things Santa will share with his penguin pal each year in this new series. A gift is tagged "1986."

Handcrafted, 4⅟₁₆" tall
Light and Motion
2200QLX703-3, $22.00 ☐

Christmas Classics — First Edition
The stage is aglow for the Sugarplum Fairy. She strikes a classic pose and waits for the "Nutcracker Ballet" to begin. Painted in pearly pastels, the stage carries the caption, "Sugarplum Fairy 1986." This series will feature scenes from classic Christmas poems, ballets, or stories.

Handcrafted, 4½" tall
1750QLX704-3, $17.50 ☐

Chris Mouse — Second Edition
A night-light gives this mouse's pinecone bower a cheery glow. His cozy retreat, molded from a real pinecone, is the perfect place for "Chris Mouse Dreams." The treetop address is "1986."

Handcrafted, 3¾" tall
1300QLX705-6, $13.00 ☐

Village Express
A train circles the peaceful mountain village, chugging over the trestle and through the tunnel, as comforting light from the buildings shines across the newly fallen snow.

Handcrafted, 3½" tall
Light and Motion
2450QLX707-2, $24.50 ☐

Christmas Sleigh Ride
The lamp sheds a romantic light on the couple gliding around the park in an old-fashioned sleigh. The bottle-brush trees and dome are sprinkled with snowflakes. Caption: "Love's precious moments shine forever in the heart."

Handcrafted, 3¾" tall
Light and Motion
2450QLX701-2, $24.50 ☐

Santa's On His Way
When you look inside this ornament, it appears as if Santa and his reindeer are magically flying above the city. A silvery hologram, fashioned through laser photography, creates the three-dimensional effect. Caption: "A time of magical moments and dreams come true...Christmas."

Panorama Ball, 3⅝" tall
Light and Hologram
1500QLX711-5, $15.00 ☐

General Store
Warmed by a potbelly stove, this old-fashioned "General Store" is bright and cozy. The woman by the counter may have come in to buy a tree after seeing the sign "Christmas Trees 50¢."

Handcrafted, 2¹¹⁄₁₆" tall
1575QLX705-3, $15.75 ☐

Christmas Classics

Chris Mouse

Village Express

Christmas Sleigh Ride

Santa's On His Way

General Store

Gentle Blessings

The animals in the stable silently gather around the cradle to watch the Baby as He sleeps. Light shines from above, shedding a warm glow on the intricately sculpted scene. Caption: "Baby Jesus, sweetly sleeping, you have blessed our world today."

Panorama Ball, 3⅝" tall
1500QLX708-3, $15.00

Keep on Glowin'!

One of Santa's elves takes time out for some fun and slides down a glowing icicle.

Handcrafted, 2⁷⁄₁₆" tall
1000QLX707-6, $10.00

Santa's Snack

Santa has raided the refrigerator! Wearing a striped nightshirt and reindeer slippers, he carries his sandwich creation back to bed. A candle in his hand lights his way.

Handcrafted, 2¹⁵⁄₁₆" tall
1000QLX706-6, $10.00

Merry Christmas Bell

Bathed in soft light, this acrylic bell is decorated with etched holiday flowers and greenery. "Merry Christmas," the universal message of the season, is etched into the center.

Acrylic, 5⁹⁄₁₆" tall
850QLX709-3, $8.50

Sharing Friendship

An etched poinsettia provides a festive accent to the gold foil sentiment stamped on this illuminated acrylic teardrop. Caption: "Friendship is a special kind of sharing. 1986."

Acrylic, 5⁵⁄₁₆" tall
850QLX706-3, $8.50

Mr. and Mrs. Santa

Reissue from 1985. (See 1985 Lighted Ornament Collection.)

Handcrafted, 3" tall
1450QLX705-2, $14.50

Sugarplum Cottage

Reissue from 1984. (See 1984 Lighted Ornament Collection.)

Handcrafted, 3" tall
1100QLX701-1, $11.00

Gentle Blessings

Keep on Glowin'!

Santa's Snack

Merry Christmas Bell

Sharing Friendship

THE 1987 KEEPSAKE MAGIC COLLECTION

In 1987, the Holiday Magic Lighted Ornament Collection was given a new name — the "Keepsake Magic Ornament Collection." In the eyes of collectors, this name change reflected the line's exciting — almost magical — innovations. But what entitled the lighted line to claim the name Keepsake, according to Hallmark, was the increased number of original designs and commemoratives, and the wide variety of features and formats. Hallmark knows that "Keepsake" has come to mean something very special to collectors.

Each "light and motion" ornament in the '87 line displays a different kind of electronic movement. In "Christmas Morning," two children slide down a bannister. Sparky, the penguin in the series ornament "Perfect Portrait," moves forward to illuminate a sculpture of Santa and then retreats to admire his work. And both the man and woman in "Loving Holiday" come out of their house to meet face to face before moving back again.

The "changing scene" ornament this year was "Angelic Messengers." Shepherds watch their flocks under a starry sky until the scene changes, filling the sky with angels. A brand-new feature was "blinking lights," which appeared in the silvery "Good Cheer Blimp."

The 1987 Keepsake Magic line also introduced Hallmark's first lighted photoholder, "Memories Are Forever." The design is festive and suitable for a photo of either an adult or child.

Baby's First Christmas
Trimmed with a lacy fabric curtain, this brightly lit window is the perfect place for Teddy to paint his announcement: "Baby's First Christmas." Baby's blocks on the sill show the date "1987."
Handcrafted, 3¾" tall
1350QLX704-9, $13.50 ☐

First Christmas Together
The igloo glows with light and love. Holding hands by a bottle-brush tree, the polar bear couple celebrates a special Christmas. A red heart displays the year "1987," and "First Christmas Together" is etched in the snow at the top.
Handcrafted, 2⅝" tall
1150QLX708-7, $11.50 ☐

Santa and Sparky—Second Edition
Santa is so pleased with Sparky's latest work of art. Sparky moves forward and lights the sculpture so Santa can see it's a "Perfect Portrait." The pedestal dates the creation "1987."
Handcrafted, 4¹⁄₁₆" tall
Light and Motion
1950QLX701-9, $19.50 ☐

Christmas Classics — Second Edition
The elegantly draped stage is set for Dickens' classic work identified in gold on the front: "A Christmas Carol." Illuminated in the center, a happy Scrooge gives gifts to Tiny Tim while Mr. and Mrs. Cratchet look on. Date on Back: "1987"
Handcrafted, 4³⁄₁₆" tall
1600QLX702-9, $16.00 ☐

Baby's First Christmas

First Christmas Together

Santa and Sparky

Christmas Classics

Chris Mouse — Third Edition

Designed to look like stained glass, this lamp sheds a lovely "Chris Mouse Glow." The little mouse has a leather tail and wears a cozy nightshirt dated "87."

Handcrafted, 4⅛" tall
1100QLX705-7, $11.00 ☐

Christmas Morning

It's early morning in this cheery Victorian home, and the tree is lit in anticipation of the children's arrival. They slide down the garland-trimmed bannister eager to open their gifts from Santa.

Handcrafted, 4⁵⁄₁₆" tall
Light and Motion
2450QLX701-3, $24.50 ☐

Loving Holiday

Light glows softly within this ornament sculpted to resemble an old-fashioned glockenspiel. The loving couple move forward to meet under the clock and then move back, knowing their encounter will be repeated. Caption: "Precious times are spent with those we love."

Handcrafted, 3⅝" tall
Light and Motion
2200QLX701-6, $22.00 ☐

Angelic Messengers

A light shines on the shepherds watching their flocks at night. Then suddenly, the sky is aglow and angels appear, bringing the joyous tidings of Christmas. Light alternates from the shepherds to the angels, creating the "changing scene" effect. Caption: "Love came down at Christmas, love all lovely, love divine. Love was born at Christmas, star and angels gave the sign."

Panorama Ball, 3⅝" tall
Light and Changing Scene
1875QLX711-3, $18.75 ☐

Good Cheer Blimp

The blinking lights on the "Good Cheer Blimp" light the way for Santa on Christmas Eve. He leans over the side of the gondola to spot his next stop. The "blinking-lights" feature appears for the first time in the Keepsake Magic line.

Handcrafted, 3¹⁄₁₆" tall
Blinking Lights
1600QLX704-6, $16.00 ☐

Train Station

At the "Train Station" the lights are on, and the ticket window is open for business. A mother and child sit inside where it's warm and cozy while the ticket taker waits for customers. Caption Over Front Door and Side Window: "Merriville." Under Front Window: "Tickets."

Handcrafted, 3³⁄₁₆" tall
1275QLX703-9, $12.75 ☐

Chris Mouse

Christmas Morning

Loving Holiday

Angelic Messengers

Good Cheer Blimp

Train Station

Keeping Cozy
Dressed in flocked long johns, Santa is warmed by the burning embers inside this potbelly stove. A little mouse is keeping warm, too.

Handcrafted, 2½" tall
1175QLX704-7, $11.75 ☐

Lacy Brass Snowflake
Fashioned with two interlocking brass snowflakes, this ornament sparkles with light. The back piece is solid with a delicately etched design. The front piece looks like filigree with its lacy etched and cut-out design.

Brass, 2½" tall
1150QLX709-7, $11.50 ☐

Meowy Christmas!
Two playful kittens frolic on a glowing translucent red heart. They're having a happy holiday time playing with the handcrafted white bow that decorates the ornament.

Handcrafted, 2½" tall
1000QLX708-9, $10.00 ☐

Memories Are Forever Photoholder
This is the first photoholder in the Keepsake Magic line. It illuminates one of your cherished photographs in a frame decorated with red and green bas-relief holly. Caption on Back: "Memory keeps each Christmas forever warm and bright."

Handcrafted, 3⅞" tall
850QLX706-7, $8.50 ☐

Season for Friendship
The bevel of this acrylic teardrop has a delicately cut design that reflects light like crystal. Christmas greenery etched at the top of the ornament is accented with gold foil berries that complement the matching foil caption: "How lovely the season when it's filled with friendship."

Acrylic, 5⁵⁄₁₆" tall
850QLX706-9, $8.50 ☐

Bright Noel
Within a glowing star, the word "Noel" shines for the holiday. This contemporary acrylic ornament captures the look of neon lighting.

Acrylic, 5½" tall
700QLX705,-9, $7.00 ☐

Village Express
Reissue from 1986. (See 1986 Lighted Ornament Collection.)

Handcrafted, 3½" tall
Light and Motion
2450QLX707-2, $24.50

Keep on Glowin'!
Reissue from 1986. (See 1986 Lighted Ornament Collection.)

Handcrafted, 2⁷⁄₁₆" tall
1000QLX707-6, $10.00

Keeping Cozy

Lacy Brass Snowflake

Meowy Christmas!

Memories Are Forever Photoholder

Season for Friendship

Bright Noel

$\mathcal{T}$HE 1988
KEEPSAKE MAGIC COLLECTION

The Keepsake Magic Collection celebrated its fifth year by offering collectors more choices than ever before. There was a greater variety of subjects...nearly twice as many designs as the 1984 debut year...and twice the number of light-and-motion ornaments as in 1986 when that innovation brightened the line.

The continuing expansion of the Keepsake Magic Collection reflects its popularity with collectors who appreciate uniqueness and intricacy of design, as well as with holiday shoppers who seek meaningful gifts that will give pleasure for years to come.

"Country Express" was a particular favorite of collectors this year. The second light-and-motion train offered by Hallmark, this ornament is also designated as one of the Artists' Favorites. Five other new light-and-motion designs joined the line in 1988, including the third and final edition of the Collectible Series "Santa and Sparky." This was also the first year that the "Baby's First Christmas" design featured light and motion. Other light-and-motion designs included "Parade of the Toys," "Skater's Waltz," and "Last-Minute Hug."

The Hallmark artists also created ornaments based on personal memories and experiences that many collectors share. The blinking light design "Kitty Capers" delights everyone who's watched a kitten play with string or yarn — or strands of Christmas tree lights! "Christmas Is Magic" evokes memories of making shadow figures on a wall or windowshade. And "Festive Feeder" is a dream-come-true for bird watchers who provide treats for their feathered friends.

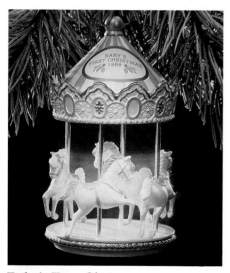

Baby's First Christmas
The carousel goes 'round and 'round to celebrate Baby's arrival. A tiny light under the blue-and-white canopy casts a magical glow on four prancing horses. The ornament is hand painted in pearly colors, and the elaborate cornice is accented with gold. Caption: "Baby's First Christmas 1988."

Handcrafted, 4" tall
Light and Motion
2400QLX718-4, $24.00 ☐

First Christmas Together
Two white mice share a holly wreath decorated with colorful handcrafted candies. The sparkly gumdrops glow with light. The caption on the back of the ornament reads, "Our First Christmas Together 1988."

Handcrafted, 3" tall
1200QLX702-7, $12.00 ☐

Santa and Sparky — Third and Final Edition
In the grand finale for the series, Santa and his penguin pal take to the stage with their magical act titled "On With the Show." As Santa steps forward to wave his wand, Sparky pops up out of the hat. The footlight is lighted, and displays the year date "1988."

Handcrafted, 4" tall
Light and Motion
1950QLX719-1, $19.50 ☐

Christmas Classics —
Third Edition
Santa's in the living room, ready to fill the stockings with care. He's opened his bag of gifts, and paused to admire the decorated bottle-brush tree. A light shines down from the second floor, where the residents are snug in their bed. Caption: "Night Before Christmas 1988." (Note: The series symbol was inadvertently omitted from this ornament.)

Handcrafted, 4½" tall
1500QLX716-1, $15.00 ☐

Chris Mouse — Fourth Edition
Wearing his favorite blue nightshirt and red Santa cap, this mouse is busily polishing his golden "Chris Mouse Star." The star is lighted and carries the year date "1988" in the center. The mouse has a leather tail.

Handcrafted, 2½" tall
875QLX715-4, $8.75 ☐

Parade of the Toys
The jack-in-the-box pops up and down, as he rides in a red wagon pulled by the toy soldier. A doll pushes a baby carriage, and three ducks join the happy procession around a lighted Christmas tree.

Handcrafted, 3½" tall
Light and Motion
2450QLX719-4, $24.50 ☐

Skater's Waltz
Sharing the fun of an old-fashioned holiday, two ice-skating couples glide gracefully around an outdoor rink. They are dressed in elaborate Victorian-style clothing. Their way is lighted by the glow from a lamppost, amidst a grove of snow-covered evergreen trees.

Handcrafted, 3½" tall
Light and Motion
2450QLX720-1, $24.50 ☐

Last-Minute Hug
It's almost time for Santa to leave on his annual journey. As he comes out one doorway, Mrs. Claus hurries out another. They'll hug, then part, beneath the porch light. Pearly snow decorates the roof of their Swiss chalet style home.

Handcrafted, 3½" tall
Light and Motion
2200QLX718-1, $22.00 ☐

Kitty Capers
This little kitten has made a delightful discovery — a strand of tiny lights that blink on and off. The glow is reflected by handcrafted, pearly white tissue paper in a red box labeled "Christmas Lights." The ornament clips to a branch on your tree.

Handcrafted, 1½" tall
Blinking Lights
1300QLX716-4, $13.00 ☐

Christmas Classics

Chris Mouse

Parade of the Toys

Skater's Waltz

Last-Minute Hug

Kitty Capers

Christmas Is Magic

Santa shows his puppy how to make a reindeer silhouette appear on the window shade. He's using the puppy's Christmas bones and the light from a table lantern. A real lace cloth covers the table. Caption: "Christmas is Magic!"

Handcrafted, 3¼" tall
1200QLX717-1, $12.00 ☐

Heavenly Glow

Holding a Christmas star, this lovely angel symbolizes the hope and joy of the season. The glowing brass ornament combines openwork designs and carefully etched patterns. It is lighted from within.

Brass, 3" tall
1175QLX711-4, $11.75 ☐

Radiant Tree

Light shimmers through ten triangular panels, which taper upward to form the sides of this richly detailed brass tree. Each panel features cut-out designs of the dove of peace. An unusual brass hanger repeats the shape of a tree. Viewed from above, the ornament is shaped like a star.

Brass, 3¼"tall
1175QLX712-1, $11.75 ☐

Festive Feeder

A cardinal, goldfinch, and bluebird enjoy a holiday feast provided by a friendly bird watcher. The lantern-style feeder has a light beneath its roof, and colorful Christmas lights on top. Tiny tracks are visible in the snow on the roof.

Handcrafted, 3" tall
1150QLX720-4, $11.50 ☐

Circling the Globe

Santa holds the all-time record for on-time delivery. His secret may be this big lighted globe he uses to chart the course for his ambitious Christmas Eve journey.

Handcrafted, 2¾" tall
1050QLX712-4, $10.50 ☐

Bearly Reaching

When it's time to turn out the lights, this little bear is ready to help. He's standing on the candle holder with a candle snuffer in hand. The lighted flame casts a golden glow. Pearly white handcrafted wax decorates the top of the candle. The ornament clips to a branch of your tree.

Handcrafted, 4" tall
950QLX715-1, $9.50 ☐

Christmas Is Magic

Heavenly Glow

Radiant Tree

Festive Feeder

Circling the Globe

Bearly Reaching

Moonlit Nap

Who needs a night-light when you can drift off to sleep on a glowing crescent moon! This little angel wears pearly white wings and a light blue gown. A bright yellow star with a red Christmas stocking swings from the tip of the moon.

Handcrafted, 2¾" tall
875QLX713-4, $8.75 ☐

Tree of Friendship

Light cascades softly down the sides of this shimmering acrylic tree. The beveled edges add depth and sparkle to the design. Delicate snowflakes and a caption are etched into the clear acrylic. Caption: "Friends decorate the holiday with Love."

Acrylic, 4¼" tall
850QLX710-4, $8.50 ☐

Song of Christmas

The cardinal — one of America's favorite songbirds — is featured in this elaborate, etched acrylic. The edges of the circular design are beveled and faceted to reflect the light. The cardinal perches on a holly branch accented with berries. Caption: "Song of Christmas."

Acrylic, 3½" tall
850QLX711-1, $8.50 ☐

Christmas Morning

Reissue from 1987. (See 1987 Keepsake Magic Collection.)

Handcrafted, 4⁵⁄₁₆" tall
Light and Motion
2450QLX701-3, $24.50 ☐

Artists' Favorites

Country Express

Right on schedule! The engine, boxcar, and little red caboose disappear into a mountain tunnel and then return. The railroad tracks are on top of a trestle which has the appearance of real wooden timbers. Lighted buildings and a bonfire in the center of town add a warm glow. Artist Linda Sickman says she designed the scene based on memories of visits to old Western towns.

Handcrafted, 3½" tall
Artist: Linda Sickman
Light and Motion
2450QLX721-1, $24.50 ☐

Moonlit Nap

Tree of Friendship

Song of Christmas

Country Express

*T*HE 1989
KEEPSAKE MAGIC COLLECTION

The Keepsake Magic line came alive with the sound of music! In addition to light and motion, two ornaments offered favorite melodies. The "Baby's First Christmas" design plays "Brahms' Lullaby," and the "Joyous Carolers" design plays "We Wish You a Merry Christmas."

The electronic motion became more "magical" and complex, and appeared in a wide variety of designs: Two mice ride a seesaw spoon in "Loving Spoonful"; an airplane soars across the sky in "Spirit of St. Nick"; a cobbler finishes a shoe in "Tiny Tinker"; a mother mouse rocks her baby in "Baby's First Christmas"; four musicians perform for you in "Joyous Carolers"; and not one but two trains circle the city in "Metro Express."

Flickering light was a new feature in '89. It adds an effective touch of realism to the romantic fireplace in the "First Christmas Together" design and to the burning embers in the whimsical "Busy Beaver" ornament.

A new light and motion Collectible Series, and a new property debuted this year. The series, called "Forest Frolics," features woodland animals. And the property is a beloved classic — "Rudolph the Red-Nosed Reindeer®." Collectors of crystal and bells were especially pleased with the sparkling "Holiday Bell." This elegant ornament is made of 24 percent lead crystal.

Baby's First Christmas
As Mama mouse rocks in her comfortable rocking chair, a touch of her foot makes the cradle rock, too. The mother (or grandmother) mouse reads "Bedtime Tales" by the soft glow of the nursery lamp until Baby is fast asleep. This design is among the first in the Keepsake Magic collection to feature music and plays "Brahms' Lullaby." Front Caption: "Baby's First Christmas 1989." Back Caption: "Christmas and babies fill a home with love."

Handcrafted, 4½" tall
Light, Motion, and Music
3000QLX727-2, $30.00

First Christmas Together
The flickering light from the fireplace casts dancing shadows inside a cozy bungalow. Two stockings, hanging from the mantel, and two tiny mugs on the hearth belong to the couple celebrating a special Christmas. The side windows are adorned with curtains molded from real lace. A heart above the fireplace holds the caption: "Our First Christmas Together," and "1989" appears on the front of the house.

Handcrafted, 3¾" tall
Flickering Light
1750QLX734-2, $17.50

Forest Frolics — First Edition
The forest was never merrier! This new series will feature woodland animals having fun and celebrating the season each year. In the first edition, a raccoon, bunny, squirrel and skunk ski on the trail that circles the lighted candy cane. A little bluebird perches on a sign that reads, "Merry Christmas! 1989."

Handcrafted, 4 7/16" tall
Light and Motion
2450QLX728-2, $24.50

Christmas Classics — Fourth Edition

Inside the stable, the "Little Drummer Boy" kneels beside the manger to play a drum-song for the newborn Baby. Light shines down from above, illuminating this favorite story. The year date "1989" appears on the cradle.

Handcrafted, 3¼″ tall
1350QLX724-2, $13.50 ☐

Chris Mouse — Fifth Edition

The light in the lantern turns this mouse's marshmallow a toasty brown as he enjoys a "Chris Mouse Cookout." The lantern, decorated with holly, is dated "1989."

Handcrafted, 4½″ tall
950QLX722-5, $9.50 ☐

Joyous Carolers

This design, the second of two musical ornaments in the 1989 Keepsake Magic line, plays "We Wish You a Merry Christmas." Standing in front of a glowing streetlight, a trio of Victorian carolers sings favorite tunes to the melody of a violin. The women's heads turn from side to side as if they are moving with the rhythm of the music. The tall gentleman moves as if he is playing the violin.

Handcrafted, 4 11/16″ tall
Light, Motion, and Music
3000QLX729-5, $30.00 ☐

Tiny Tinker

An elfin cobbler puts the finishing touches on a shoe for one of his friends. The light from his lantern shows him where to hammer every gold-toned nail. His bench, crafted to look like wood, displays his name: "Tiny Tinker." A toy locomotive rests on the back of the bench waiting for the elf's attention.

Handcrafted, 3″ tall
Light and Motion
1950QLX717-4, $19.50 ☐

Rudolph the Red-Nosed Reindeer®

The most famous reindeer of all is ready to guide Santa on Christmas Eve. His red nose glows to light the way, but Santa has some additional help this year. The sleigh is equipped with blinking lights.

Handcrafted, 2½″ tall
Blinking Lights
1950QLX725-2, $19.50 ☐

Loving Spoonful

Two ingenious mice have created a mouse-sized seesaw out of a spoon and a sugar bowl filled with glowing sugar crystals. The mice, fashioned with leather tails, ride up and down throughout the holiday. Caption: "Sugar."

Handcrafted, 3½″ tall
Light and Motion
1950QLX726-2, $19.50 ☐

Christmas Classics

Chris Mouse

Joyous Carolers

Tiny Tinker

Rudolph the Red-Nosed Reindeer®

Loving Spoonful

Holiday Bell

An intricately faceted bell, created in 24 percent lead crystal, sparkles with light. Two lacy snowflakes decorate the sides, and the date "1989" is printed on the front in gold. The shimmery brass cap was designed especially for this ornament.

Lead Crystal, 3½" tall
1750QLX722-2, $17.50 ☐

Busy Beaver

On a frosty night, an enterprising beaver warms his paws over the flickering fire in the barrel. He's selling "Fresh Cut Trees" to his pals in the forest. A bunny is hiding in one of the trees on the back of the design.

Handcrafted, 2⅞" tall
Flickering Light
1750QLX724-5, $17.50 ☐

Backstage Bear

Preening before his mirror, a little bear dresses in his Santa costume for his stage debut. The mirror, which actually reflects the bear's image, is framed by tiny lighted bulbs. Someone has written a message across the top: "Beary Christmas!" Golden stars on the bear's coffee mug and on the back of the ornament indicate that this fellow has a bright future. His "SCRIPT" is an updated version of a familiar poem: "Beary Christmas to all and to all a good night."

Handcrafted, 3⅜" tall
1350QLX721-5, $13.50 ☐

The Animals Speak

A beloved Christmas story is illustrated inside a lighted panorama ball. An angel listens as the animals speak on the night the Holy Child is born. The town of Bethlehem and the Christmas Star can be seen in the background. The figures are painted in soft colors, and the caption appears in gold: "The animals rejoiced and spoke, the star shone bright above, for on this day a child was born to touch the world with love."

Panorama Ball, 3⅝" tall
1350QLX723-2, $13.50 ☐

Angel Melody

This baroque-shaped acrylic ornament has been delicately etched and faceted to reflect the light. Wearing a flowing gown, the angel in the center plays her trumpet to herald great tidings of comfort and joy.

Acrylic, 5 ⁷⁄₁₆" tall
950QLX720-2, $9.50 ☐

Unicorn Fantasy

A gazebo provides the fanciful setting for this beautifully sculpted unicorn. His pearly white coat and silvery hooves and horn shimmer with the light as he brings his magical world to your tree.

Handcrafted, 4½" tall
950QLX723-5, $9.50 ☐

Holiday Bell

Busy Beaver

Backstage Bear

The Animals Speak

Angel Melody

Unicorn Fantasy

Moonlit Nap
Reissue from 1988. (See 1988 Keepsake Magic Collection.)

Handcrafted, 2¾" tall
875QLX713-4, $8.75 ☐

Kringle's Toy Shop
Reissue. (See 1988 Added Attractions.)

Handcrafted, 3⅝" tall
Light and Motion
2450QLX701-7, $24.50 ☐

Artists' Favorites

Metro Express
It's Christmastime in the city! Two trains, traveling one after the other on two separate levels of track, circle the lighted city. Sculptor Linda Sickman, who created this ornament, says, "The two trains carry commuters to snow-covered skyscrapers, and bring shoppers to see the holiday lights." You can see two additional trains in tunnels at the bottom of the design.

Handcrafted, 3½" tall
Artist: Linda Sickman
Light and Motion
2800QLX727-5, $28.00 ☐

Spirit of St. Nick
With all of his experience flying every Christmas, Santa would make a terrific barnstormer, says Ed Seale, sculptor of this unique ornament. The scene evokes the early days of aviation. While two people watch from below, Santa's biplane swoops and soars over the barn and lighted house. A path in the snow spells, "Merry Christmas!" and the banner behind the plane reads, "Spirit of St. Nick."

Handcrafted, 4" tall
Artist: Ed Seale
Light and Motion
2450QLX728-5, $24.50 ☐

Metro Express

Spirit of St. Nick

$\mathcal{T}$HE 1988 KEEPSAKE MINIATURE COLLECTION

Collectors will remember 1988 as the year that Keepsake Miniature Ornaments first appeared in Hallmark retail stores — and quickly disappeared to become cherished collectibles.

The new miniature collection was presented as a complete line, expressed in a wide range of formats including handcrafted, ball, brass, acrylic, and wood. Three dated, commemorative captions were issued: "Baby's First Christmas," "First Christmas Together," and "Mother."

The first editions of four miniature Collectible Series debuted, introducing a charming "Old English Village," nostalgic "Rocking Horse," friendly "Penguin Pal," and playful "Kittens in Toyland."

Two ornaments were miniature versions of favorite Keepsake designs from years past. They are "Jolly St. Nick" and "Sneaker Mouse." The miniature "Skater's Waltz" ornament was adapted from a popular Keepsake Magic Ornament design.

Commemoratives

Baby's First Christmas
Attached to a pearly white star dated "1988," this nostalgic wood-look swing gives Baby an ideal place to view the holiday festivities. The caption on the blanket confirms that it's "Baby's 1st" Christmas. Baby wears a red handcrafted bow.

Handcrafted, 2½" tall
600QXM574-4, $6.00 ☐

Mother
A red puffed-heart design, symbolizing love, is topped with mistletoe. The golden inscription reads, "Mother 1988."

Handcrafted, 1¼" tall
300QXM572-4, $3.00 ☐

First Christmas Together
The popular country motif is expressed in this straw wreath, wrapped with red and green fabric ribbons. The wreath is decorated with dried flowers and a heart made of real wood. Caption: "Our First Christmas 1988."

Wood, Straw, 1¾" tall
400QXM574-1, $4.00 ☐

Love Is Forever
A delicate acrylic oval conveys the sentiment, "Love is forever." The caption is stamped in gold foil, and the sparkling clear ornament is faceted to reflect the light.

Acrylic, 1" tall
200QXM577-4, $2.00 ☐

Baby's First Christmas

Mother

First Christmas Together

Love Is Forever

Friends Share Joy

Holy Family

Jolly St. Nick

Skater's Waltz

Sweet Dreams

Three Little Kitties

Snuggly Skater

Happy Santa

Friends Share Joy

This graceful acrylic is faceted on both the front and back for maximum brilliance. The message, "Friends Share Joy," is stamped in gold foil on the clear acrylic.

Acrylic, 1 ¼" tall
200QXM576-4, $2.00 ☐

Holiday Traditions

Holy Family

The reverence and joy of the First Christmas are portrayed with intricate detail and careful hand-painting in this miniature Nativity scene.

Handcrafted, 1 ¾" tall
850QXM561-1, $8.50 ☐

Jolly St. Nick

This miniature ornament is patterned after and carries the same name as the Special Edition in the 1986 Keepsake line. It depicts the jolly old elf in the style popularized by cartoonist Thomas Nast in the 1800s. St. Nick is holding a tiny Christmas stocking, doll, and pull-toy.

Handcrafted, 1 ⅜" tall
800QXM572-1, $8.00 ☐

Skater's Waltz

An elegantly attired couple whirls across the ice on a wintry day. The blades on their skates are painted a silvery color. The design is adapted from a favorite Keepsake Magic Ornament.

Handcrafted, 1 ⅜" tall
700QXM560-1, $7.00 ☐

Sweet Dreams

An angel with tiny white wings sits on the lap of a friendly crescent moon. Both are sound asleep. The pearly, golden moon wears a handcrafted stocking cap.

Handcrafted, 1 ½" tall
700QXM560-4, $7.00 ☐

Three Little Kitties

Arriving in a real willow basket, these frisky little kittens are sure to make Christmas merry. Two petite, red fabric bows on the basket handle suggest that this trio is a gift for someone special.

Handcrafted, Willow, ¹⁵/₁₆" tall
600QXM569-4, $6.00 ☐

Snuggly Skater

Teddy bear can hardly wait for Christmas morning fun. He's snuggled into a white, high-top figure skate. His skate is laced in red and decorated with a real pompom. The silvery blade is carefully crafted to resemble metal.

Handcrafted, 1 ⅛" tall
450QXM571-4, $4.50 ☐

Happy Santa

The only ball ornament in the Keepsake Miniature line this year, this frosted glass design is topped with silvery, filigree leaves. Santa carries a bag of toys with a panda peeking out.

Frosted Glass, ¾" diam.
450QXM561-4, $4.50 ☐

Little Drummer Boy

The appealing Christmas legend of the little boy who gave the only gift he could offer — a song from his drum — is charmingly captured in this miniature ornament. The rosy-cheeked lad wears a green jacket and a red cap.

Handcrafted, 1 ¼" tall
450QXM578-4, $4.50 ☐

Country Wreath

Two little teddy bears nestle inside a handcrafted wreath, which was carefully molded from real twigs. The miniature ornament is decorated with tiny red berries. A red and green fabric ribbon forms a bow at the top of the wreath.

Handcrafted, 1 ½" tall
400QXM573-1, $4.00 ☐

Sneaker Mouse

Adapted from a favorite 1983 Keepsake Ornament, this mouse may be dreaming of running to meet Santa. He's chosen a red and white sneaker, with laces of real cord for his bed.

Handcrafted, ½" tall
400QXM571-1, $4.00 ☐

Joyous Heart

In this wooden ornament, three blocks twirl about inside a heart-shaped frame. The country-style heart is decorated with green holly leaves and red berries. Red letters on the blocks spell out the caption, "JOY."

Wood, 1 ⅛" tall
350QXM569-1, $3.50 ☐

Candy Cane Elf

All caught up in holiday fun, the elf is suspended by the hem of his green smock. His red tights match his Santa cap and the stripes on the peppermint cane.

Handcrafted, ⅞" tall
300QXM570-1, $3.00 ☐

Folk Art Reindeer

Reminiscent of an old-fashioned pull-toy, this wooden ornament is carefully hand-painted in deep colors. The reindeer has wide, green antlers and a decorative saddle to match.

Wood, 1 ⅛" tall
300QXM568-4, $3.00 ☐

Folk Art Lamb

The scalloped silhouette of this snow-white lamb suggests a coat of curly wool. His ears are fashioned of fleecy black fabric, and he rides a colorful pull-cart painted in pink and aqua colors.

Wood, 1" tall
275QXM568-1, $2.75 ☐

Gentle Angel

A peaceful portrait of an angel kneeling in prayer is featured on a lovely etched acrylic teardrop. The faceted edges of the ornament sparkle in the light.

Acrylic, 1 ½" tall
200QXM577-1, $2.00 ☐

Little Drummer Boy

Country Wreath

Sneaker Mouse

Joyous Heart

Candy Cane Elf

Folk Art Reindeer

Folk Art Lamb

Gentle Angel

Brass Star

Brass Angel

Brass Tree

Old English Village

Kittens in Toyland

Rocking Horse

Penguin Pal

Brass Star

Look closely at this lacy silhouette, and discover an intricate series of star-shaped patterns. The elaborate design is etched in shimmering brass.

Brass, 1¼" tall
150QXM566-4, $1.50 ☐

Brass Angel

An angel in a flowing gown raises a heavenly trumpet to proclaim the joy of the season. The delicate filigree design is etched in gleaming brass.

Brass, 1¼" tall
150QXM567-1, $1.50 ☐

Brass Tree

Light dances on, around, and through this glowing etched brass Christmas tree. It is intricately detailed from the ornaments on the branches to a star at the top.

Brass, 1¼" tall
150QXM567-4, $1.50 ☐

Collectible Series

Old English Village — First Edition

This new series reflects the warmth and charm of a country village at Christmastime. This year's "Family Home" is exquisitely detailed with tiny windowpanes, and decorated with wreaths on the bay window and door. Upstairs, the homeowner opens a window to extend a friendly greeting. Pearly snow covers the roof, and the year date "1988" appears over the door.

Handcrafted, 1¼" tall
850QXM563-4, $8.50 ☐

Kittens in Toyland — First Edition

Toyland — what a happy place for a playful kitten! This orange and white one has found a green locomotive and climbed aboard for the first adventure of the series. The train is accented with silvery trim.

Handcrafted, ¾" tall
500QXM562-1, $5.00 ☐

Rocking Horse — First Edition

Adapted from the popular Keepsake Ornament series, this dappled "Rocking Horse" will lead the parade for others to come in this new series. The year date "1988" appears in gold on his red rockers, and his saddle and bridle are painted in bright holiday colors.

Handcrafted, 1⅛" tall
450QXM562-4, $4.50 ☐

Penguin Pal — First Edition

This cheerful fellow is the first in the series, and the first in his flock to finish his holiday shopping. He's delivering a gift package decorated with a handcrafted red bow. And he's dressed for the occasion, in a red Santa hat and green muffler.

Handcrafted, 1" tall
375QXM563-1, $3.75 ☐

$\mathcal{T}$HE 1989
KEEPSAKE MINIATURE COLLECTION

This year's line offered collectors nearly 40 percent more miniature ornament designs than the 1988 debut offer. A majority of the designs were fashioned in the popular handcrafted format, but a variety of other formats were represented as well.

The collection included the first cameo design in an ornament for "Mother," and the first dimensional brass design in an ornament called "Brass Snowflake." Ceramic and porcelain appeared in the "First Christmas Together," "Merry Seal," and "Strollin' Snowman" designs. Wood returned in '89 in the "Puppy Cart" and "Kitty Cart" ornaments, as did acrylic in ornaments named "Bunny Hug," "Holiday Deer," and "Rejoice." Three handcrafted designs are combinations of materials: the "Baby's First Christmas" ornament has an acrylic cloud; the "Special Friend" design includes a willow wreath; and the "Lovebirds" ornament features two brass birds. This design is also a Twirl-About. The birds rotate inside a wreath. The "Folk Art Bunny" features movement as well. His front and hind legs move as if he were running.

Two new Collectible Series made their premiere in '89. The first one stars the North Pole's most famous couple, "The Kringles," in a design that resembles hand-carved wood. And the other series starts a train called "Noel R.R." The first edition is a "Locomotive" which will be followed by different types of railroad cars. The 1989 line also offered the first miniature Special Edition ornament, "Santa's Magic Ride." In this design, an exquisitely detailed unicorn carries Santa on an enchanted Christmas journey.

Commemoratives

Baby's First Christmas
A bunny, a wreath, and a stocking with a teddy bear inside dangle from a frosted acrylic cloud in this mobile for Baby. The caption on the cloud reads, "Baby's 1st Christmas." The stocking is dated " '89."

Handcrafted, Acrylic, 1 ⅜" tall
600QXM573-2, $6.00 ☐

Mother
A serene swan, sculpted in snowy white, is silhouetted against a blue background in a unique cameo design. Bezeled in chrome, the ornament carries captions stamped in silver foil. Front: "Mother." Back: "With Love at Christmas 1989."

Cameo, 1¼" diam.
600QXM564-5, $6.00 ☐

First Christmas Together
The snow white bisque finish of this ceramic ornament emphasizes the bas-relief detail of the delicate design. Inside the wreath, the circlet carries the caption in gold: "Our 1st Christmas 1989."

Ceramic, 1 ⅜" tall
850QXM564-2, $8.50 ☐

Lovebirds
Two lustrous brass birds are framed by a heart of Christmas greenery and holly berries in this romantic Twirl-About ornament. Etched on both sides, the brass birds can be rotated inside the wreath.

Handcrafted, Brass, 1 ⅛" tall
600QXM563-5, $6.00 ☐

Baby's First Christmas

Mother

First Christmas Together

Lovebirds

Special Friend

Sharing a Ride

Little Star Bringer

Santa's Roadster

Load of Cheer, Slow Motion

Merry Seal

Starlit Mouse

Little Soldier

Special Friend

A handcrafted Christmas tree, topped with a bright yellow star, carries the caption for this design: "Special Friend 1989." The wreath is made of willow and is tied with a yarn bow.

Handcrafted, Willow, 1 ⅜" tall
450QXM565-2, $4.50 ☐

Holiday Traditions

Sharing a Ride

Safe and secure on the elf's lap, a teddy bear enjoys a ride on the swing. The elf's facial features, including his flowing beard, have been meticulously sculpted and painted.

Handcrafted, 1 ¼" tall
850QXM576-5, $8.50 ☐

Little Star Bringer

Gowned in shimmery blue, a gentle angel flies on pearly wings to deliver her basket of stars. The star she holds in her hand is dated " '89."

Handcrafted, 1 ¼" tall
600QXM562-2, $6.00 ☐

Santa's Roadster

Santa's got some snazzy new wheels! The car has a silvery front grill and bumpers, and it carries a personalized license plate: "1989."

Handcrafted, ¹⁵/₁₆" tall
600QXM566-5, $6.00 ☐

Load of Cheer

The golden ball ornament is as big as the elf. But that won't prevent this sturdy fella from carrying it to Santa. The ball is dated " '89."

Handcrafted, ⅞" tall
600QXM574-5, $6.00 ☐

Slow Motion

Who needs a sleigh and reindeer when you have a turtle to ride! The chipmunk delivers a teeny pack of gifts — perhaps some nuts for his friends. He wears a Santa cap, and his slow but trusty steed wears a red cap with antlers.

Handcrafted, 1" tall
600QXM575-2, $6.00 ☐

Merry Seal

Fashioned in fine porcelain, a white baby seal wears a red bow trimmed with holly for Christmas. The texture of his coat and flippers has been sculpted into the design.

Hand-Painted Fine Porcelain, ⅞" tall
600QXM575-5, $6.00 ☐

Starlit Mouse

Sitting on a glowing yellow acrylic star, this cheerful white mouse watches over the world celebrating Christmas. He has a little leather tail.

Handcrafted, 1 ³/₁₆" tall
450QXM565-5, $4.50 ☐

Little Soldier

Wearing his best "dress" blue and white uniform, a rosy-cheeked soldier performs a drum solo in the Christmas parade. His uniform is decorated with touches of gold.

Handcrafted, 1 ⅜" tall
450QXM567-5, $4.50 ☐

Acorn Squirrel

An acorn makes a perfect holiday hideaway for a lucky squirrel. He's hanging a wreath outside and telling his friends that a real acorn was used to mold his home.

Handcrafted, 1 ⅜" tall
450QXM568-2, $4.50 ☐

Happy Bluebird

Carrying a sprig of holly in his beak, a bluebird flies south. He wears a Santa cap for the trip, in case he meets the jolly old elf on the way.

Handcrafted, ⅞" tall
450QXM566-2, $4.50 ☐

Stocking Pal

Snug in his rosy stocking, a teddy bear is ready to be somebody's Christmas present. The ornament has been sculpted with careful attention to details such as the texture of the bear's coat and the folds in the stocking.

Handcrafted, 1" tall
450QXM567-2, $4.50 ☐

Scrimshaw Reindeer

Originally created from whalebone or ivory, scrimshaw works of art are prized for their beauty and rarity. This regal reindeer has been designed to look like a scrimshaw sculpture.

Handcrafted, ¹⁵⁄₁₆" tall
450QXM568-5, $4.50 ☐

Folk Art Bunny

Styled in the tradition of American folk art, this bunny is sculpted and painted to look like wood. His front and hind legs will move if you want him to run.

Handcrafted, 1" tall
450QXM569-2, $4.50 ☐

Brass Snowflake

Two shimmering brass snowflakes interlock to form a dimensional, multi-sided ornament. The lacy design was created through precise and delicate etching.

Dimensional Brass, 1 ⅜" tall
450QXM570-2, $4.50 ☐

Pinecone Basket

Wrapped with an embroidered fabric ribbon, a basket is filled with tiny pinecones. Actual miniature pinecones were used to create the mold for these. The handle is red fabric ribbon.

Handcrafted, ⅞" tall
450QXM573-4, $4.50 ☐

Strollin' Snowman

Taking a jaunty stroll in the crisp December air seemed like a good idea to this fine porcelain snowman. He wears a green scarf, matching red boots and cap, and two tiny buttons.

Hand-Painted Fine Porcelain, 1 ¼" tall
450QXM574-2, $4.50 ☐

Brass Partridge

A beloved symbol of the season, the partridge in a pear tree is interpreted in a glowing filigree design etched in brass.

Brass, 1 ¼" diam.
300QXM572-5, $3.00 ☐

Acorn Squirrel

Happy Bluebird, Stocking Pal

Scrimshaw Reindeer

Folk Art Bunny

Brass Snowflake

Pinecone Basket

Strollin' Snowman

Brass Partridge

Cozy Skater, Old World Santa

Roly-Poly Ram, Roly-Poly Pig

Puppy Cart

Kitty Cart

Holiday Deer

Bunny Hug

Rejoice

Cozy Skater
This mouse doesn't mind the frosty weather because he's wearing a warm green scarf with red trim and matching red mittens. The skates have metal blades.

Handcrafted, 1 ⅜" tall
450QXM573-5, $4.50

Old-World Santa
This Santa ornament has been crafted to resemble turned wood. A variety of European collectibles made out of this style of wood were popular in the early 1900s. Santa carries a bottle-brush tree.

Handcrafted, 1 ⅜" tall
300QXM569-5, $3.00

Roly-Poly Ram
A whimsical, rounded ram wears a handcrafted green ribbon and red heart. He's warm during the winter because he's been sculpted with a thick curly coat.

Handcrafted, ⅞" tall
300QXM570-5, $3.00

Roly-Poly Pig
A cute little ball of a porker carries a handcrafted golden star. His markings are similar to those of Spotted Poland pigs.

Handcrafted, ⅞" tall
300QXM571-2, $3.00

Puppy Cart
Made of wood, a Dalmatian pup is ready to journey 'cross town. His custom-designed pull-cart has a brass pull-ring attached at the front.

Wood, 1 ¼" tall
300QXM571-5, $3.00

Kitty Cart
A black and white kitten waits for someone to give her a ride in her specially painted pull-cart. The ornament is fashioned of wood and has a brass pull-ring at the front of the cart.

Wood, 1 ⅛" tall
300QXM572-2, $3.00

Holiday Deer
A faceted acrylic teardrop is the setting for this proud stag. The design, etched into the acrylic, has the intricate detail of elegant cut crystal.

Acrylic, 1 ½" tall
300QXM577-2, $3.00

Bunny Hug
It was love at first sight! The child etched onto this faceted acrylic oval gives his bunny friend a warm Christmas hug. The design has been etched to display subtle shadings and nuances of expression.

Acrylic, 1 ¼" tall
300QXM577-5, $3.00

Rejoice
This lustrous ornament features the beauty of calligraphy and a caption that expresses the loving message of the season. The caption "Rejoice" and the holly design are stamped in gold foil and framed by an oval of acrylic facets that sparkle with the light.

Acrylic, 1" tall
300QXM578-2, $3.00

Holy Family
Reissue from 1988. (See 1988 Miniature Ornament Collection.)

Handcrafted, 1 ¾" tall
850QXM561-1, $8.50

Three Little Kitties
Reissue from 1988. (See 1988 Miniature Ornament Collection.)

Handcrafted, ¹⁵/₁₆" tall
600QXM569-4, $6.00

Country Wreath
Reissue from 1988. (See 1988 Miniature Ornament Collection.)

Handcrafted, 1 ½" tall
450QXM573-1, $4.50

Collectibles Series

Noel R.R. — First Edition
Dated "1989," a special "Locomotive" is on the right track for this new series. Each year, a different type of railroad car will be added to complete the holiday train. The ornament, fashioned with revolving wheels, is painted with bright colors and touches of gold to accentuate detail.

Handcrafted, 1″ tall
850QXM576-2, $8.50   ☐

The Kringles — First Edition
The season's happiest twosome will make an appearance every year of this new series. In the first edition, the jolly old elf hides a green package behind his back for the Mrs. It's sure to be something she had on her list! The ornament is sculpted and painted to look like hand-carved wood.

Handcrafted, 1 ⅛″ tall
600QXM562-5, $6.00   ☐

Old English Village — Second Edition
The shopkeeper stands in the doorway to welcome customers into her "Sweet Shop." Second in the series, this ornament is charmingly detailed with timber trimmings, pearly snow on the roof, and a tiny wreath in the window. A sign on the front advertises "Sweets." The address is "1989."

Handcrafted, 1 ¼″ tall
850QXM561-5, $8.50   ☐

Penguin Pal — Second Edition
The second penguin in the series is lookin' cool and enjoying a tasty candy cane. He wears a dashing green bow tie and a red Santa cap.

Handcrafted, Acrylic, 1 ⅜″ tall
450QXM560-2, $4.50   ☐

Rocking Horse — Second Edition
A handsome palomino with flowing white mane and tail prances on blue rockers dated "1989." His saddle and trappings are Christmas green and red with accents of gold.

Handcrafted, 1 ⅛″ tall
450QXM560-5, $4.50   ☐

Kittens in Toyland — Second Edition
This tan and white kitten travels in style. She's put on a blue stocking cap with a white handcrafted pompom to go for a ride in her brand-new red scooter.

Handcrafted, 1″ tall
450QXM561-2, $4.50   ☐

Noel R.R.

The Kringles

Old English Village

Penguin Pal

Rocking Horse

Kittens in Toyland

Special Edition

Santa's Magic Ride
Santa races through the forest on a magical unicorn with golden hooves and horn. The carefully sculpted details of this ornament, such as the unicorn's flying tail and Santa's flowing red coat, create a vision of grace and motion. Santa clasps his pack of gifts in one hand and holds onto the unicorn's mane with the other as he takes his wondrous ride.

Handcrafted, 1 ³/₁₆″ tall
850QXM563-2, $8.50   ☐

Santa's Magic Ride

THE HALLMARK KEEPSAKE ORNAMENT COLLECTOR'S CLUB COLLECTION

Since its founding in 1987, the Hallmark Keepsake Ornament Collector's Club has offered members a variety of exclusive ornaments. Each of the annual Membership Kits included an ornament called the "Keepsake of Membership." This design was the Club's special gift to all members. Members were also given the opportunity to order a "Members Only" ornament each year through their Hallmark retailers. In addition to these ornaments, some members received exclusive Club miniature ornaments in their kits. In 1988, the Keepsake Miniature Ornament was given to members who renewed early or who purchased a multi-year membership. In 1989, every member was sent the miniature design.

Because these ornaments were fashioned for an especially valued group of collectors — Club members — the Hallmark artists created designs that reflected the joy of collecting as well as the spirit of the season. The 1989 "Wreath of Memories," for example, featured tiny reproductions of popular Keepsake Ornaments from past years.

Limited Edition ornaments, considered by many to be the most collectible ornaments of all, were offered exclusively to Club members in 1988 and 1989. Ordered through Hallmark retailers, these designs were among the most beautifully designed in the Keepsake Collection.

Wreath of Memories

1987

Keepsake of Membership — Wreath of Memories

The Club's first ornament — an elaborate handcrafted wreath — was designed to welcome Charter Members and celebrate the tradition of decorating with Keepsake Ornaments. It marked the first time that tiny reproductions of favorite Keepsake designs from previous years were used on a new ornament. Intricate details help collectors identify "Rocking Horse" and "Clothespin Soldier" among the designs. The year date "1987" appears on the front of the wreath. The caption "1987 Charter Member" appears on the back, along with the official Club logo engraved in brass.

Handcrafted, 3⅛" tall
QCX580-9   ☐

Members Only Ornament — Carousel Reindeer

This fanciful reindeer prancing inside a hoop symbolizes both the history and the evolution of the Keepsake Ornament line. Although reminiscent of the appealing "Nostalgia" ornaments of the 1970s, the "Carousel Reindeer" is more elegant and contemporary — a reflection of the Hallmark artists' flair for fresh, innovative designs. The caption "1987 Charter Member" appears on the front of the ornament, and the year date "1987" on the back. The official Club logo is printed in gold on the bottom of the hoop.

Handcrafted, 3¾" tall
800QXC581-7, $8.00   ☐

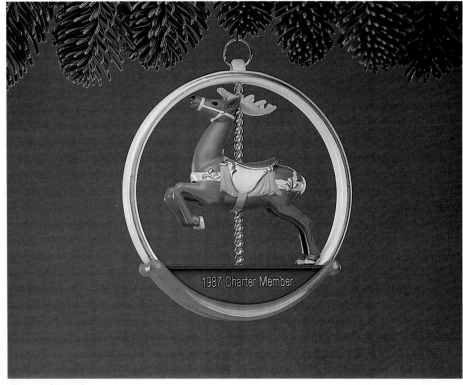

Carousel Reindeer

1988

Keepsake of Membership —
Our Clubhouse

A little mouse swings open the door to welcome members to the Club's second year. He's placed a wreath on the door and candles in the windows of the clubhouse. Inside, a decorated bottle-brush tree, teddy bear, and gift package are waiting. Pearly white snow covers the clubhouse roof, and a sign over the door reads, "Club Members Only." The year date "1988" appears on the back of the ornament, and the official Club logo is printed on the bottom.

Handcrafted, 2 ½" tall
QXC580-4   ☐

Members Only Ornament —
Sleighful of Dreams

Ready for a journey into a wintry wonderland, this members only ornament is handcrafted and hand painted to resemble an old-fashioned wooden sleigh. Golden bas-relief designs portray favorite Keepsake Ornaments from years past including "Tin Locomotive," "Cookie Mouse," "Clothespin Soldier," and "Santa's Deliveries" from the Collectible Series "Here Comes Santa." A lap blanket crafted of plaid ribbon completes the inviting design. The year date "1988" appears on the front of the sleigh. The official Club logo is engraved in brass on the back.

Handcrafted, 2⅛" tall
800QXC580-1, $8.00   ☐

Keepsake Miniature Ornament —
Hold On Tight

An adventurous mouse takes a magic carpet ride, holding tight to a tiny green leaf. His red-and-white striped cap has a real yarn pompom. This miniature ornament was a special gift exclusively for those Club members who renewed their membership early or purchased a multi-year membership. The Club's official logo is printed on the bottom of the leaf.

Handcrafted, ¹⁵/₁₆" tall
QXC570-4   ☐

Limited Editions

Holiday Heirloom —
Second Edition

Suspended in flight above a sparkling 24 percent lead crystal bell, two silver-plated angels hold a silver-plated star. The star-shaped pattern is repeated by the silver-plated clapper inside the bell. The edition size is limited to 34,600 pieces. The year date "1988" is debossed on the front of the star. The edition size "Ltd. Ed. 34,600" is debossed on the back.

Lead Crystal, Silver Plating, 3½" tall
2500QX406-4, $25.00   ☐

Our Clubhouse, Sleighful of Dreams

Hold on Tight

Holiday Heirloom, Angelic Minstrel, Christmas is Sharing

Angelic Minstrel

Designed in the classical tradition and fashioned in fine porcelain, this elegant angel strums a golden lyre to welcome the holiday season. She wears a lovely blue gown, edged and accented with gold, and comes complete with her own wood display stand. The edition size is limited to a maximum of 49,900.

Hand-Painted Fine Porcelain, 5" tall
2950QX408-4, $29.50   ☐

Christmas is Sharing

Two rabbits share the quiet beauty of the season. Finely textured, white bone china conveys a subtle impression of their furry coats, as well as the pine needles and bough. Golden berries enhance the design. The caption reads: "Christmas is sharing. Bone China, Limited Edition of 49,900 Max., Number: (hand-written number)."

Hand-Painted Bone China, 2¼" tall
1750QX407-1, $17.50   ☐

1989

Keepsake of Membership — Visit From Santa

Santa has the entire Collector's Club roster on his special delivery list. He's bringing a sled to every member, personalized with the member's name. A gift inside his bag carries the year date "1989."

Handcrafted, 4" tall
QXC580-2 □

Members Only Ornament — Collect a Dream

Snug in a leafy hammock, this mouse dreams of Keepsake Ornaments. Club members will recognize his book: "My Keepsake Ornament Treasury 1989." The leaf displays the Club logo, "Hallmark Keepsake Ornament Collector's Club," and is fashioned with hooks at both ends so it can hang between two branches.

Handcrafted, 1¾" tall
900QXC428-5, $9.00 □

Visit From Santa, Collect a Dream

Limited Editions

Christmas is Peaceful

Two owls perch on a snow-covered branch in this lovely scene created in bone china. A limited edition of 49,900 pieces, the ornament has been painted and individually numbered by hand. A gold cord and golden berries add sparkle to the subtle colors of the design. Caption: "Christmas is peaceful. Bone China, Limited Edition of 49,900 Max., Number: (hand-written number)."

Hand-Painted Bone China, 2½" tall
1850QXC451-2, $18.50 □

Noelle

This elegant cat is dressed for a Christmas party with Club members. Created in fine porcelain and painted by hand, "Noelle" wears a red bow decorated with a sprig of holly and a real brass jingle bell. The ornament, issued in a limited edition of 49,900 pieces, comes with a specially designed wooden display stand.

Hand-Painted, Fine Porcelain, 3¾" tall
1975QXC448-3, $19.75 □

Holiday Heirloom — Third and Final Edition

The melodic tones of the 24 percent lead crystal bell announce the end of the series. The bell is suspended from a silver-plated design of a Christmas tree and a group of old-fashioned toys. Also plated in silver, the bell clapper is a gift box. The year date "1989" is debossed on a child's ball on the front of the ornament. The edition size "Limited Edition of 34,600" is embossed on the back.

Lead Crystal, Silver Plating, 2½" tall
2500QXC460-5, $25.00 □

Sitting Purrty

Keepsake Miniature Ornament — Sitting Purrty

A pretty little kitty, wearing a red stocking cap with a tiny handcrafted bell at the tip, sits in her own custom-made mug. The mug carries the captions: "1989" and "Hallmark Keepsake Ornament Collector's Club." This ornament was a special gift for all 1989 members.

Handcrafted, 1¼" tall
QXC581-2 □

Christmas is Peaceful, Noelle, Holiday Heirloom

KEEPSAKE ORNAMENTS: THE ADDED ATTRACTIONS

Collectors notice everything. Through the years, they have discovered several Keepsake Ornaments that were not part of the regular line. These designs were not included in the Keepsake Ornament brochures or displayed with the other Keepsake Ornaments. To say the least, collectors have been intrigued.

To clear up the mystery surrounding these precious odds and ends, I have added the following section to this *Collector's Guide.* It includes the Keepsake Ornaments that have been featured in Hallmark gift and promotional programs such as the "Musical Collection" or "Open House" events. Grouped together, these ornaments make quite an interesting mini collection.

Musical Ornaments

The 1982 designs were offered in the Hallmark "Gift Collection," and the 1983 designs in the "Hallmark Musical Collection." All but the "Twelve Days of Christmas" ornament came packaged with an acrylic display stand.

1982

Baby's First Christmas
Baby has a merry time with all the new Christmas toys. The blocks spell out the first word in the caption: "Baby's First Christmas 1982." Melody: "Brahms' Lullaby."

Musical, Classic Shape, 4½" tall
1600QMB900-7, $16.00 ☐

First Christmas Together
A sleigh ride in the snow is the perfect way to spend that memorable first Christmas. Caption: "First Christmas Together 1982." Melody: "White Christmas."

Musical, Classic Shape, 4½" tall
1600QMB901-9, $16.00 ☐

Love
Pinecones and holiday greenery decorate a festive ornament that offers a loving melody and message of the season. Caption: "Love puts the warmth in Christmas 1982." Melody: "What the Worlds Needs Now Is Love."

Musical, Classic Shape, 4½" tall
1600QMB900-9, $16.00 ☐

Baby's First Christmas, First Christmas Together, Love

1983

Twelve Days of Christmas
This French blue and white bas-relief design was included in the 1984 Keepsake Ornament collection. Melody: "Twelve Days of Christmas."

Musical, Handcrafted, 3 ¾" tall
1500QMB415-9, $15.00 ☐

Baby's First Christmas
Dressed in Santa sleepers, the babies on this ornament crawl up and down and all around the candy canes that spell out the caption: "Baby's 1st Christmas 1983." Melody: "Schubert's Lullaby."

Musical, Classic Shape, 4½" tall
1600QMB903-9, $16.00 ☐

Friendship
Muffin celebrates Christmas with her little friends. Caption: "It's song-in-the-air time, lights-everywhere time, good-fun-to-share time, it's Christmas." Melody: "We Wish You a Merry Christmas."

Musical, Classic Shape, 4½" tall
1600QMB904-7, $16.00 ☐

Nativity
The Three Kings bring gifts for the Holy Child in this brightly painted Nativity scene. Caption: "The star shone bright with a holy light as heaven came to earth that night." Melody: "Silent Night."

Musical, Classic Shape, 4½" tall
1600QMB904-9, $16.00 ☐

Twelve Days of Christmas, Baby's First Christmas

Friendship, Nativity

Early Promotional Ornament

In 1982, Hallmark offered collectors a specially designed brass ornament for $3.50 with the purchase of Hallmark merchandise. This was the first time an ornament of this quality was offered as a promotion. The packaging did not carry the Keepsake name.

Dimensional Ornament

A 24 karat gold tone coating adds sparkle to this dimensional brass ornament. In the design, a Victorian couple enjoys a nighttime ride in their one-horse open sleigh. Behind them, a village lies sleeping on Christmas Eve. The back oval features both die-cut shapes and etching. Extending forward from the oval, the cut-out sleigh is etched to show detail.

Dimensional Brass, 2 3/8" tall
No Stock Number, $3.50 retail price ☐

Early Promotional Ornament

Open House Ornaments

Special Keepsake Ornaments were created for the "Open House" events Hallmark dealers held as a festive start to the holiday season.

1986

Santa and His Reindeer

Santa's sleigh is packed, and his reindeer are ready to fly between two branches of your tree, suspended by hooks at both ends of the red cord harness. The ornament can also be displayed on a table or mantel.

Handcrafted, 2" tall and 14" wide
975QXO440-6, $9.75 ☐

Santa and His Reindeer

Coca-Cola® Santa

Reproduced on porcelain white glass, three nostalgic Coca-Cola paintings show that Santa always has time for his favorite drink! Caption: "Memories are reflections of the yesterdays we'll always love. Merry Christmas."

Porcelain White Glass, 2 7/8" diam.
475QXO279-6, $4.75 ☐

Old-Fashioned Santa

Crafted to look like hand-carved wood, this Old World Santa carries a bag filled with intricate sculpted toys. A little kitten rides in his pocket.

Handcrafted, 4 1/2" tall
1275QXO440-3, $12.75 ☐

Santa's Panda Pal

This lovable flocked panda dresses just like Santa. His red and white knitted hat is topped with a pompom.

Handcrafted, 2 1/4" tall
500QXO441-3, $5.00 ☐

Coca-Cola® Santa, Old-Fashioned Santa, Santa's Panda Pal

1987

North Pole Power & Light
This hard-working elf uses his shiny metal wrench to light your tree for Christmas. Always ready for an emergency, he carries three colorful replacement bulbs in his pack in case a light goes out.

Handcrafted, 3″ tall
627XPR933-3, *$10.00 value,*
$2.95 retail price ☐

1988

Kringle's Toy Shop
Two elves are busy making Christmas toys in the lighted window of the famous toy shop named "Kringle's." The elves hammer and saw all day long, while passersby, like the two children in the design, watch in fascination.

Handcrafted, 3⅝″ tall
Light and Motion, $24.50
2450QLX701-7 ☐

North Pole Power & Light

Kringle's Toy Shop

SANTA CLAUS – THE MOVIE™ Ornaments

Two Keepsake Ornaments were part of a varied group of Hallmark gifts centering on this film. The "Elfmade" emblem appeared on the back of each design stamped in gold foil.

1985

Santa's Village
The movie's magical portrait of Santa's Village is reproduced in this wintry photograph set in a brass bezel. The caption reads, "Merry, Merry Christmas."

Lacquer-Look, 2¼″ tall
675QX300-2, *$6.75* ☐

Santa Claus
The sleigh is filled to overflowing with brightly wrapped packages for good girls and boys. Holding the reins, Santa is about to begin his magical journey. Framed in brass, the photograph was taken directly from the movie.

Lacquer-Look, 3½″ tall
675QX300-5, *$6.75* ☐

Santa's Village, Santa Claus

Gold Crown Ornament

"Gold Crown" is the name of a special Hallmark promotional program. Participating stores offered groups of exclusive gifts and collectibles. The 1986 Gold Crown program included a porcelain Keepsake Ornament.

1986

On The Right Track
Carefully painted by hand, this fine porcelain Santa puts the finishing touches on a toy train. He wears brass spectacles, and his boot carries the artist's signature, "P. Dutkin."

Hand-Painted Fine Porcelain, 4¾" tall
1500QSP420-1, $15.00 ☐

Baby Celebrations

In 1989, Hallmark offered the first "Baby Celebrations" collection of baby gifts and shower partyware. Included are four Keepsake Ornaments. Two of the designs are captions not included in the Keepsake line: "Baby's First Birthday" and "Baby's Christening Keepsake." The other two are identical to the "Baby's First Christmas" satin ball ornaments in the 1989 Keepsake offer. All of the ornaments are packaged in special "Baby Celebrations" boxes. The 1989 collection will be offered year-round in a limited number of Hallmark Gold Crown stores.

1989

Baby's Christening Keepsake
This new commemorative can be displayed throughout the year. Bezeled in chrome, the smooth acrylic oval is adorned with a silver foil caption and teddy bear. Caption: "Baby's Christening Keepsake 1989."

Acrylic, 3¾" tall
700BBY132-5, $7.00 ☐

Baby's First Birthday
A cheery teddy bear clown carries a big number "1" to announce a very important birthday. The ornament comes with an acrylic stand for year-round display. Caption: "Baby's 1st Birthday 1989."

Acrylic, 4½" tall
550BBY172-9, $5.50 ☐

Baby's First Christmas—Baby Girl
Identical to 475QX272-2, (See 1989 Annual Collection.)

Pink Satin, 2⅞" diam.
475BBY155-3, $4.75 ☐

Baby's First Christmas—Baby Boy
Identical to 475QX272-5. (See 1989 Annual Collection.)

Blue Satin, 2⅞" diam.
475BBY145-3, $4.75 ☐

On the Right Track

Baby's Christening Keepsake, Baby's 1st Birthday

COLLECTIBLE SERIES

A Collectible Series is a group of ornaments that share a specific design theme or motif, such as the vehicle in the "Here Comes Santa" series. These ornaments are issued one per year for a minimum of three years. Between 1973 and 1989, Hallmark issued forty official Collectible Series. Thirty appeared in the Keepsake Ornament line, four in the Keepsake Magic line and six in the Keepsake Miniature line.

Series ornaments are very popular with collectors, and much time and effort go into collecting every edition. The longest-running series was the Betsey Clark ball ornament group that ended with the thirteenth edition in 1985. The "Holiday Heirloom" series, started in 1987 and retired in 1989, was the first to be issued in a limited edition. Thirteen series were added in 1988 and 1989.

Beginning with the Collectible Series ornaments offered in 1982, all series editions are identified with the words, "(number) in a series" or a tree-shaped symbol ▲ with the edition number inside. The symbol is especially helpful in identifying dated series designs and in pinpointing their year of issue.

Hark! It's Herald: 1989

Keepsake Ornament Collectible Series

Hark! It's Herald
Herald, the talented star of this series, plays a different musical instrument every year. The whimsical name of the series, a word play on the familiar carol, mirrors the warm humor of this happy elf.

1989   675QX455-5   Hark! It's Herald

Christmas Kitty
It's Christmas...and the kitties in this series love to dress up in their holiday best. Every edition offers a different kitty, fashioned in fine porcelain and painted by hand.

1989   1475QX544-5   Christmas Kitty

Winter Surprise
The penguins inside the peek-through eggs in this series create a new winter surprise each year. They have a merry time in their winter world whether they're decorating a Christmas tree, playing in the snow, or celebrating the holiday.

1989   1075QX427-2   Winter Surprise

Christmas Kitty: 1989, Winter Surprise: 1989

CRAYOLA® Crayon

There's no limit to the ingenuity of the animals in this bright series. They fashion colorful objects and toys out of CRAYOLA® Crayons and even the crayon box!

1989   875QX435-2   Bright Journey

The Gift Bringers

Beloved Christmas legends from around the world are illustrated in the five editions that make up this series. Each ornament features a classic "Gift Bringer" beautifully illustrated on a glass ball.

1989   500QX279-5   St. Nicholas

CRAYOLA® Crayon: 1989, The Gift Bringers: 1989

Mary's Angels

The angels in this series are designed by Hallmark artist Mary Hamilton, who is known for her charming depictions of children. Each angel has her own special flower name and appears with an acrylic cloud. The cloud carries the artist's signature, "Mary."

1988   500QX407-4   Buttercup
1989   575QX454-5   Bluebell

Mary's Angels: 1988, 1989

Porcelain Bear

For teddy bear lovers especially, an annual porcelain edition of a lovable bear named Cinnamon. Each bear is carefully painted by hand.

1983   700QX428-9   Cinnamon Teddy
1984   700QX454-1   Cinnamon Bear
1985   775QX479-2   Cinnamon Bear
1986   775QX405-6   Cinnamon Bear
1987   775QX442-7   Cinnamon Bear
1988   800QX404-4   Cinnamon Bear
1989   875QX461-5   Cinnamon Bear

Porcelain Bear: 1988, 1989

Porcelain Bear: 1983, 1984, 1985, 1986, 1987

Nostalgic Houses and Shops: 1984, 1985

Nostalgic Houses and Shops: 1988, 1989

Nostalgic Houses and Shops: 1986, 1987

Nostalgic Houses and Shops

The Nostalgic Houses and Shops series was introduced in 1984. Each piece is carefully researched so that detailing is both authentic and accurate.

1984	1300QX448-1	Victorian Dollhouse
1985	1375QX497-5	Old-Fashioned Toy Shop
1986	1375QX403-3	Christmas Candy Shoppe
1987	1400QX483-9	House on Main St.
1988	1450QX401-4	Hall Bro's Card Shop
1989	1425QX458-2	U.S. Post Office

Mr. and Mrs. Claus

Santa and his lovely spouse appear in your
home to show how they celebrate
Christmas in the Claus household.

1986	1300QX402-6	Merry Mistletoe Time
1987	1325QX483-7	Home Cooking
1988	1300QX401-1	Shall We Dance
1989	1325QX457-5	Holiday Duet

Mr. and Mrs. Claus: 1986, 1987

Mr. and Mrs. Claus: 1988, 1989

Betsey Clark: Home for Christmas

The second Betsey Clark ball series
features the artist's lovable children
celebrating Christmas around the home.
The glass balls are 2 ⅞" in diameter, smaller
than those in the first Betsey Clark series.

1986	500QX277-6	Home for Christmas
1987	500QX272-7	Home for Christmas
1988	500QX271-4	Home for Christmas
1989	500QX230-2	Home for Christmas

Betsey Clark: 1986, 1987

Betsey Clark: 1988, 1989

Reindeer Champs: 1986, 1987

Reindeer Champs: 1988, 1989

Reindeer Champs

Santa's team of reindeer champions appears in a series that features a different sport each year.

1986	750QX422-3	Dasher
1987	750QX480-9	Dancer
1988	750QX405-1	Prancer
1989	775QX456-2	Vixen

Here Comes Santa

The Here Comes Santa collection proves that Santa is capable of using any mode of transportation to make his Christmas Eve deliveries.

1979	900QX155-9	Santa's Motorcar
1980	1200QX143-4	Santa's Express
1981	1300QX438-2	Rooftop Deliveries
1982	1500QX464-3	Jolly Trolley
1983	1300QX403-7	Santa Express
1984	1300QX432-4	Santa's Deliveries
1985	1400QX496-5	Santa's Fire Engine
1986	1400QX404-3	Kringle's Kool Treats
1987	1400QX484-7	Santa's Woody
1988	1400QX400-1	Kringle Koach
1989	1475QX458-5	Christmas Caboose

Here Comes Santa: 1979, 1980, 1981

Here Comes Santa: 1982, 1983, 1984, 1985

Here Comes Santa: 1986, 1987

Here Comes Santa: 1988, 1989

Windows of the World: 1985, 1986, 1987

Windows of the World: 1988, 1989

Windows of the World

A series which depicts international celebrations of Christmas by children, including holiday greetings in a different language each year.

1985	975QX490-2	Feliz Navidad
1986	1000QX408-3	Vrolyk Kerstfeest
1987	1000QX482-7	Mele Kalikimaka
1988	1000QX402-1	Joyeux Noël
1989	1075QX462-5	Fröhliche Weihnachten

Frosty Friends

Each design in the Frosty Friends series depicts a form of winter-wonderland fun in Santa's North Pole neighborhood.

1980	650QX137-4	A Cool Yule
1981	800QX433-5	Frosty Friends
1982	800QX452-3	Frosty Friends
1983	800QX400-7	Frosty Friends
1984	800QX437-1	Frosty Friends
1985	850QX482-2	Frosty Friends
1986	850QX405-3	Frosty Friends
1987	850QX440-9	Frosty Friends
1988	875QX403-1	Frosty Friends
1989	925QX457-2	Frosty Friends

Frosty Friends: 1980, 1981, 1982, 1983

Frosty Friends: 1984, 1985, 1986

Frosty Friends: 1987, 1988, 1989

Rocking Horse

This ever-popular toy, cherished by generations of children, has found favor in a new form. Each year the Rocking Horse series features a different steed with flying mane and tail of yarn.

1981	900QX422-2	Dappled
1982	1000QX502-3	Black
1983	1000QX417-7	Russet
1984	1000QX435-4	Appaloosa
1985	1075QX493-2	Pinto
1986	1075QX401-6	Palomino
1987	1075QX482-9	White
1988	1075QX402-4	Dappled Gray
1989	1075QX462-2	Bay

Rocking Horse: 1988, 1989

Rocking Horse: 1981, 1982, 1983

Rocking Horse: 1984, 1985, 1986, 1987

Twelve Days of Christmas

This acrylic series depicts Hallmark's interpretation of each of the twelve days in the favorite Christmas carol.

1984	*600QX348-4*	*Partridge in a Pear Tree*
1985	*650QX371-2*	*Two Turtle Doves*
1986	*650QX378-6*	*Three French Hens*
1987	*650QX370-9*	*Four Colly Birds*
1988	*650QX371-4*	*Five Golden Rings*
1989	*675QX381-2*	*Six Geese A-Laying*

Twelve Days of Christmas: 1984, 1985

Twelve Days of Christmas: 1986, 1987

Twelve Days of Christmas: 1988, 1989

Collector's Plate: 1987, 1988

Collector's Plate

The heartwarming artwork on this series of miniature fine porcelain collector's plates depicts the excitement, joy, and anticipation children experience at Christmas.

1987	800QX481-7	Light Shines at Christmas
1988	800QX406-1	Waiting for Santa
1989	825QX461-2	Morning of Wonder

Collector's Plate: 1989

Retired Collectible Series

Betsey Clark

The Betsey Clark series is the oldest and longest-running series in the Keepsake Ornament Collection. Starting in 1973 (the year Hallmark introduced its ornaments nationally) and ending with the final Betsey Clark ball ornament in 1985, a total of thirteen ornaments appeared in the series. Other Betsey Clark formats offered have included satin balls, cameo ornaments, handcrafted designs and hand-painted porcelain angels. The series designs shown here are:

1973	250XHD110-2	Christmas 1973
1974	250QX108-1	Musicians
1975	300QX133-1	Caroling Trio
1976	300QX195-1	Christmas 1976
1977	350QX264-2	Truest Joys of Christmas
1978	350QX201-6	Christmas Spirit
1979	350QX201-9	Holiday Fun
1980	400QX215-4	Joy-in-the-Air
1981	450QX802-2	Christmas 1981
1982	450QX215-6	Joys of Christmas
1983	450QX211-9	Christmas Happiness
1984	500QX249-4	Days are Merry
1985	500QX263-2	Special Kind of Feeling

Betsey Clark: 1973, 1974, 1975

Betsey Clark: 1976, 1977, 1978, 1979

Betsey Clark: 1980, 1981, 1982

Holiday Heirloom

This series marks several firsts. It is the first limited edition series and the first to feature lead crystal and a precious metal. It is also the first to have two editions — the second and third — available only through the Hallmark Keepsake Ornament Collector's Club. Each ornament combines an intricately sculpted silver-plated design with a 24 percent lead crystal bell in an edition limited to 34,600 pieces. The series ended in 1989.

1987	2500QX485-7	Holiday Heirloom
1988	2500QX406-4	Holiday Heirloom
1989	2500QXC460-5	Holiday Heirloom

Holiday Heirloom: 1987

Betsey Clark: 1983, 1984, 1985

Holiday Heirloom: 1988, 1989

Bellringer: 1979, 1980, 1981

The Bellringers

Holiday bells have a touch of whimsy in this unique series that brings a new interpretation to this traditional design motif. Made of fine porcelain, the bells have different handcrafted clappers each year. The sixth and last of The Bellringers series was produced in 1984.

1979	1000QX147-9	The Bellswinger
1980	1500QX157-4	The Bellringers
1981	1500QX441-5	Swingin' Bellringer
1982	1500QX455-6	Angel Bellringer
1983	1500QX403-9	Teddy Bellringer
1984	1500QX438-4	Elfin Artist

Bellringer: 1982, 1983, 1984

Art Masterpiece

This padded satin series offers reproductions of religious fine art masterpieces from around the world. The series ended in 1986.

1984	650QX349-4	Madonna and Child and St. John
1985	675QX377-2	Madonna of the Pomegranate
1986	675QX350-6	Madonna and Child with the Infant St. John

Art Masterpiece: 1984, 1985, 1986

Collectible Series continued

Norman Rockwell

The art of Norman Rockwell is known and loved by all, and this delightful series of cameos presents the artist's vision of Christmas in a beautiful dimension. In addition to the cameo series, Rockwell artwork has been featured on glass and satin ball ornaments since 1974. The ninth and final ornament was issued in 1988.

1980	650QX306-1	Santa's Visitors
1981	850QX511-5	The Carolers
1982	850QX305-3	Filling the Stockings
1983	750QX300-7	Dress Rehearsal
1984	750QX341-1	Caught Napping
1985	750QX374-5	Postman and Kids
1986	775QX321-3	Checking Up
1987	775QX370-7	The Christmas Dance
1988	775QX370-4	And to All a Good Night

Norman Rockwell: 1980, 1981, 1982

Norman Rockwell: 1983, 1984, 1985

Norman Rockwell: 1986, 1987, 1988

Miniature Crèche: 1985, 1986, 1987

Miniature Crèche

A series of unique Nativities fashioned in different media such as wood and porcelain. The last edition, a *retablo*, appeared in 1989.

1985	875QX482-5	Wood and Woven Straw
1986	900QX407-6	Fine Porcelain
1987	900QX481-9	Multi-Plated Brass
1988	850QX403-4	Acrylic
1989	925QX459-2	Handcrafted

Miniature Crèche: 1988, 1989

Wood Childhood Ornaments

These nostalgic wooden ornaments from yesteryear feature special authentic touches such as wheels that turn and bows made of fabric. The 1989 ornament concluded the series.

1984	650QX439-4	Wooden Lamb
1985	700QX472-2	Wooden Train
1986	750QX407-3	Wooden Reindeer
1987	750QX441-7	Wooden Horse
1988	750QX404-1	Wooden Airplane
1989	775QX459-5	Wooden Truck

Wood Childhood Ornaments: 1984, 1985, 1986, 1987

Wood Childhood Ornaments: 1988, 1989

Tin Locomotive

The Tin Locomotive series, introduced in 1982, is of interest to train, tin, and ornament collectors alike. The series, retired in 1989, depicted eight models of locomotives inspired by trains from the early days of American rail transportation.

1982	1300QX460-3	Tin Locomotive
1983	1300QX404-9	Tin Locomotive
1984	1400QX440-4	Tin Locomotive
1985	1475QX497-2	Tin Locomotive
1986	1475QX403-6	Tin Locomotive
1987	1475QX484-9	Tin Locomotive
1988	1475QX400-4	Tin Locomotive
1989	1475QX460-2	Tin Locomotive

Tin Locomotive: 1982, 1983

Tin Locomotive: 1984, 1985

Tin Locomotive: 1986, 1987

Tin Locomotive: 1988, 1989

Holiday Wildlife: 1982, 1983, 1984

Holiday Wildlife

The Holiday Wildlife series, introduced in 1982, is especially appealing to bird watchers who appreciate skillful and true-to-life artistic representations of beautiful birds. The paintings are reproduced on a white, porcelain-like insert and are framed and backed in natural wood. The series was retired in 1988.

1982	700QX313-3	Cardinalis Cardinalis
1983	700QX309-9	Black-Capped Chickadees
1984	725QX347-4	Ring-Necked Pheasant
1985	750QX376-5	California Quail
1986	750QX321-6	Cedar Waxwing
1987	750QX371-7	Snow Goose
1988	775QX371-1	Purple Finch

Holiday Wildlife: 1988

Holiday Wildlife: 1985, 1986, 1987

Thimble

Especially popular with thimble collectors, this whimsical series shows how versatile a thimble can be! The series concluded in 1989.

1978	250QX133-6	*Mouse in a Thimble*
1979	300QX131-9	*A Christmas Salute*
1980	400QX132-1	*Thimble Elf*
1981	450QX413-5	*Thimble Angel*
1982	500QX451-3	*Thimble Mouse*
1983	500QX401-7	*Thimble Elf*
1984	500QX430-4	*Thimble Angel*
1985	550QX472-5	*Thimble Santa*
1986	575QX406-6	*Thimble Partridge*
1987	575QX441-9	*Thimble Drummer*
1988	575QX405-4	*Thimble Snowman*
1989	575QX455-2	*Thimble Puppy*

Thimble: 1988, 1989

Thimble: 1978, 1979, 1980, 1981, 1982, 1983

Thimble: 1984, 1985, 1986, 1987

Clothespin Soldier: 1982, 1983, 1984, 1985, 1986, 1987

Clothespin Soldier

The Clothespin Soldier series features a soldier wearing a different uniform each year. The final ornament was issued in 1987.

1982	500QX458-3	British
1983	500QX402-9	Early American
1984	500QX447-1	Canadian Mountie
1985	550QX471-5	Scottish Highlander
1986	550QX406-3	French Officer
1987	550QX480-7	Sailor

SNOOPY® and Friends: 1979, 1980

SNOOPY® and Friends

SNOOPY®, in a three-dimensional format, made his debut in 1979 in an exciting peek-through ball ornament. The "window" in this ball ornament allows you to peek in on SNOOPY's® holiday antics. The 1983 edition is the final ornament in this series.

1979	800QX141-9	Ice-Hockey Holiday
1980	900QX154-1	Ski Holiday
1981	1200QX436-2	SNOOPY® and Friends
1982	1300QX480-3	SNOOPY® and Friends
1983	1300QX416-9	Santa SNOOPY®

SNOOPY® and Friends: 1981, 1982

SNOOPY® and Friends: 1983

Carrousel

The Carrousel series depicts fun and frolic on a colorful, rotating carrousel. This is one of the series most sought after by collectors. The 1983 design was the final edition.

1978	600QX146-3	*Antique Toys*
1979	650QX146-7	*Christmas Carrousel*
1980	750QX141-4	*Merry Carrousel*
1981	900QX427-5	*Skaters' Carrousel*
1982	1000QX478-3	*Snowman Carrousel*
1983	1100QX401-9	*Santa and Friends*

Carrousel: 1978, 1979, 1980

Carrousel: 1981, 1982, 1983

Keepsake Magic Ornament Series

Forest Frolics: 1989

Forest Frolics

A happy group of endearing woodland animals makes the forest a merry place. They play and celebrate the season in ornaments that feature light and motion.

1989   2450QLX728-2   Forest Frolics

Christmas Classics

This series of lighted three-dimensional scenes illustrates beloved Christmas stories, ballets, books, poems, and songs.

1986	1750QLX704-3	The Nutcracker Ballet – Sugarplum Fairy
1987	1600QLX702-9	A Christmas Carol
1988	1500QLX716-1	Night Before Christmas
1989	1350QLX724-2	Little Drummer Boy

Christmas Classics: 1986

Christmas Classics: 1987

Christmas Classics: 1988

Christmas Classics: 1989

Chris Mouse

This is the first series to feature light. The little mouse sitting by the candle and the other mice in following years both decorate and light your tree.

1985	1250QLX703-2	Chris Mouse
1986	1300QLX705-6	Chris Mouse Dreams
1987	1100QLX705-7	Chris Mouse Glow
1988	875QLX715-4	Chris Mouse Star
1989	950QLX722-5	Chris Mouse Cookout

Chris Mouse: 1985

Chris Mouse: 1986

Chris Mouse: 1987

Chris Mouse: 1988

Chris Mouse: 1989

Retired Collectible Series

Santa and Sparky

Santa and his penguin pal Sparky share the fun of Christmas in this first "light and motion" series. This series ended in 1988.

1986	2200QLX703-3	Lighting the Tree
1987	2200QLX701-9	Perfect Portrait
1988	1950QLX719-1	On With the Show

Santa and Sparky: 1986

Santa and Sparky: 1987

Santa and Sparky: 1988

The Kringles: 1989

Noel R.R.: 1989

Old English Village: 1988, 1989

Kittens in Toyland: 1988, 1989

Rocking Horse: 1988, 1989

Penguin Pal: 1988, 1989

Keepsake Miniature Ornament Series

The Kringles
The most celebrated couple in the North Pole shares the merriment of the season in this series of ornaments designed to look like hand-carved wood.

1989   600QXM562-5   The Kringles

Noel R.R.
The colorful "Locomotive" was the first car to make a Christmas journey in this miniature ornament train series. It picks up a different type of railroad car on every annual trip.

1989   850QXM576-2   Locomotive

Old English Village
The details and architecture of the houses, buildings, and shops in this series capture the charm of a country village in England. The ornaments evoke the joy of the season and the warmth of home.

1988   850QXM563-4   Family Home
1989   850QXM561-5   Sweet Shop

Kittens in Toyland
Each year a different kitten has a holiday filled with fun playing with his Christmas gifts. The kittens especially like to ride on the wonderful toys they receive from Santa.

1988   500QXM562-1   Kittens in Toyland
1989   450QXM561-2   Kittens in Toyland

Rocking Horse
A beloved childhood toy and Keepsake Ornament design appears in this series of noble rocking steeds.

1988   450QXM562-4   Rocking Horse
1989   450QXM560-5   Rocking Horse

Penguin Pal
Christmas is the favorite season of these dapper penguins, partaking in the holiday's festivities in each year of the series.

1988   375QXM563-1   Penguin Pal
1989   450QXM560-2   Penguin Pal

ABOUT THE AUTHOR

The author, Clara Johnson Scroggins, became an avid collector in 1972 shortly after the death of her first husband. It was then that she discovered the second edition Reed and Barton "Sterling Cross" ornament. She began seeking the first edition and found her quest to be far greater and more challenging than she expected. By the time the 1971 "Cross" was hers, so were ninety percent of all Christmas ornaments made by silver companies, as well as those issued by museums, mints, and department stores in the United States and abroad.

She has collected Hallmark ornaments since 1973 as well as those of other manufacturers since their beginnings. After amassing more than 50,000 ornaments several years ago, she ceased counting and started depending upon ledgers and computers to keep her collections current.

Mrs. Scroggins, a meticulous historian, is considered by many to be the premier authority on contemporary ornaments. She has been the subject of cover stories for both the *Franklin Mint* and *The Plate Collector* magazines, and has been interviewed by hundreds of newspapers and television talk shows nationwide. Her collection was filmed in her home by the "700 Club" and was shown in sixty-five countries.

The author of a collector's guide on silver ornaments, and four editions of the *Hallmark Keepsake Ornament Collector's Guide,* Mrs. Scroggins is also a columnist for several collectors' publications. She travels year-round on the lecture circuit, speaking to collectors' groups, fraternal organizations, and appearing at retail gift shows and ornament shows.

She is a former broadcast journalist, and has interests in art, antiques, and rare books. She resides with her husband, Joe, in Houston, Texas, and has one son. She will soon be a grandmother for the second time.

INDEX

NOTES

NOTES